TRAVOLTA

TRAVOLTA

◇ ◇ ◇ ◇ ◇ ◇

Dave Thompson

TAYLOR PUBLISHING COMPANY
Dallas, Texas

Published by Taylor Publishing Company
           1550 West Mockingbird Lane
           Dallas, Texas 75235

Library of Congress Cataloging-in-Publication Data

Thompson, Dave.
    Travolta / Dave Thompson
        p.   cm.
    Filmography: p.235
    Discography: p.242
    ISBN 0-87833-949-3
    1. Travolta, John, 1954– . 2. Actors—United States—Biography.
I. Title.
PN2298.T73T48   1996
791.43'028'092—dc20
   [B]   96–21440
                                             CIP

Printed in the United States of America

10   9   8   7   6   5   4   3   2   1

Contents

◇◇◇

Acknowledgments
◇◇◇

First, I'd like to thank my agent, Madeleine Morel; my editor, Macy Jaggers; and a large chunk of my inspiration, Amy Mueller—this book could not have been written without her enthusiasm, excitement, and an almost demonic appreciation of the truly special moments . . . uouugghh.

My wife Jo-Ann, who only once turned down my Bee Gees records and only threw ice at the mirror ball; she also proofread the text, so big thanks for that, and made innumerable suggestions, which helped out immeasurably.

Snarleyyow and K-Mart, whose little kitty brains have yet to grasp the concept of opposable thumbs; Ella and Sprocket; Stephanie F. Ogle and Cinema Books in Seattle; the Rock Shop in Hollywood; Geoff Monmouth; Barb East; Gaye and Tim; Anchorite Man and the mysterious Orifice . . . . Bat-ears, for whom nothing is ever good enough but soda comes a close second; and Nutkin, whose beaming smile at least keeps them happy at the bus stop.

One thing I will never get over is the sheer weight of enthusiasm that this project aroused, as people I'd never have imagined would care suddenly appeared in white suits and smart Cuban heels; I don't believe I mentioned this book to anybody who didn't react with excitement and an anecdote.

Too many to mention, and there'll always be one I forget (probably you, Zak), I'd like to thank them all for their good wishes. There were moments, midway through one or two of those movies, when it really helped to know that so many folk cared.

A veritable room full of people offered more tangible assistance, everything from dog-eared newspapers to the latest glossy magazine, from personal memories to potent observations; again, I don't want to name you because I know I'll leave someone out, but if you think you should be in here, you are. There's also a couple of people who talked to me on the condition I rendered them anonymous—er, what were their names again?

Finally, I would like to acknowledge the small forest's worth of books and magazines that I consulted during my researches. My thanks to the relevant authors and publications (and again, apologies for any omissions):

The John Travolta Scrapbook, Suzanne Munshower (Sunridge Press, 1978); *Travolta to Keaton*, Rex Reed (William Morrow, 1979); *Danse Macabre*, Stephen King (MacDonald & Co, 1981); *The Kid Stays in the Picture*, Robert Evans (Hyperion, 1994); *By All Means Keep on Moving*, Marilu Henner (Simon & Schuster 1994); *Quentin Tarantino: The Cinema of Cool*, Jeff Dawson (Applause Books, 1995); *Olivia: More Than Physical*, Gregory Branson-Trent (CGP, 1995); *Complete Directory to Prime Time TV Shows*, Brooks/Marsh (Ballantine, 1995).

Advocate (April 4, 1995); *Chicago Tribune* (various issues); *Cinescape* (February 1996); *Dance Magazine* (August 1983); *Details* (February 1996); *Entertainment Weekly* (various issues); *Film Threat* (February 1996); *GQ* (October 1995); *Harpers Bazaar* (July 1983); *Interview* (August 1994); *Life* (July 1980); *Loaded* (March 1996); *Los Angeles Times* (various issues); *McCalls* (July 1978, April 1980, July 1983); *National Enquirer (May 8, 1990); The New York Times* (various issues); *New York Daily News* (various issues); *Newsweek* (December 19, 1977; May 29, 1978; June 9, 1980; September 19, 1994); *People* (various issues); *Playboy* (March 1996); *Premier* (September 1993, November 1994); *Redbook* (February,1993, April 1993); *Rolling Stone* (June 15, 1978; August 18, 1983; December 28, 1995; February 22, 1996); *Seventeen* (October 1976); *Spy* (Jan/Feb 1996); *Teen* (February 1979); *Theater Crafts* (May 1986); *Time Out* (February 21, 1996); *Time Magazine* (July 26, 1976; December 19, 1977; April 3, 1978; May 6, 1991; October 16, 1995); *US* (December 1995, January 1996); *Variety* (various issues); *Vogue* (October 1994); *Working Woman* (August 1983).

TRAVOLTA

○○○

Introduction

Many actors and actresses be-
come stars; that is, after all, what the movie business is all about. Few of
these stars, however, are able to take the next step, beyond stardom,
beyond even superstardom, and onward until they have so transcended
their milieu that they not only represent a person at the peak of their
profession, but they also become synonymous with the era in which
they reached that peak.

James Dean did it. Although he starred in just three movies (and
died after just two), Dean manifested a vision of 1950s America that
neither history nor hindsight will ever dilute. At screenings of his final
film, *Giant*, grief-stricken teens cried out "come back Jimmy, we're
waiting for you." Forty years later, there are still people waiting, which
is why the commemorative postage stamp the United States Postal
Service honored him with in 1996, the anniversary of his death, was
awaited with a fervor that made philatelists of the entire nation.

If Dean was the king of the 1950s, Marilyn Monroe was his
queen. Like Dean, she is remembered not for the parts she played but
for all that she represented. The scene in *Seven Year Itch* in which her
skirt is blown aloft by the air from a vent in the sidewalk infuriated her
husband, Arthur Miller, but it captivated a generation and lodged in

1

the imagination of every successive age. Even today, Monroe remains the poster girl of the twentieth century.

There are others, too. A tiny tramp waddling awkwardly off into the sunset: Charlie Chaplin need only flicker into view to conjure up the image of the silent movies of Hollywood's infancy. Clark Gable remains the suave spirit of the thirties; Errol Flynn, the swashbuckling soul of the roaring forties. Jayne Mansfield barely made a decent movie in her life, but with death she became immortal, the last of the glamour queens, the sixties' sexiest siren.

And most recently of all, Winona Ryder has already established herself as the epitome of "Generation X" of the 1980s. Even though her own career has long since steered her clear of the typecasting graveyard that might have ensnared a lesser talent, there are still moments—midway through *Beetlejuice*, in lacey black and Goth-chick splendor, or the end of *Heathers*, lighting a smoke off her exploding ex-boyfriend—that are already seared into collective memory.

Yet not one of these names, these dreams, even comes close to the one-man, one-decade fusion that practically defines the term Hollywood iconography. The image is so much a part of its own age that even today, the scene still plays itself out irresistibly in the mind's eye.

The camera glimpses, then is glued upon, a figure in white polyester and platform shoes. Nik Cohn, whose writings fathered the figure, once described him as a human timepiece, cryogenically frozen at four o'clock.

The right arm points vertically to the ceiling, the left aims diagonally downward. And if you suspend reality then close in on the face comically locked in a look of eternal surprise, as the years fast-forward, *Saturday Night Fever*'s Tony Manero becomes *Pulp Fiction*'s Vincent Vega, and as the eyes narrow slightly, the lips barely part. "You're mine, I own you."

He's speaking to costar Danny DeVito, of course, but he could also be talking to the mid-seventies. They *are* his, he does own them, and there is no one else in Hollywood past or present who could make a similar claim on time. On any time.

That was then, this is now.

Today, John Travolta is a million miles (and a good fifty pounds) away from his *Saturday Night Fever* days. He is a living legend, but he has eluded the confines of that legend to concentrate simply on living.

He knows the perils of living in a legend.

"You look at Dean, Jayne Mansfield, Buddy Holly, whoever," he told *Vogue* magazine in the early 1990s. "Their record for survival is not so hot. If they even made it past thirty they were ahead of the game. And here I was, zooming forty, with all my family and friends around me, my health and my hair, and lots of other good stuff besides."

But still the legendary image persists around him—and despite him. When John appeared on television's *Saturday Night Live* in the aftermath of *Pulp Fiction*'s stupendous success, his earlier role became the show's running joke. Every time John stepped forward, the studio band struck up his old movie's theme, "Staying Alive."

When that same song was reprised by Eurodisco sensation N-Trance for a 1995 hit single, the record sleeve replicated the old four o'clock stance, and the band shot an accompanying video in which one member did nothing but strike the requisite pose.

It is more than an image, it is an icon. But for the man who created it, it has been as much a millstone as a milestone. It's not been an obstacle to being taken seriously—with critic Pauline Kael on his side and director Francois Truffaut on his team, acceptance had already prostrated itself at his Cuban-heeled feet. Rather, it's made it difficult for him to be taken at all.

If an actor is bigger than the movie he is in, that is fair enough; today, the lowest grade star can get his name above the title. But if an actor is bigger than both the movie and the role, there are problems. The essential point of acting is to suspend belief, to convince the viewers to believe that the actor is suddenly somebody else. If that exercise fails, the movie fails—not on the weaknesses of the actual performance but on the strengths of the audience's own expectations.

The star determines the nature of the characters in his films. They absorb him, accepting the gifts he has brought them. But they also give him gifts of their own, imbibing reality with their own fictional qualities. It's the process that made it seem perfectly reasonable for a California chapter of the Gary Cooper fan club to have campaigned for the actor to run for President in 1936 on the strength of his performance in *Mr. Deeds Goes To Town*. After all, he had no trouble dealing with the politicians there.

Maybe if John Travolta had cut a less dashing figure in his early roles—in *Saturday Night Fever*, in certain elements of *Carrie* and *Welcome Back, Kotter*, and in the hit musical *Grease*—if he had simply turned up and done his job, then spent the rest of his time disavowing his budding image, he might have saved himself a lot of trouble.

But he didn't, and looking back on the pit his own honesty dug him, it is a miracle that he was even able to live with what he created. The fact that he has also been able to escape it scarcely bears believing.

But it was belief that propelled John forward, that stopped him from sinking into the mire that has enveloped so many other of Hollywood's biggest hit men, that kept his head above water while a string of his movies sank without trace. Belief in himself, belief in his talent, and belief above all that there is always something worth believing in.

1

○○○

A Family of Actors

In 1950, with just over 23,000 people, neatly planned, tree-lined streets, and a bustling downtown shopping area, Englewood was the typical New Jersey commuter town. Perched on the brim of the Hudson River, in full view of Manhattan's concrete jungle, the comfortably middle-class Englewood enjoyed the best of both worlds. It was a suburb with a city skyline, a split-level town within fifteen minutes of a multistory metropolis.

It had its problems, of course. Block-busting landlords shattered generation-old neighborhoods, converting one-family houses into ten-family rabbit hutches and stirring unknown new ingredients into an already seething melting pot.

But if you refrained from peeling back the layers, growing up in Englewood was like growing up in any television sitcom city. When nighttime rolled up the sidewalks and the pastel-painted doors slammed a unified good night, those sitcoms would enter Englewood's parlors, the blue flicker from the TV screen seeming strangely enchanting and reassuring. The world outside was a long way away. Pops always came home from work at the same time, and mom always had a steaming dinner waiting on the table.

That was the world that Salvatore Travolta had always dreamed of creating—and had fought tooth and nail to maintain. Family was important to Sal, more important than anything else he could name.

His own father and mother had always been home when he got in from school, and he never forgot how important it was to know that they would always be there when he needed them. He wanted his children to enjoy that same security.

The Travolta family was second generation Italian-American, the offspring of Neapolitan-Sicilian immigrants. According to family legend, Sal's paternal grandfather arrived at Ellis Island an orphan. He was promptly dispatched to an orphanage, where he was rechristened Travolta. A lively child, quick and electrifying, the name was apparently appropriate: in one Italian dialect it means "high voltage."

That tale may or may not be accurate, but regardless of the truth, Grandfather Travolta lived up to his new name. It was he who opened the tire store that Sal still ran almost half a century later. He had scraped together the money to keep it going as the Depression loomed through the late 1920s, when even the rich folk had to stop buying little luxuries for their motor cars. Most weeks he could make ends meet, so his wife worked in a sweatshop to give them a little extra. In the evenings, she came home to hand-make clothes for their four children. That Trojan work ethic was just one of the valuable legacies they would hand down to succeeding generations.

In 1929, when Sal was a seventeen-year-old promising semi-professional football player, he met the girl who would become his wife. Helen Burke was a vivacious Anglo-Irish lass, famed in the neighborhood for so many talents that it was impossible to believe they all fit into her tiny frame. An expert swimmer, for instance, Helen held the record for swimming the fastest across the Hudson River back in the days when it still was a river and not simply a raging torrent of industrial sludge.

Typically modest, however, it was not the feat itself that would remain one of her favorite personal anecdotes but her mother's reaction to it.

"There were hordes of photographers waiting on the other side," she would laugh, "and when I got home my mother said, 'Why is your hair wet?'

"'Because I swam across the Hudson.'

"'Well, you'd better dry it before you catch cold.'"

When she wasn't in the water, Helen was happiest on the stage.

She was a member of a teenage singing group called the Sunshine Sisters, darlings of local Hackensack radio, with their chirpy repertoire of period hits. She also acted with a local stock company. In later years, she would laughingly recall how her fellow budding thespians would compare her to Barbara Stanwyck, the stunning, sultry star of *The Locked Door* and *Mexicali Rose*.

According to Sal, however, it was no laughing matter. Helen, he swore, was an extraordinarily talented actress. He even offered her the opportunity to follow in Stanwyck's footsteps and move to Hollywood to make movies herself, but she turned it down. The Great Depression was in full swing, a time when even the most well-to-do families needed all the breadwinners they could get. Hollywood was too fickle and uncertain for the levelheaded Helen to want to take a chance upon. Besides, she and Sal were engaged to be married. Even though it would be a few years more before they wed, Helen, like Sal, already valued hearth and home more than fame and fortune.

Her youngest child, John, has never ceased singing her praises. "She was a drama teacher, speech teacher, and an actress herself. She was in summer theater, she was on radio shows. She was really remarkable and influenced all of us."

In 1937, with America having at last emerged into the rejuvenated world of President Roosevelt's New Deal, Helen and Sal finally wed. "They really adored each other," John reflects. "My father thought my mother was the living end, that she was the best actress, the best director, and had the most style, presence, and personality of anyone he had ever known. They had a very hot relationship. Even after they'd been married twenty-seven years, you could walk into their bedroom in the morning—like I sometimes did as a kid—and there they'd be, nestled in each others' arms, their bodies totally locked together. They were really into each other."

Marriage and the responsibilities of raising what swiftly became a large Catholic family curtailed Helen's active participation in show business, just as it had ended Sal's sporting life. The couple's first child, Ellen, was born in 1941. Sam arrived in 1944, Margaret in 1946, Anne in 1949, and Joey in 1951. When Helen learned shortly before her forty-second birthday that she was pregnant again, she could not have been more surprised—nor more afraid.

Even by contemporary standards, she had already been past her child-bearing prime when Joey came along. Although she tried her hardest not to appear concerned, the rest of the family did their best to make sure she took things easy, splitting the chores and giving her hell when they found her up and about. Still, when baby John was born on February 18, 1954, he was so frail and tiny that Helen spent most of his first year fretting that he would not make it. "I'd call the doctor every week and ask, 'Will Johnny survive?'"

"Once we had those kids," Sal later remarked, "my life became unimportant; theirs were the important lives. Helen and I wore second-hand clothes. It didn't matter; we weren't out to make a show. The main thing was, the kids saw pop wasn't putting on a hundred-dollar suit while they went without. They knew nobody was getting more than anybody else, and they knew nobody was loved more than anybody else. One of us was always at home; I could have belonged to a dozen organizations, but I didn't. I don't think I spent more than ten nights out in all the time the kids were growing up."

John agrees. The old Victorian house on its (now denuded) tree-lined street was always full of love, "and that was the most important commodity." As for the other, more material demands of raising a family, he continues, "we always had enough, but we were by no means well-off." So by the time they reached twelve or thirteen, the Travolta children were out working. "We didn't want to be a burden on our parents," says John.

Margaret earned the big money, a hundred dollars a week as a waitress. Twenty bucks would go to her parents, and she would always save a little for her youngest siblings. "We have an expression in Italian, 'Even the little ones want,'" reflected her father. He remembered Margaret handing John a couple of dollars every week with a smiling, "Here you are, brat." John's own first job would be as a box boy in a local supermarket. Even as he bagged groceries, however, his mind was always elsewhere, just as it had been since he was very young.

Not once while they were growing up did the Travolta children hear their parents try to steer them in any direction but the one they chose for themselves. Sal was proud of that. "We never said, 'Why don't you become a priest like your cousin Frankie?' We never told [them] to be a doctor or a lawyer." But with his and Helen's past professions and ambitions so close to their hearts, the children never needed to look far for their own destinies.

"The result was like dominoes," John describes. "The oldest of [the] children got interested in acting, and the next, and the next one. It was the accepted thing in our family to perform. It was looked up to. You were either interested in sports because my father was an athlete, or you were interested in theater. It went one way or the other. So you weren't the black sheep of the family as long as you were interested in one of them."

Ellen, the oldest of the children, was the first to reach out for the golden ring. When she was seven, she appeared on that longest-running of daytime talent shows, "Star for a Day," singing "If I Knew You Were Comin', I'd 'ave Baked a Cake." For the rest of the Travolta children, Ellen would always be a tough act to follow, but John could barely walk before he was doing his best to usurp her.

When he was two, he saw a performance of *Peter Pan* on television and was promptly persuaded that he, too, could fly. Climbing as high up the stairs as he dared, usually no higher than the third step, he would flap his arms and launch himself into the air, coming down with a crash flat on his stomach. Then he'd stand up, and go right back and do it again.

Two years later, it was Jimmy Cagney who caught his eye, and John kept the entire family entertained during a TV rerun of *Yankee Doodle Dandy*, improvising the old master's dance steps. Not long after, Helen enrolled her youngest in a tap-dancing school run by Fred Kelly, the brother of the dancing actor Gene.

As John's horizons widened, so did his repertoire. "As a kid, I'd mimic all the actors in all the musical comedies on Broadway. It was fun." He studied television with a devout passion, and if anyone he knew made the big trip up to Broadway for a play, John would demand an account more precise than the most fastidious critic could ever deliver.

But it wasn't only the onstage routines that he memorized. One day, Helen offered the four- or five-year-old John a part in a stage production she was arranging at the local high school. These were regular events in the Travolta household, and all the children had done a turn, starting off at the bottom of the bill and working their way up as their age allowed.

John, however, had very different ideas about how things should be done. So what if he was the youngest? It was talent that counted, not years, and Helen had barely finished outlining his role than she was watching, absolutely mortified, as her youngest son unleashed his first-ever display of artistic pique. Brother Joey was also appearing in the show, and John wanted a role as big as his. And if he couldn't have one—well, she could just have her show without him. Then he stormed upstairs to pout furiously at his black teddy bear, Audi.

"I always had to think before I said anything even faintly critical to Johnny," Helen shuddered. "His feelings were so easily hurt. If I raised my voice to him, he'd run upstairs to his room and slam the door. Then, like the good little actor he was, he'd yell down, 'I'm throwing myself out the window.'"

Her heart in her mouth, Helen would tear upstairs only to find him hiding behind his dresser.

In 1960, when he was six, John was given his first taste of the greasepaint when he flew out to Boston on his own to join sister Ellen in the road company of Ethel Merman's *Gypsy*.

"*Gypsy* had all these kids in it," John remembered. "The cast had school in the theater, and they were studying their books in the theater, not in a school. At night they got to perform and I thought, 'I want to be with those kids!'" Already, he had decided what he wanted to do with his life. "Acting's just so darned entertaining to me, to create different walks and different voices and different accents and different characterizations and different thoughts. I don't know why it entertains me, but I just love being other people and pretending I'm them. It's somewhat satisfying to design it to a level that you'll buy it and I can affect you."

But as he boarded the plane at nearby Teteboro Airport, clutching his sandwiches in one hand, his hat in the other, and puzzling out how he was expected to wave goodbye to his parents as well, it was hard to say what was the biggest thrill: his destination or the act of getting to that destination. For in that marvelous way of organizing ambition that children alone seem to possess, he had also decided he wanted to be a pilot.

Night after night, as he lay awake in his bed, John would listen to the planes whose flights out of New York took them directly over the Travolta house. He thrilled to the roar of their engines, charting in his own mind the battle for supremacy between jet and propeller, and dreaming of the day when he, too, might be able to fly.

It was that conflict that established the late 1950s as such an exciting time in the history of aviation, and John's fascination with flight has never left him.

"I wanted to be a pilot. I was in New Jersey and there was a path over my house, where the planes from La Guardia runway seemed to reach two thousand feet by the time you looked up. Every day, every ten minutes, there was either a DC-17 or DC-6, and it would lumber across the sky. I can remember wanting to be on them, wondering what the people were like sitting on them. From every standpoint, I fantasized about being part of aviation. It entertained me for years. I'd go to the airport and watch my sisters go off to do different shows."

The appeal is obvious. The world of airplanes and theaters offered him a way out of the mundane conformity of Englewood, New Jersey. Ellen smiles as she takes the blame for the two becoming so inextricably linked in her younger brother's mind. "My acting career symbolized travel to him." She even used to save her flight tickets for him, encouraging his dreaming with tales of glamorous stewardesses, glossy in-flight magazines, and the sheer exhilaration of watching through the cabin windows as the ground floated further and further away until it was lost beneath the clouds.

Now it was John's turn to experience that magic, and he was determined to savor every last second of it. More than thirty years later he let out a hint of his fervor in *Propeller One-Way Night Coach*, a short novel he wrote and self-published in 1992.

"The excitement ran through my body like nothing I had ever felt before. Knowing that within minutes I would be airborne for the first time was comparable to nothing."

The protagonist of *Propeller One-Way Night Coach* is three years older than John was at this time, but still John would acknowledge that the book was "kind of an autobiography, only not exactly."

Of course, joining the *Gypsy* company proved just as memorable as flying out to meet it. Night after night, John would stand beside the stage, and Ellen always laughed when she caught sight of him mouthing the words to the songs and mimicking the cast's dance steps. In fact, he memorized them so perfectly that by the time he got home he could treat the rest of the family to the entire performance single-handedly, all the while playing his copy of the *Gypsy* soundtrack album until he actually wore it out—no easy feat in those days of thick vinyl and deep grooves.

As he grew, John's life continued to revolve around the twin dreams of flight and the theater. At the nearby parochial school he attended, the nuns all but despaired of the boy who could barely do his multiplication tables because his head was already full of numbers—the seating capacity of the DC-6, the number of weeks *Gypsy* spent on the road. They were exasperated by the boy who could not retain a few lines of scripture but could recite entire movie scripts without a fault, and who spent the entire day itching to get out of class so he could work twice as hard at home.

His bedroom was filled with model aircraft: an entire history of aviation hanging by threads from the ceiling and occupying every shelf not already stuffed with books and articles about aircraft. Outside, the backyard resounded with the noise of John marshalling his friends into a series of impromptu plays and performances. The basement echoed with the tapping of his feet on the floor as he danced until he was dizzy.

On other occasions, when his brothers and sisters were all out of the house, John would haul Helen down there as well, with the plea, "Ma, let's play act." Helen would dutifully drag out the big old trunk in which she kept all her old stage costumes, and the two of them would set to work.

"My father built a theater complete with curtains in the basement," sister Margaret remembered. "Almost every night we would do musicals, and our parents would be the audience. They were always praising us, whether we were good or bad. It was interesting because you always felt like there was a show going on, which meant there was always a little bit of vying for attention."

John usually won. "He was my mother's last child," Margaret continues, "and she knew she wasn't going to have any more. So to her, this was a little blessing in disguise. We all kowtowed to John pretty much. He was a little bratty, but no more than any other kid."

"To be perfectly honest with you," John corrects her, "I was spoiled to death." He recalls how every Sunday, Sal would set the day aside so that he and John could do something together.

"Every Sunday we worked on a project, whether it was a go-cart, an airplane, building a new basement, a new attic, a new fence, building a deck around the pool, building a barbecue. We always had a project to do. We were partners in creating a better atmosphere in our house. It normally had to do on some level with carpentry, because that was his hobby. Some of these projects would take a year because that was his only day off. Mom would kind of get mad because I would take him away from her on the day off."

One of these projects was the miniature bowling alley they erected in the basement, which John would charge his friends two cents each to play on. He sold refreshments as well—hotdogs and sauerkraut, and soda that cost him a nickel, but he sold for a dime. There were prize competitions: ten free sodas to anybody who could knock down all ten milkbottle pins. But Sal proudly boasted that no one ever collected; "John always came out ahead of the game," he chuckled.

Late in 1961, American youths were smitten by the greatest craze since baton twirling—a new dance called the Twist. It erupted, like so many other societal blights, from the danceclubs of New York City. For a couple of months, you could not turn around—let alone towel your back dry—without being mistaken for doing the Twist. Records were released insisting people Twist and, indeed, Twist Again; entire movies were filmed around the exhortation, "Hey! Let's Twist!" And throughout suburban America, Twist competitions dominated any place where teens gathered to listen to music. Englewood was no exception.

John made his public debut shortly after his eighth birthday at just such a gathering. The Church Social Club was playing host to a local dance band, and the culmination of their act would be a solo Twist—performed, as the announcer put it (and John blushingly recalls), by "Little Johnny Travolta."

"That was it. 'Ladies and Gentlemen, the Englewood, N.J. Yearly Fireworks presents that dance craze, the Twist, danced by Little Johnny Travolta.'"

John, who spent weeks practicing in readiness for his big day, expected the dance to be over in a couple of minutes. Instead, to his mounting horror, the band seemed to take an almost sadistic delight in keeping their young performer gyrating.

"That poor kid looked so trapped and so exhausted," Helen looked back. "I kept gesturing to him, 'Johnny, it's okay, you can walk off the stage.' But he didn't dare stop." For persistence alone, John was elected Twist champion of Englewood.

The Twist died a natural death as swiftly as it had arrived, probably while John was still trying to get off stage. But in the blinking of an eye, it found itself superceded by other obsessions, most of them springing from the increasingly vibrant musical scene. In the years since rock 'n' roll first burst onto the scene in the year of John's birth, music had ceased to be a mere teen distraction; now it was a teenage obsession, and John was as caught up in it as anyone.

The soul sounds of the Motown label spun full-bloodedly out of his sisters' transistor radios, teaching John that there was even more to dancing than he had ever known—"a sound," as he put it, "to move to and feel." He spent Saturday afternoons in front of *American Bandstand*, with its never-ending conveyor belt of hot pop sounds paternally presented by the eternally grinning Dick Clark. And there was the Sunday night, nine days before John's tenth birthday, that he joined seventy-three million other people to watch Ed Sullivan unwittingly fire the first shot of what would become the British Invasion by introducing the Beatles to prime-time America.

John, no less than most of the western world, was utterly smitten by the Fab Four. It didn't matter that the *New York Herald-Tribune* summarized the group's appeal as "seventy-five percent publicity, twenty percent hair and five percent lilting lament," nor that the *Washington Post* saw them as nothing more than "a mass placebo" for a country still in mourning for the three-months dead President Kennedy. The Beatles represented something new, something dynamic, something America couldn't have resisted even if it had wanted to. During the first week of April 1964, the Beatles occupied the top five places on the American chart; a week later, they had an astonishing fourteen records on the Top 100.

John bought them all. "Maybe I wasn't a ten on the 'Nutty Fan Richter scale,'" he reflected, "but I was a solid eight. I had every album, every magazine, I tried to get to see them." He even persuaded his parents to let him have his hair styled in a Beatles-fashion "mop top," and when the nuns issued him with the heaviest ultimatum in their arsenal, "change your hair or change your school," Sal and Helen sided with their son. John was transferred to public school.

Even in the fifth grade, public school was very different from the Catholic education John had previously endured. Discipline seemed somehow slacker: there was no inhibiting uniform, and if he clowned around in class, the ensuing punishment did not necessarily incorporate an eternity burning in hell's fiery pits.

The school was "maybe fifty percent black," John remembers. Right away, that was the clique John found himself drifting toward. "I loved the black people, and they loved me because I could dance and was funny to them. The white kids never laughed at me, only the black kids. So it was the first time I was accepted by the masses. Like the blacks, I simply called things as they were."

He threw himself into living what he calls "a dual life": a rabid Beatles fan on one hand, venerating the baby-faced Paul McCartney, and a solid gold Motown freak on the other, copping dance steps from television's *Soul Train*. One of his school friends, Jerry Wurms, later recalled, "We were taught to dance by the blacks. Somebody in the corridors or outside always had a radio, and somebody was always dancing."

John agreed. "Whatever new dance came to school, I learned it. I think the blacks accepted me because I cared about them accepting me. They seemed to have a better sense of humor, a looser style. I wanted to be like that." Years later, he would acknowledge, "All the qualities that make me uniquely appealing to the masses are the black qualities I have as a person—my sense of humor, my dancing, my openness sexually with my movements."

In 1966, when John was twelve, Actors Studio, the New York acting academy, arrived in Englewood to hold some workshops. Brando, Pacino, and De Niro had all passed through Actors Studio's ranks, and Helen wrangled John in as an observer.

"The first time I visited class, I came in when some of the studio people, the advanced students from New York, were in the middle of doing a scene. After a couple of minutes they broke character to ask the director a question and I was stunned. I didn't know they'd been acting. That's how believable they were."

What struck John the most about the experience, however, was how easy it was to share in it. He learned he could duplicate what he saw those people do in class as soon as he saw it. He didn't mean he could simply imitate them, either. "I always did have this ability to observe people, watch them awhile, and then very quickly absorb their essence and then reproduce it. Nobody told me to do that."

After all, that was how he used to spend his evenings, "hanging out in the park on summer nights, sitting by the sewer, underneath the street lamp. Just watching. Studying the action and kind of biding my time."

John joined the group, and shortly after, he made his acting debut in an Actors Studio production of Frank Gilroy's *Who'll Save the Plowboy?* He had only two or three lines, his mother proudly remembered, "but he said them so meaningfully."

With such a successful experience behind him, John continued his schooling but with an increasing lack of interest. Enrolled at Englewood's Dwight Morrow High, he was a keen sportsman but scarcely a committed academician. The teachers, he complained, simply didn't want to know him. They thought they could see right through the charming kid with a ready smile and the bristling conversation. John, for his part, couldn't understand their problem. He tried to communicate with them on "a more adult level"; the staff just figured he was mouthing off.

"I didn't like high school in general," he later remarked. "My family couldn't afford to send me to a private school," he added, as though that could have altered his opinion. He was convinced that he could break into show business; he just needed the time to pursue his aims, time that the daily grind of schooling stole away from him. Math or *MacBeth*, that was the question. And John knew the answer before he could walk.

Besides, he would ask *Time* readers a few years later, "How do you go back to school and make anybody understand how it was to be with those theater people, watching the sun come up over the cigarettes and glasses of wine?"

Any curricular interests he did find appealing were drawn from the movies. History, for instance, fascinated him briefly when he discovered the Depression-era world of the legendary bankrobbers Bonnie Parker and Clyde Barrow—but only as they were portrayed on screen by Warren Beatty and Faye Dunaway. Indeed, he was so entranced that he dropped eighteen dollars at a local thrift store for a double-breasted suit, a black shirt, and a white tie, and then coerced Margaret, suitably decked out like Dunaway, to pose alongside him clutching a toy machine gun. John convinced himself that one day he would be up there alongside Beatty himself.

From an early age, then, John worked to refine his proficiency at what he would later help to define—the art of being cool. Of course, he is quick to point out, he learned just as early not to let it go to his head.

"Every time I thought I was being cool," John laughed later, "something would happen." On one occasion, when he was thirteen, he was at the pool, bragging to the others about some big-shot audition he'd just attended. His chances were good, he was going to be a star, and just to prove his point, he executed a beautiful dive—into the shallow end of the pool. One broken nose later . . . .

Still, he was accepted by the people whose approval meant the most to him, as he proved one afternoon when he and the rest of the school football team were returning from a road game.

A group of African-American players were entertaining themselves with a few choruses of the James Brown showstopper, "Say It Loud, I'm Black and I'm Proud." John waited for a lull in the song, then threw in his own lyric: "Say it light, I'm white and outtasight."

The year was fast shaping up to be a momentous one. Not only did he appear on stage for the first time, he got his first kiss as well. "She was sixteen . . . a black girl who introduced me to reefer. She said, 'Did you ever soul-kiss?' and I said, 'no, I don't think so,' and she said, 'well come on over here and let me try it with you.' So we kissed."

Reefer would become a part of John's life only briefly. "From sixteen to eighteen I did marijuana, but it always made me sick—physically ill." Drugs in general turned him off, and in later years he would reminisce sadly about the handful of overdoses that so savagely cauterized Dwight Morrow High.

"I remember the most popular athletes being killed . . . and they were guys with really incredible abilities. It was an outside force that sort of came in and contaminated the whole school. I knew I didn't like it, I knew it wasn't going to help me, and I felt uncomfortable even thinking about it."

Kissing, on the other hand, thrilled him from the start.

"1967-68 was my favorite teenage year. I was thirteen. I flew on airliners a lot, that made me happy; I went to see my sister do summer stock and went to ball games in Chicago and St Louis. And I was discovering girls, and that was good."

That winter, John started dating his first serious girlfriend, Jerry Wurms' sister, Denise. She looked like Ali McGraw, he recalls, and was only four inches shorter than his already impressive six feet. More importantly, though, "she was the first girl that was brave enough to be, like, overtly crazy about me. I dug that. I had sought after girls that weren't responding to me the way I expected, and this girl was responding to me exactly like I expected."

Helen Travolta remembered, "Denise came home from school with him every day. They'd make snacks together, study together, listen to music on the radio. He just adored her." Denise and John were still going steady three years later.

Through the summer of 1970, John achieved a dream he had nurtured for almost a decade when he appeared in a summer stock production of *Gypsy*. He moved from that to the role of Hugo Peabody in a similar production of *Bye Bye Birdie*, earning fifty dollars a week, and he was already congratulating himself on his progress when even greater praise came from a smartly dressed gent who had just stepped out from the audience.

He introduced himself as Bob LeMond, a New York theatrical agent, and as he handed over his card, it was all John could do to stop himself from bolting. Inside his head, he knew this was it; this was his big break. But even deeper, a cynicism he didn't even know he possessed laughed at the sheer cliché of the entire affair—the young aspirant stepping off the stage into the firm handshake of the high-rolling big wheel with a cigar clenched in his teeth. "Sign with me, kid, I'll make you a star." Even the movies had grown out of that storyline.

But here it was happening, and all the way home that evening the scene played and replayed in his head. It was still playing there four weeks later when John finally plucked up the courage to pick up the phone and punch the number on LeMond's business card.

If John was nervous about renewing contact with LeMond, the agent had been just as concerned about whether he would ever hear from him again.

"When John came on stage, everyone else looked like they should go home," LeMond revealed of that night in New Jersey summer stock. It was a matter of presence and talent, and this kid, this John Travolta, had them both in abundance. "He brings an incredible honesty to his work," LeMond raved.

Acquiring an agent fueled John's next dream, his most audacious one yet. With summer nearing its end, another school year rolled ever closer—and he was dreading it. There was an alternative, though, and lying awake at night, or talking on the phone with LeMond, John slowly formulated his next step. Finally, he went to his parents and told them what was on his mind. He was sixteen. It was time to drop out of school and go into acting full time.

"I decided I was good enough to compete with the professionals," John says simply. He adds with classic understatement, "I told my father about my wishes—and he was shocked."

However, Sal also knew that John was unhappy, that he was desperate to get on with what was really shaping up to be a promising career. He promised to think it over; after he and Helen spent some time on the phone with LeMond, as the school gates prepared to creak open again, he sat John down and delivered his decision.

"My father said that I could leave school for a year—and if everything worked out and I could make money, I wouldn't have to go back. But he made me promise that if I didn't succeed, I would go back to Dwight Morrow the next year." John would be the first of the Travolta kids not to complete his schooling.

John hightailed it across the George Washington Bridge the first chance he could. Moving in with sister Ann, who had relocated to the city herself, John now found himself ensconced with a bunch of fellow struggling actors in what he remembers as a condemned building with a broken elevator and temperamental heating. He didn't care. "I was seventeen, I had just quit school, and New York was like a gigantic playground."

2

◇◇◇

Broadway Bound

Throughout John's first year in New York City, 1971, Bob LeMond worked hard to justify the faith that John, and perhaps more importantly, John's parents, had shown in him. He quickly discovered, though, that John really didn't need that much work. Usually, the boy sold himself.

"He was a dream," LeMond reflected. "He got the first part I ever sent him up for, and he's never been turned down since."

That first job was a commercial for h.i.s. slacks, and John recalls, "I went from getting fifty dollars a week to getting a check for over $1,000. That was unreal." He invested his new riches wisely, taking acting and voice lessons, and studying dance under a tutor named Luigi. But the money wasn't everything. "I was really excited. To see yourself on television was really something neat."

Other commercials quickly followed; over the next five years, John estimates, he must have appeared in almost forty commercials. One, for Mutual of Omaha, he credits for bringing him to the attention of Hollywood producers long before he made his first movie. Another, a soap ad shot in a school changing room, was gleefully unearthed by a cackling Jay Leno when John guested on *The Tonight Show* in February 1996.

John didn't have it all his own way, of course. Confident that even this early on, he was ready to break out of the commercials treadmill, LeMond sent John to the auditions for Jerry Schatzberg's gritty tale of New York street life, *Panic in Needle Park*. It was only a small part, and John failed to get it. So much for "never" having been turned down!

But neither John nor LeMond was particularly worried. Somehow, there was always something else waiting around the corner.

Reasoning that with his experience rooted in live theater work, he would be better off setting his sights on Broadway, John auditioned for, and was accepted by, an off-Broadway production of Ovid's *Metamorphoses*. When that was over, he jetted off to spend the summer of 1971 in stock at the Allenbury Playhouse in Pennsylvania, with roles in *She Loves Me* and Sandy Wilson's musical comedy *The Boyfriend*. Then it was back to New York for another round of readings and auditions.

One of the most notable auditions in light of John's later career was for rock impresario Robert Stigwood's Broadway production of *Jesus Christ, Superstar*. Already a major hit in London, where it helped spring the songwriting team of Tim Rice and Andrew Lloyd Weber on an unsuspecting world, *Jesus Christ, Superstar* was still at the audition stage, and already it was creating waves across the surface of America's Religious Right. Any part in such a high-profile play would be a step in the right direction. But John was turned down flat.

Robert Stigwood later explained, "We thought he was too young to fit in with the rest of the cast." And for John, as 1971 slipped through the hourglass, it would have been little consolation had he known that Stigwood would remember his name.

Once again, however, there was no time for despair. There was something just around the next corner, and as fall fell into place, John finally struck Broadway paydirt.

Director Michael Flanagan was casting a revival of the old-time Broadway standard-bearer, *Rain*, the story of Sadie Thompson, a young lady of extraordinarily weak morals, and her enforced meeting with a correspondingly devout missionary, the Reverend Alfred Davidson. John was accepted for the admittedly minor but nevertheless visible role of Private Griggs, one of the military men passing through Joe Horn's tumbledown hotel store on the South Seas island of Pago Pago.

Written by Clemence Randolph and John Colton but based on

British writer W. Somerset Maugham's short story "Miss Thompson," the original play was launched in 1922. For its time, it was a truly daring enterprise. Miss Thompson's barely disguised sexuality—brought to bear on a holy man of all people—was so shocking that when *Rain* pitched tent in Philadelphia for its pre-Broadway tryout, it was all but run out of town. Sophisticated New York, however, adored it, and *Rain* would run on Broadway for another five years.

Time and changing attitudes, unfortunately, had done few favors to this once risqué epic. What was once saucy now seemed arch, if not absurdly melodramatic, and this painstakingly faithful revival did not attempt to remedy that. As *The New York Times'* Clive Barnes remarked in his opening night review, "It takes a 1922 text and unflinchingly stages it in a 1922 manner, and lets the laughs and the sighs fall where they will."

That, unfortunately, was mostly on deaf ears. Despite both Madeleine Le Roux, as Sadie, and James Cahill, as the missionary, turning in excellent, well-received performances, *Rain* opened at the Astor Place Theater on Lafayette Place, March 23, 1972 . . . and closed on March 28, after precisely seven performances.

John was horrified, but for Bob LeMond, *Rain's* failure was a fortuitous break. John's television appearances, though they still boasted nothing more extravagant than a handful of local commercials, had proved to him that the boy was remarkably televisual. He was a natural on the screen, and the camera, to borrow a cliché, really did love him.

But New York was no place to put that into practice. John had barely returned Private Griggs' uniform to the wardrobe department when Lemond hit him with his next career move. He should move to California.

John heard him out, then nodded. Sister Ellen was already out there and would be happy to put him up while he sorted himself out. Just a few weeks shy of the second anniversary of his departure from Dwight Morrow, John boarded a plane to Los Angeles, bound for a new life, maybe even a new world.

It wouldn't be easy, he knew. Indeed, when he first arrived in L.A., he was so frightened that he carried a bottle of Maalox around in his pocket simply to calm himself down. But he was determined to make a go of it, and within a couple of weeks he all but felt like a native. Soon he was happily admitting to everyone, "I like California better than New York. No matter where you live out there, there's always sunshine outside, and a palm tree under your window."

He scarcely dreamed that no sooner had he arrived on one coast, than he would be hurling back to the other once again.

Born in the humble surroundings of Chicago's streetcar-based Kingston Mines Theater, Jim Jacobs and Warren Casey's *Grease* appeared to lead a charmed life.

No one knows how many plays, locally successful and seemingly deserving, never leave their tiny birthing place, fading into the obscurity of distant thespian memory and a few yellowed regional reviews. Almost from the outset, however, *Grease* was attracting attention, and when the husband and wife production team of Kenneth Waissman and Maxine Fox came upon it, they had no doubt that *Grease* was precisely the sort of vehicle they'd been searching for.

Although the couple were very much the new kids on the Broadway block, they had close to two decades of experience between them, despite the fact that Waissman was only thirty and his wife of five years a mere twenty-eight.

Their first joint production took off three years before, with Sal Mineo's off-Broadway version of *Fortune and Men's Eyes*, a critically successful study of homosexuality inside a Canadian prison. Two years later, *And Miss Reardon Drinks a Little*, starring Julie Harris, won over audiences as well as reviewers, earning its investors a healthy sixty percent return and raising the duo's profile even further.

But when they announced that they were planning to follow up these successes with *Grease*, seasoned Broadway observers merely sighed. This, many insisted, is where their bubble would burst.

"All the experts told us not to [do it]," Waissman recalled. "They said '50s music is dead, the clothes were awful, nobody would want to look at any of it again."

He couldn't understand their skepticism. His generation, the postwar baby boomers, constituted the biggest consumer group in the country, and *Grease* spoke directly to them. Of course they would flock to see it.

Of course they wouldn't, his detractors replied. Why? Because nobody under forty would even set foot on Broadway.

But Waissman and Fox weren't convinced. Even if their critics' claims were true, the couple countered, what was the explanation? Did younger generations shun Broadway because they didn't like it? Or because they didn't like what Broadway habitually had to offer?

Jesus Christ, Superstar notwithstanding, little offered in 1972 seemed to have been even vaguely targeted at a younger crowd. Eugene O'Neill's *Mourning Becomes Electra* was playing at the Circle in the Square; Shakespeare's *Much Ado About Nothing* was preparing for its four-hundredth birthday at the Winter Garden; and there was a pseudo-rock musical adaptation of *Two Gentlemen of Verona* at the St. James just to prove that the Bard could bop. Patrick MacNee was starring in *Sleuth* at the Music Box, and Neil Simon's latest effort, *The Prisoner of Second Avenue* was just opening at the Eugene O'Neill. Was it any wonder that "the kids" didn't care?

Grease was different. Explaining what she hoped would prove to be its trump card, Maxine Fox continued, "*Grease* is extremely explicit about how painful it is to be an adolescent. It's a sociological statement. But mostly, it's fun." It was also authentic—despite an almost laughably low budget of $110,000.

Greased Lightning, the 1957 Chevy around which a great chunk of the action revolves, for example, was actually a golf cart modified with a fiberglass mold. "But it had to move like greased lightning," designer Douglas Schmidt recalled. "You can't give the audience a second to realize how silly all this is!"

It was silly, but that was part of the show's appeal. *Grease* was an exuberant love story set amid the fixtures and fittings of late-1950s Americana. There, boy meets girl on holiday, then meets her again at Rydell High School. But things have changed. The boy now is the leader of his gang, cool, suave, hip. And the girl? She's a sap, prim and proper, straight and narrow. The path of true love seldom runs true, but as *Grease* wove its way through the world of teen-angst etiquette and peer-pressure panic, Danny and Sandy's hearts weren't following a path, they were facing a veritable obstacle course.

The basic stage set reflected the show's preoccupations. Douglas Schmidt, the resident designer at the Lincoln Center's repertory theater, framed the action with a series of enormous reproductions of genuine fifties-era high school yearbook photographs, joking that if you wanted to be involved in *Grease*, you had to hand over your photograph first. No one was exempt, either, and that included the producers.

Waissman cringed at the directive. Casting his mind back to the day his own yearbook picture was taken, he could still remember sitting at the kitchen table staring in horror at the proofs splayed before him. "I kept saying 'these are disgusting!' until my mother got tired. 'Will you just pick one?' she said. 'You'll never have to look at it again.'" In 1976, he complained, "I've been looking at it for four years. I've looked at it on Broadway, in London, in Mexico City . . . "

The cast members appeared no less authentic. At a time when fifties revivalism still meant the faintly music hall routine of the rock band Sha Na Na, *Grease* singlehandedly repopularized drainpipe trousers and poodle skirts (all delightfully redesigned for the play by Carrie Fishbein Robbins), unearthed a near-forgotten cache of classic fifties rock songs, and almost incidentally forged a fashion that would not go away for another five years.

Indeed, for a time, *Grease* had the field completely to itself. It would be another year before *American Graffiti*, with its now bedazzling cast of Ron Howard, Harrison Ford, Penny Marshall, and Richard Dreyfuss, hijacked that same air of period innocence and carried nostalgia boldly into America's heartland, priming the pump both for *Grease's* annual tours and for Howard's return in *Happy Days*. And by the mid-1970s, with the pre-Vietnam era storming the media from stage, screen, and TV, it was difficult to believe that the clocks really hadn't been turned back two decades.

At the outset, *Grease* was not only different, it was actually considered controversial. The play premiered at New York's Royale Theatre on Valentine's Day, 1972, and immediately it was in critical trouble.

"Greased Lightning," Jacobs and Casey's ode to the automatic, systematic, hydromatic, hotrod that Danny's gang, the T-Birds, had produced from a beaten-up rust bucket, positively oozed with bad language and innuendo; and *Playbill* magazine's Chris Chase encountered at least one theatergoer who complained that "half the people playing high school kids looked thirty-five to her, and anyway, it was a bad idea to glorify teenaged punks who wore oil-slicked hair."

Not all *Grease's* problems could be so easily ignored as those complaints. As Waissman and Fox had predicted, nobody expected the older generation to understand *Grease*; what was worrying was when *Variety* suggested that the kids weren't particularly keen either, reporting that *Grease* was playing to a two-thirds empty theater at a time when Waissman's own figures indicated that the Eden was two-thirds full.

In early May 1972, Waissman filed a $700,000 damages suit against *Variety* only to have his suit denied by the courts because his papers fell short of "establishing actual malice" in *Variety*'s reporting. For the record, *Grease* went on to produce a five-hundred percent profit for all concerned. As New York's *Daily News* pronounced, it was "a lively and funny musical—as well as the dancingest one in town—that brings back the look and sound of the teenage world of the late 1950s with glee. It's a winner."

By the end of *Grease*'s first year on Broadway, six of the original cast had moved on. For Waissman and Fox, life was suddenly turning into a never-ending stream of auditions, not only to replace existing cast members but also to compile new companies for Broadway and beyond. *Grease* was going on tour.

"Our standards are very high," Waissman confirmed. For each company of *Grease*, he and Fox, choreographer Patricia Birch, and director Tom Moore would audition an average of two thousand actors and actresses, "to find the sixteen freshest and most versatile people around. Each one has to be an excellent actor and singer, and also a fairly good dancer. So it's no accident that network executives are waiting in the wings, ready to swoop up our discoveries as soon as their contracts expire."

By 1978, television and cinema was full of *Grease* alumni. Adrienne Barbeau, who played Rizzo, ringleader of the Pink Ladies, was now starring in the long-running hit series *Maude*. Modern-day Hollywood regulars Barry Bostwick (the original Danny), Jeff Conaway, Richard Gere, Treat Williams, and Marilu Henner had all served time in *Grease*. So had seventies soap stars Ilene Kristen (*Ryan's Hope*), Meg Bennett and John Driver (*Search For Tomorrow*), and Candice Early (*All My Children*), *Mary Hartman Mary Hartman*'s Michael Lembeck, *Phyllis*'s Garn Stephens, and *Soap*'s Ted Wass. Alan Paul, who played both Teen Angel and Johnny Casino, went on to further musical fortune as a member of the highly successful singing group Manhattan Transfer. And then, of course, there was John Travolta.

John auditioned for *Grease*'s first, thirteen-city, road show in Los Angeles, much to Bob LeMond's undisguised chagrin. He was convinced that John's future assuredly lay in movies and television. No way should he be wasting his time on stage.

John, concerned only with working and not really caring where it came from, disagreed. "He didn't want me to do *Grease*," John recalled. "He said 'I would rather you stay in California and become a film star.' That was unreal. I was going to do what I knew best." Broadway still seemed a far more reassuring world, "and it drove [Bob] nuts."

It drove him even nuttier when he learned that *Grease*'s behind-the-scenes crew also disagreed with him.

Choreographer Patricia Birch recalled, "when I saw John audition, I said to myself, 'There's something there.' He's a wonderfully imaginative performer and tremendously cooperative when you've earned his trust."

Kenneth Waissman, too, knew John was the right choice. "John showed up one day at the auditions for our first national touring company," Waissman recalled. "His only experience at that time had been some summer stock in New Jersey." (Sensibly or otherwise, John had failed to mention the ill-fated Rain in his career resume!)

"But Tom Moore recognized his unique qualities and superior acting talent, so we cast him as Doody"—the youngest and klutziest of the T-Birds gang and possibly the hardest part of all. With *Grease* having already garnered a rabid cult following, in the eyes of its audience there really was only one Doody: James Canning, the Chicago actor who had played the part since *Grease*'s infancy at Kingston Mines.

Without doubt, *Grease* was going to keep John out of the Hollywood spotlight—even at a time when LeMond believed he was just about ready to step into it. The boy had only just found his feet in L.A., and already he had scooped his first part. John Travolta's prime-time television debut, in *Owen Marshall—Counsellor at Law*'s second season episode, "A Piece Of God," was scheduled for broadcast on December 14. And where would John be? Two weeks into a month of rehearsals, preparing for the opening night of *Grease*'s two-week stint at the Schubert Theater in Boston.

Grease opened on schedule December 23. It traveled with a then largely unknown cast. Jeff Conaway played Danny; Barry Pearl was

Sonny; Pamela Adams was Sandy; Judy Kaye was Rizzo; Ellen March was Frenchie; and in the role of Marty, a curvy, redheaded actress named Marilu Henner. John noticed her immediately, and the attraction was mutual.

"From the moment we met," Henner later reflected, "we adored each other." She and John were the youngest members of the cast by several years, he was eighteen, she twenty, and "once we started talking, we never stopped laughing. It was like rediscovering a long-lost sibling. Before the first day of rehearsal was over, we were linked, we were buddies."

Like John, Marilu Henner came from a large family, the third of six children growing up in Chicago. Like John, too, her father worked in the motor trade, managing a car dealership, while her mother ran a dance school out of the family garage. Such similarities brought them even closer together.

Marilu continues, "Both of us come from big families, Catholic backgrounds, and our mothers were the major influences in both our lives. They were positive, forceful women who gave us the greatest feelings about show business and made us believe that we could do anything in the world we wanted to do.

"Our families also helped us both develop a strong sense of sharing, of communal responsibility. As one of six kids you learn very quickly that you've got to consider the greater needs of the group. You also learn other kinds of strength. If you can survive all that sibling competition, you know you can survive anything. So, partly because of our amazingly similar environments, Johnny and I understood each other right from the start."

Marilu was studying political science on a scholarship to the University of Chicago when she joined *Grease*, taking the role of Marty—"a voluptuous, Jayne Mansfield-type bombshell," as she put it—in the Kingston Mines version of the show. She quit school to join the national touring company and fell for Travolta as hard as he fell for her.

Yet for the first nine months, their friendship was purely platonic. "John's spontaneous," Marilu later remarked, "but he's not impulsive." John was still involved with Denise Wurms, and his commitment to that relationship certainly made an impression on Marilu. It proved, she believed, that he was "definitely a one-woman man, very selective. He's not the kind of person you worry about at a party." Or if he's away on the road, leaving you at home alone.

Denise, too, impressed her. They met a couple of times, once when Denise flew out to visit John on the road, and once when John invited Marilu back to L.A. with him, during a weekend off from the show. "She was a doll," Marilu remembered. "It made sense they were together." But she also sensed that their relationship was not as strong as it could have been. The long separation was taking its toll, on Denise if not on John. "Things were becoming iffy," Marilu later remembered. "But they were very much involved in each other's lives."

In fact, things were even more "iffy" between John and Denise than Marilu realized. John reflects, "For five years I was with her, never going out with another girl. That's pretty hard to do when you're a teenager and want to see what's around, but I thought ours was a life-time thing."

John's life on the road changed that. "Our relationship couldn't take the separation. She was too pretty to stay home waiting for me, and she started going with other guys. And one day she broke up with me."

John was devastated. The show was in the Midwest when he got the fatal call, and without a word to anybody, he got on the next plane home, determined to reason with Denise. It was useless. He flew back to *Grease* the next day, completely shattered. According to sister Ellen, he would see Denise just once more—when *Grease* hit San Francisco. Backstage at the premiere, she rushed up to tell him her own big news. She was engaged to be married.

Slowly tracking across the country, through Philadelphia, Columbus, Baltimore, Indianapolis, Toronto, Detroit, and Denver, *Grease* returned John to Los Angeles in July 1973. Bob LeMond was all but waiting for him at the airport. He had landed John an audition for the second lead in the new Jack Nicholson movie, *The Last Detail.*

It was a strong part, a larcenous young sailor who the veteran Nicholson would be transferring from one brig to another, and the only real competition was from Randy Quaid, the kid out of *What's Up Doc?*

John, LeMond was certain, was a shoo-in for the part.

John gave the audition of his life, then headed up to San

Francisco for an "away-from-it-all" weekend with Marilu. The pair had long since got into the habit of taking short breaks together, jetting around the country on their half-fare student stand-by cards, then staying at the cheapest tolerable place they could find. In San Francisco, it was the Travel Lodge, and it was there, with John still newly, rawly, single, that they had their first—as Marilu puts it—"big moment."

The following day, July 16, 1973, John called LeMond. He'd been promised an answer from *The Last Detail* people. Had it come in yet? John knew the answer even before LeMond spoke. It was no.

"It was a great role, and I wanted it very much," John admitted later. Unfortunately, although he knew that he could have acted the part "and done it just as well," Randy Quaid *was* the part and would get the Academy Award nomination to prove it.

He put down the phone and shrugged. "Oh well, let's go to Las Vegas instead." Marilu still laughs at the memory. "Johnny's idea was that when you're disappointed, don't throw a pity party, get out of town. Throw a new reality into the mix." He got back to L.A. to find his consolation prize awaiting, a small part in an episode of *The Rookies*, ABC's weekly glimpse into the life of three trainee cops. The episode, "Frozen Smoke," would be broadcast October 1, 1973.

John quit *Grease* shortly before it moved on to Marilu's hometown of Chicago, very gently breaking up with Marilu at the same time. "We went steady for a while and I thought I was crazy about her," John reflected. "But it never reached the serious stage. We went together during the run of the play, but when it was over, so were we." His career, Marilu would remark years later, always came first.

"When we were together, he was like, 'Oh God, I love you, love your body, love sleeping with you.' But he was also going, 'I have to worry about my career; we're still technically on the road, and who knows what's going to happen in September?' With L.A. feeling like home to him and like the road to me, he slammed on the brakes."

"This is the longest I've done a show," John shuddered as he came off the road. "Nine months. And it's difficult, even though this is the kind of show that's fun. To try and have fun for nine months is just as difficult as trying to hold a heavy thought thing. It can work both ways. You've got to work up a technique to make it look as if you are having fun."

It was almost relaxing, then, to throw himself once again into the hurly-burly of auditions and screen tests, and he was still hustling in October when Marilu joined him in Los Angeles for a brief visit that included an invitation to dinner with Tom Moore, *Grease's* director.

Moore was already thinking about his next project, a World War II-era nostalgia play called *Over Here*, but that was the furthest thing from his guests' minds as they enjoyed the evening. Indeed, when Moore apologized that there was nothing for either of them in the new project, Marilu recalled, "We were like, 'Hey, no problem. Neither of us was dying to be in it anyhow.'" As it turned out, they would both experience a significant change of heart over the next couple of months.

Even with an initial cost of $650,000—or almost six times more than *Grease*—*Over Here* would suffer from none of the uncertainty that had lain in ambush for its predecessor. Still the youngest producers on the block—Waissman was now thirty-two, Fox twenty-nine—they were also the hottest and the hungriest. That combination attracted Richard and Robert Sherman, the musical brains behind one of the previous decade's most enduring soundtracks, *Mary Poppins*, and the authors of what would become *Over Here*.

According to Fox, the arrival of the Shermans' tape, a mere (but fully orchestrated) eighteen bars of music, took Waissman and Fox completely by surprise. "We weren't even considering doing another work at the time," she revealed, "and certainly not another piece of nostalgia."

But the Shermans' big band tape was immediately captivating, Waissman was swift to explain. "By a process of word association, we went from big band to World War II to the Andrews Sisters." Then it was just a short step to *Victory Canteen*, another Sherman musical, which had starred Patty Andrews in Los Angeles, three years before.

Waissman and Fox had seen *Victory Canteen* during its short L.A. lifetime, and as their conversations with the Shermans developed, it turned out that they were all thinking along similar lines—a Broadway revival of *Victory Canteen*.

According to Richard Sherman, however, "they decided *Victory Canteen* wasn't big enough in scope, so they brought in a new writer, Will Holt, [who] fashioned a book that was a salute to the big band era." Over the next five months, Holt and the Shermans talked almost daily on the telephone, piecing together the script and a total of seventeen songs, while Waissman did his own homework. Having made his name as a producer with an unerring eye for period detail, it was essential that he retained that eye this time around.

But while *Grease* had required him merely to relive his own adolescence, this new play demanded more—Robert Sherman, after all, was the only World War II vet on the entire production team. Waissman spent his nights ploughing through every issue of *Life* magazine published between 1940 and 1945 while listening to every big band record he could get his hands on.

"But right from the beginning, we knew [the play] would have to be presented from the viewpoint of the seventies." That would separate it from *Victory Canteen*; that is what would give it an edge over any other piece of nostalgia on the circuit—including *Grease*.

Casting *Over Here* required as much hard work as it did intuition. "We've come to believe," explained Waissman, "that economy in musicals today means performers who are multitalented, who can act, dance, and sing." It only made sense that he would turn to his now-experienced school of ex-*Greasers* for support both onstage and off.

Once again, for instance, Douglas Schmidt would be overseeing the sets, centering the action beneath three enormous curved proscenium arches plastered with colored poster art. He was joined by costume designer Carrie Fishbein Robbins; musical director Louis St. Louis; choreographer Patricia Birch, who truly outdid herself with a wonderful aquacade swim act performed on treadmills; and director Tom Moore, the man who had spotted John's talent back in the *Grease* auditions.

Again, Moore brought John into the project. Reading the finished script, he realized that he had completely misjudged the new play's requirements. There was a part for him, a young soldier named Misfit, and John read for the role in December. Coincidentally, he auditioned in Los Angeles at almost the same time that Marilu wandered into New York rehearsals. At Tom Moore's prompting, she jokingly sang "Goody Goody," the only 1940s stage song she knew.

The arrival of Treat Williams as another soldier, Utah, completed the illusion—Rydell High was now officially the first school in American history to stage its reunion before its pupils had even been born, dancing to the music their parents had grown up with.

With the backroom crew and the supporting cast in place, it was time to assemble the stars, and again Waissman and Fox knew exactly who they wanted. Throughout the war years and beyond, the Andrews Sisters—*Victory Canteen* star Patty, and her sisters Maxene and LaVerne—were all but synonymous with entertainment in America. "We were such a large part of everybody's life in the Second World War," Patty emphasized. "We represented something overseas and at home—a sort of security."

Since the war, however, things had changed. LaVerne had died in 1967, and the following year Maxene dropped out of show business to become Dean of Women at Tahoe Paradise College in Lake Tahoe. The school went bust in 1971, and Maxene drifted slowly back in to focus, drawn, she laughed, by the knowledge that for all the Andrews Sisters' accomplishments, there was one thing they had never done— Broadway. *Over Here* offered the opportunity to rewrite that piece of their history.

They had starred in twenty-two movies and appeared countless times on radio, television, the theater, and night clubs. But Broadway had never been interested. It was, Maxine cursed, "too snobbish and cliquish. They separate Broadway from vaudeville and records, which was what we were associated with." Now, after thirty-five years, as journalist John Wilson joked, they would finally get to cross the road "from the stage door of the Paramount [where] they packed the house five or six times a day. . . to the stage door of the Schubert." Even this late in life, *Over Here* was simply too good an opportunity to pass up.

So was the chance to puncture a few of their own legends. Over the years, the Andrews Sisters had made nine-hundred records, which between them sold close to one-hundred million copies. But not one of them even came close to the kind of songs the Sherman Brothers had written for them. One, "The Good Time Gal," was nothing short of a cautionary tale about the short-term pleasure and long-term pain involved in catching syphilis. "In our day," Maxene laughed, "people were scared to even talk about things like that!" The sisters loved it. In fact, the only cloud on the horizon was the absence of LaVerne. As far as Waissman and Fox were concerned, the public knew the Andrews Sisters as a trio. How could they go out as anything else?

That, Waissman would admit, became "one of our most difficult assignments, finding the right person to play the third Andrews Sister. Patty and Maxine were a little anxious about the idea at first, but we assured them that the voice would be perfectly matched before we decided on one. The girl we had in mind would also have to be able to act, dance, and be a talented comedienne."

That was a rare combination, he knew, and one that kept the production team busy through the course of two thousand auditions. Finally, however, they discovered Janie Sell, and rehearsals could begin in earnest.

It was pure coincidence, but once again, Waissman and Fox had tapped an incipient public mood. In May 1973, with *Over Here* still in the preproduction stage, the most modern of vaudeville superstars, Bette Midler, scored her first major hit single with a revival of the Andrews Sisters' own signature tune, "Boogie-Woogie Bugle Boy." Five months later, riding on the wave of affection Midler had uncovered, two compilations of the sisters' own original recordings, *The Best of the Andrews Sisters* and inevitably, *Boogie-Woogie Bugle Girls*, made the lower reaches of the national album charts. For the cast and team of *Over Here*, there could have been no greater portents.

Over Here is set on a train traveling from the West Coast to New York to join the ship that will carry the passengers to wartime Europe. The two De Paul Sisters (Maxene and Patty Andrews) are a singing group hoping to recruit a third member before they reach New York.

This turns out to be Mitzi (Janie Sell), a glamorous central European singer-dancer who just happens to double as a German spy tracking the company of military recruits who are also aboard the train—that number includes Misfit, Sarge (William Newman), Lucky (John Mineo), and Utah (Treat Williams).

Mitzi's radio transmitter is concealed in her lipstick case, and although several people suspect her motives, she is not unmasked until the play's end, when she is challenged to prove she's a patriotic American. She obliges with the second verse of the "Star-Spangled Banner," and of course, no real American knows the second verse of the "Star-Spangled Banner."

Also aboard the train are Donna (Marilu Henner), a waitress on her way to a new job at a defense plant, an automobile executive (William Griffis), and sundry civilians, many of whom are to be roped into a morale boosting radio broadcast live from the moving train. This is John's biggest moment, performing "Dream Drummin'/Soft Music," and Kenneth Waissman later pointed out just how crucial that moment would prove. "Some TV producers heard his voice on the cast album, and came to see him in the show and signed him up."

Over Here was in rehearsal for two months, before it moved to Philadelphia for a month of previews.

It was a disaster. Douglas Schmidt's complicated three-level stage, complete with a treadmill and hydraulic lift, "had to work like a Swiss watch," Marilu Henner wrote. "It came together more like Swiss cheese."

Audience reactions to the play were already confused; when the mechanical equipment started to echo that confusion with just two weeks remaining before the show's Broadway opening, there was no alternative. The entire performance, from the songs to the choreography, needed to be given a complete overhaul. Complicated routines were dumped and replaced with new, equally complicated ones. One of Marilu Henner's favorite moments, a passionate clinch with Treat Williams, was dropped, together with one of the best songs, "Scuttlebutt." The cast was still coming to terms with this new routine when they discovered that *Over Here* was to play host to its most important visitor yet—Bette Midler was in the audience.

Everything went according to plan. The play was approaching its finale, the showstopping few minutes when the orchestra treadmilled its way across the stage, the Andrews Sisters rose over the top in a sea of sequins, and John led them all through a wild, Gene Krupa-type drum number. Smiles of relief were already appearing on the faces of the cast; they'd done it.

Donna, Marilu Henner's waitress, made her way around the stage taking everybody's dream order, which was then enacted according to some vast, Busby Berkeley-esque game plan. One customer dreamed of being Esther Williams, and the stage exploded into the aquacade.

Another who wanted to be Miss America was instantly whisked away to the most glamorous pageant of all time. A third fancied herself as Sonja Henie, the Norwegian ice-skating star who catapulted the sport into the spotlight when she captured ten individual championship titles between 1927 and 1936.

Finally, Donna skated over to Misfit. "Okay, that's one Esther Williams, one Sonja Henie, one Miss America. So, what's your dream?"

"I dunno."

"Well, if you're gonna dream, dream big."

Seated at a table, John began gently drumming on the formica surface, and started to sing, "I'm dream drumming . . ." That was the cue for the action to begin; this night, it was also the cue for all hell to break loose.

The complex sequence of steps that should have been rehearsed until the cast could do them in their sleep was still unfamiliar. People missed their marks and bumped into one another. The orchestra, instead of treadmilling slowly across the stage, suddenly seemed to cartwheel wildly. Midstage, John was torn between total horror and absolute mortification; he started to improvise, and continued improvising even as the curtain fell on the final act, when a rapturous roar from the theater let the horror-stricken cast know that at least the audience had had a good time. And then he fled.

At two in the morning, Marilu's telephone rang. It was John.

"Where are you?"

"The airport. I'm going home. I'm quitting the show."

"How?" she asked him. "There's no flights to L.A. until morning."

"Oh. I never thought of that."

Faced with a long, lonely night at a freezing Philly airport, John agreed to return to the hotel—and the show. "Could you wait up for me, though? I don't have any money for the cab fare."

Over Here opened at New York's Schubert Theater March 6, 1974, and with all the difficulties finally smoothed away, it immediately enthralled the critics. Its score, bristling with songs that, as *The New York Times* critic put it, "you almost recognize but don't quite," was irresistible. The larger-than-life evocation of the wartime era, from the hokey plot on down, won a delighted "silly, lively pastiche" headline from New York's *Daily News. Time* went even further, joyously labelling *Over Here* "so slick and cheerfully witless that it will doubtless endure on Broadway."

And so it did, for nine months at least. The original cast album, recorded in one day at CBS' 30th Street Studios, was a hit. And when honors time came around, *Over Here* picked up four Tony nominations—for Best Musical, Best Director, Best Costume Designer, and Best Choreographer—and won a fifth, as Janie Sell waltzed away with a well-deserved Best Supporting Actress in a Musical award.

It was a glorious time. John had all but moved back to New York, regularly popping over to Englewood to visit his family before returning to the brownstone in the West eighties that he and Marilu shared, their affair back on the front burner.

They were like a couple of kids. When they went out, they were as likely to skip down the street as walk, acting out their own private street theater. Evenings indoors together were spent listening to music—the soundtrack to *Last Tango In Paris* was a big favorite—and feasting on a diet that apparently alternated between tuna melts and guacamole.

And with his mornings free between waking up and the matinee shows, John finally grasped the opportunity to indulge his greatest passion. He started taking flying lessons at Teteboro Airport, working toward his license to pilot a single engine plane. The day he qualified, he explained rapturously, was the most thrilling moment in his life.

"I love the feeling of controlling a machine that seems somehow against the rules of nature, hurling itself six hundred miles through the air at high altitudes it shouldn't be at. It's kind of like mastery over nature, the art of landing, the art of taking off, the art of a perfectly coordinated turn, and the comfort of being in a new universe here on earth. I'm getting a little esoteric about it, but it's true. These are the things I love about it and I love how extroverted it makes me. It makes me look not inward but outward. It makes me feel like I can concentrate on something else rather than look inward."

Marilu could not help but get swept up in his passion, to the exclusion of everything else, the couple's friends would jokingly complain. "They were euphoric, like Jack and Jill on speed," actor Burt Reynolds, a mutual friend, once observed. "They'd dance for fifty hours at a time. They'd just happy you to death. You just wanted to tell them to go away, get a life."

Unfortunately, that was what John himself was thinking. Broadway was great, but Bob LeMond was right. It was time to return to L.A. to pick up the threads of the television and movie career that

LeMond still swore awaited him. In September, three months before the play's scheduled closing, he quit *Over Here*, and Marilu openly admits, "I missed him terribly."

"Marilu and I have always been friends," John would reflect years later. "We've been able either to sleep with each other or not, depending on what is going on. Most of the time when we're hanging out we are, but there have been times when we're involved with other people. We're people who will get back together between other relationships." Right now, John's other relationship was with Hollywood.

Marilu was not the only thing John was leaving behind in New York. During his run in *Over Here*, he was invited to appear alongside Rita Moreno in Terence McNally's new Broadway play, *The Ritz*, set to open at the Longacre Theater in January 1975. It was good money as well. Six hundred dollars a week, John reflected, "was the most money I had ever heard of," and for a while he was sorely tempted.

This time, however, Bob LeMond refused to take "no" for an answer. Every time John's phone rang, he knew it would be LeMond, constantly badgering him, "Let's try Hollywood and see what happens."

Still thinking of *The Ritz*, John tried to argue. "I've never turned down anything this big, man." But LeMond had given in too often in the past. This time, he was adamant.

"So I went [back] to California and took the gamble," John smiled later. "And four months later, I got the Kotter show."

In fact, he suddenly found a lot of work falling his way. Their own relationship unsoured by John's break-up with Denise, her brother, John's old high school friend Jerry Wurms, had joined him in Los Angeles, and was transporting John to auditions on the back of his motorcycle.

Little more than a month after John left New York, he was back in town to shoot a commercial. He won another of his walk-on prime-time parts, appearing in one episode of the long-running medical series, *Medical Center*, "Saturday's Child." And he landed his first movie role, a small, virtually mute and certainly unrecognizable, part in *Devil's Rain*, an atrocious film with an astonishing cast.

Filming on location in Mexico throughout January 1975, John found himself suddenly rubbing shoulders with the near-legendary horror director Robert Fuest (creator of *The Abominable Dr. Phibes*) and with stars the caliber of Ernest Borgnine, Ida Lupino, and William Shatner. All seemed quite happy placing their own reputations on hold as they turned out for this sleeper to alternately kill or be killed. John was one of those to be killed, dissolving into a sticky puddle while pouring his heart into his lines: "Blasphemer! Blasphemer!"

It was a tiny part, and by the end of the year, he'd all but forgotten it. "I had a couple of lines," he shrugged, "but I was so completely disguised by the makeup that I don't consider I really existed in that."

Bob LeMond simply shrugged, "Don't worry. We'll get you noticed next time."

3

◇◇◇

Barbarino Is Born

T he Celebrity Center rises out of the architectural mosaic of Hollywood Boulevard like a monster awakening from a rococo dream, its eight floors of garrets and turrets soaring into the city smog.

It was originally built in 1929 for Eleanor Ince, the widow of Hollywood Western pioneer Thomas Ince; according to the Hollywood tours that point out the building today, Ince was shot and killed by publishing magnate William Randolph Hearst when he mistook him for Charlie Chaplin, who Hearst believed was having an affair with his wife.

Hollywood history prefers to believe that Ince merely drank and ate himself to death at a party aboard his yacht in 1924. Either way, it's an archetypal Hollywood story, and in the monument his friends erected to his memory, Ince remains enshrined in Hollywood hyperbole.

The Celebrity Center has long since passed out of the Ince family's hands. Today it is owned by the Church of Scientology, whose leadership describes it somewhat modestly as a clubhouse-*cum*-church for one of the most exclusive and powerful groupings in modern Hollywood—showbiz Scientologists.

For outsiders, it is hard to know what to make of Scientology. Its detractors paint it as a cult, offering exaggerated comparisons to such apocalyptic doom-mongerers as David Koresh's Branch Davidians and Jim Jones's People's Temple. It faces criticism from bodies as disparate as the IRS and the Cult Awareness network.

Its supporters, on the other hand, argue just as convincingly in its favor. They point not only to personal growth but also to personal success as evidence that Scientology, the Science of the Mind, benefits its practitioners. And nowhere is this doctrine more pronounced than in the membership of the Celebrity Center.

The Celebrity Center first began taking shape in 1955, about a year after the Church itself developed out of founder L. Ron Hubbard's self-help blockbuster *Dianetics: The Modern Science of Mental Health*. Project Celebrity was Hubbard's own brainchild, a manifesto that called upon Scientologists to introduce the Church to the rich and famous to "forward the expansion and popularization of Scientology through the Arts." Attached to Project Celebrity was a list of sixty-three names, including Walt Disney, Pablo Picasso, Ernest Hemingway, and Liberace.

Not one of that original list joined; indeed, many of them were dead before the Celebrity Center finally got off the ground and started operating out of a rented building at 1809 West Eighth Street in 1969. Neither were its earliest recruits examples of the caliber of entertainer Hubbard was anxious to attract. One early convert, Bobby Lipton, was merely the brother of *Mod Squad* (and more recently, *Twin Peaks*) star Peggy Lipton.

Slowly, however, the numbers—and the attendant cachet—swelled. Actress Karen Black became involved in the early 1970s. Screenwriter/director Ernest Lehmann followed after he worked with Black on the movie *Portnoy's Complaint* and saw how unflappable she was during even the greatest crisis. She ascribed her calm to Scientology.

"It was nice being around a lot of people who felt it was bad form to be gloomy and self-absorbed," Lehmann explained to *Premiere* magazine. "They were very cheerful, upbeat, which is not something you see much in the film community." He went on to describe the Celebrity Center itself as "more of a social thing than anything else, with cocktail parties and art exhibits. If you had nothing to do, you'd drop in."

John Travolta dropped in in January 1975.

He was introduced to Scientology by actress Joan Prather, whom he met and began dating on the *Devil's Rain* set. Joan, as John once described her, was "the most beautiful girl I'd ever been with—blue eyes, dark hair, and she had a lot of spirit." She had been involved with Scientology for some time, and when John mentioned one day that he had a cold, she offered to perform "an assist," a healing method developed by Scientology.

"You address the whole body," John explained, "but you go to the areas that are most bothersome. It really helped me. And then I had a sore throat and she did another process on me, and the sore throat went away. So then I knew, something's really working here." Still, not until he and Joan broke up was John prepared to embrace the philosophy fully.

The split had left him shattered. "I was really heartbroken. She was really it for me, and I would have married her," he lamented. Joan, however, was understandably wary. Like Marilu Henner before her, she was well aware of the strength of John's dedication to his career, of the fact that no relationship could ever hope to compete with the real love of his life.

So much was happening in both of their careers—she had just won a part in the teen-exploitation movie *Smile*—that it was better to wait. Now she was gone, and from where John stood, it seemed Scientology alone offered him an escape from his pain.

"I went to an analyst for seven months. The only real value I got out of it was the first day when I had so much to say, and it poured out of me. But after that, I didn't find that much relief." He was twenty-one years old, he complained, and "I'd spent that many years holding things back, not being able to speak.

"I'd get very depressed for no reason. Psychoanalysis wasn't for me, but Scientology made sense right away because it seemed like a means of self-help. A meter shows you when you're responding to a bad experience in your past; you find the source of pain, acknowledge it, deal with it. That seemed to me very logical, and I was right. I get answers that way."

This meter, an E-Meter (for Engram) as it is known, lies at the heart of Scientology. Engrams, according to Hubbard's teachings, are essentially the points of negativity that affect a person's mood. These Engrams are addressed during what Scientologists call the Auditing process—a form of therapy in which traumatic past experiences are relived until one learns to accept them. Controversy and cynicism have, of course, been attached in varying degrees to the efficacy of this system, but the fact remains, coming to terms with a painful experience is often tantamount to beating it.

John described the Auditing process to journalist Barbara Grizzuti Harrison in an interview for *McCall's*. "Basically you sit opposite [the Auditor] with what we call an E-meter, a little oval-shaped machine that has a motor and a needle that registers when you hold it. You just go through what you haven't said to people that you should have, what you did to people, what upsets I have with people that bother me.

"There are three . . . 'rods'—rods means basics. Okay: things get out of whack when you flaunt your rods—upsets with people that involve a breaking of affection with them, a breaking of communication with them, a breaking of your point of view versus my point of view, your reality versus my reality. That's really the basics, what Scientologists call ARC—affinity, reality, communication. So you discuss it.

"An auditor might say, okay, did you have an ARC break? So I might say, yeah, I had an ARC break with my brother. Okay, was it a break in affinity, was it a break in reality, was it a break in communication? You go one at a time. Suppose you say it was a break in communication. Now the E-meter registers. But you have to confirm it, agree with it. It's harder work than dancing!"

John has never denied the benefits he has received from Scientology. "Before, if people said negative things about me, I would cave in easily. Being a man, that wasn't a very appealing quality. Some people would say, 'The boy is too sensitive,'" and John would believe them, taking that criticism to heart.

Scientology taught him that it was not his sensitivity that was at fault, but the people around him who played on it. "Many times, I had suppressive people around me who would cave me in on purpose. I was sort of like a minefield."

Ken Rose was a member of the Celebrity Center staff at the time of John's arrival. Although he has since left the Church and

Scientology officials have publicly counselled caution in accepting his comments, he remembers, "There was tremendous excitement about [John] at the time."

Although he still seemed a long way from stardom, John was no longer an unknown. He had played on Broadway, he'd been seen on television, and he had a manager, Bob LeMond, who never stopped hustling for him. Plus, he coupled his talent with some very good looks. A still-astonished world had already seen the effect of the Osmond Brothers' devotion to the Mormon Church. Interest, membership, and public awareness of the Mormon faith had rocketed through the ceiling when the Osmonds made it big; maybe John would prove an equally impressive ambassador for Scientology.

Never comfortable with proselytizing or with over-publicizing his personal life and beliefs, John never did give Scientology the Osmond treatment. But that is not to say he has kept the Church's benefits to himself. "The more you understand yourself, the more you can understand others. It helps enhance your life so you can handle things you otherwise might not be able to."

Neither would he openly credit Scientology with the fame that within a year of his joining the Church had completely overtaken his life. "My big break was bound to happen. I spent years planning for it." However, he did admit that "if success had come earlier, I doubt if I would have been able to handle it. Scientology has helped me cope with the pressure and responsibility I now find in my life.

"It's helped me so much. I don't know why people are afraid of it. It's given me a better quality of life, a better sense of survival, and hope for mankind. I don't have a swelled head either, and I suppose a man in my position could easily become egotistical."

Certainly, he would have had good cause to get big-headed. Just four months after he returned to Los Angeles from New York, he landed a regular part in one of the most talked-about new television shows on the fall schedule. The audition line for the coveted part had stretched halfway around the block. The show was called *Welcome Back, Kotter*, starring one of the television men of the moment, comedian Gabe Kaplan.

Kaplan and Alan Sacks first came up with the idea for *Kotter* in 1974. Kaplan's fame had already spilled across a hit album, *Holes and*

Mellow Roles, while regular appearances on the Johnny Carson show had cemented his reputation as an uproarious stand-up comic.

Kaplan's best routines were autobiographical, revolving almost exclusively around his schooldays in a certain Miss Shepherd's remedial class at Erasmus High in Bensonhurst, a neighborhood in Brooklyn.

This scenario became the basis for *Welcome Back, Kotter*, fleshing out the onstage routine with real actors to portray the characters who appeared in Kaplan's most popular stories. Kaplan himself would star, portraying a hip high school teacher being introduced to the next generation of the neighborhood hoodlums he himself had once run with.

It was an intriguing idea, and by the end of the year, ABC producer James Komack had taken Kaplan and Sacks up on it. The decision paid off. After the premise of the show had been further developed, it was decided that *Welcome Back, Kotter* would focus, in addition to Kaplan, on one particularly mismatched gang of maladjusted youths, the Sweathogs. The gang included Vinnie Barbarino, the sensual, tough guy; Juan Epstein, the fast-talking street kid; the ingratiatingly smooth Freddie "Boom Boom" Washington; and a walking mass of raw nerves and neuroses, Arnold Horshack.

Komack explained his vision of how this tumultuous potpourri would relate: "*Welcome Back, Kotter* is basically the story of a borderline delinquent from a poor section, stuck in an inept school system, who somehow makes his way and gets his teacher's degree. And where does he end up? Right back in the school he struggled to escape, teaching social studies and remedial reading. The kids haven't changed. They're still poor, estranged from society, and as apt to insult a teacher as say hello to one."

He liked to think of the show as "a 1975 *Blackboard Jungle*, or an updated version of the *Dead End Kids*. What we want to show [is] what goes on in a classroom in a poor section of town.

"And I can promise you this. *Welcome Back, Kotter* will be the real thing, the way a poor school is now. The language won't be pretty, but it'll be honest." Or at least as honest as a prime-time network slot would allow.

There was never any doubt that it was Kaplan's show. "*Kotter* is not a show," Kaplan himself stressed. "It's my life. Kotter is the make-believe teacher I wanted to have in Brooklyn." And one of his future "pupils," Lawrence-Hilton Jacobs (Washington), agreed. "Gabe created the show and his dream became reality."

All of that, however, was before the show's premiere. Thereafter, *Kotter* was simply, "the show that stars John Travolta."

John, of course, considered none of this as he made his way to the auditions for the role of Vinnie. Even if he had known the effect *Welcome Back, Kotter* would potentially have on his life, he was too busy concentrating on making the right impression to have cared.

"I got so excited about the part because it was well-written, and I immediately identified with the kind of person it was, almost like a stereotype person back east," he recalls. "He was easy to do. I just knew that character. I knew that Vinnie had a certain number of characteristics that I remembered from people I had grown up with, who were close to me or whatever, and I used their traits in the characterization for the audition."

He blessed his old talent for "storing things up about people," the same talent that had served him so well at that Actors Workshop session in Englewood. Whenever he had a character to create, he simply reached inside himself to "this whole reserve of behavior and mannerisms. You remember the guys you knew who are like the guy you're playing. You build a character that way. The last thing you do is add your own emotion to the script. That part's the most important of all; it's like inside a character's facade, I live. I really come alive when I'm doing that."

At the same time, after he read Vinnie's character description, Travolta claimed, "In no way are we alike. I was a clown in school, but I certainly was not a leader. I wasn't that tough. As for girls, maybe I'd have one girlfriend. But Vinnie has a lot. I wouldn't know how to handle them! I was an athletic kid and was interested in flying airplanes. Vinnie's interests are very different from mine."

Neither did he think of himself as being the macho type that Vinnie certainly was. Onstage, he had always been cast in the meekest of roles—Private Griggs in *Rain*, Doodie in *Grease*, Misfit in *Over Here*. Even as he waited to be called in to read for Vinnie Barbarino, John didn't think the producers would believe he could play the role. "I remember at the audition I said to myself, 'Gee, if I can pull this one off, I'm doing pretty well.'" But the moment James Komack spotted him, he knew he'd found his Vinnie.

He also knew he'd tapped a well of sensitivity that was going to give Vinnie a dimension the character's creators had never imagined. It struck him the first time he asked John where he learned to act so well. "I remember the look in his eyes . . . 'My mom's been teaching me since I was a baby.'"

Bristling with experience, the cast came together quickly. The delightful Marcia Strassman, who played Kotter's long-suffering wife, Julie, had enjoyed a season in *M*A*S*H* as Nurse Margie Cutler. Ron Palillo (Arnold Horshack) had spent the past seven months appearing in a New York theater company; and Lawrence-Hilton Jacobs (Washington) and Robert Hegyes (Epstein) both had bit-part movie careers behind them—Jacobs in *The Gambler* and *Death Wish* and alongside Hegyes in *Serpico*.

Not surprisingly, the amiable cast soon gelled. John, Jacobs, and Kaplan soon became a feared basketball team on the studio lot; John and Marcia Strassman, meanwhile, were soon linked as the show's off-set love interest. Such unity was rare, but even rarer were the pressures brought to bear on it as *Welcome Back, Kotter*'s first season progressed.

ABC did its best to make the new show feel at home: *Welcome Back, Kotter* was scheduled to premiere at 8:30 P.M. Tuesday, September 9, sandwiched between the twin peaks of *Happy Days* and *The Rookies*, and up against President Ford's favorite show, the truck driving adventure *Movin' On*, and another season debutant, the short-lived *Joe and Sons*.

Unfortunately, early September 1975 also saw several American cities embroiled in a major battle in the war against racism: the desegregation of schools was set to explode a political and civil powder keg. In one of the worst-affected regions, ABC's Boston affiliate had already announced that it would not be carrying *Welcome Back, Kotter*, explaining that a show about rebellious students in an integrated high school might not go down too well in the city (the series would be broadcast instead on a local independent). And as showtime drew closer and the so-called Bussing Riots intensified, pressure started bearing down on the network from elsewhere, demanding that Komack either tone down or dress up his original concept.

Hoping to defuse what was an extraordinarily prickly situation for any new TV comedy to be faced with, ABC also opted against opening the series with a pilot episode that had already been received exceedingly well in media previews. Though it strongly delineated the characters and the kind of situations that comprised *Kotter*'s world, network executives felt that it was simply too liberal to be screened during the current crisis.

Unfortunately, the pilot was also the episode in which Kotter meets his class for the first time and in which the necessary introductions are all carried out. The morning after the show's network premiere, *Variety*'s reviewer "Bok" could barely control his disappointment.

Describing the pilot as "explosively funny," Bok condemned, "without the shock value of Kaplan's introduction to the four uproariously obstreperous misfits who will be his students. . . the cutting edge of the *Dead End Kids-Blackboard Jungle* confrontation was missing in the episode aired. Consequently, the motivations and interrelations of the four students were unknown qualities, [and] potential viewers who have been hearing how promising the series was might well wonder what all the shouting was about."

The replacement episode, which was originally intended for the show's fifth week, revolved around Kotter's attempt to prove the humanity of his charges by entering them in a debate against the school's "good" students. The subject at hand is "humans are naturally aggressive," and the Sweathogs, living proof of that notion, wipe the floor with the opposition simply by provoking their foes' star into attacking them.

In the context of what had already been shot, "The Great Debate" was actually a very good episode. But cold-calling a nation that had been led to believe that *Welcome Back, Kotter* promised something more than a dysfunctional remake of *Room 222*, it stopped short. *Kotter* was nailed firmly to the cross of infamy. Commented Leslie Halliwell, the doyen of British television critics, "The studio audience makes it seem funnier than it is: the characters are really a bunch of morons."

Commenting upon the Boston affiliate's decision not to air the program, *The New York Times* television critic, John O'Connor opined, "after tonight the station has a better excuse. The show stinks. When the laugh track sounds as if it is on the verge of a nervous breakdown, the show is in trouble. *Welcome Back, Kotter* is in trouble."

Or it would have been, perhaps, if Vinnie Barbarino had not risen so quickly above the detritus of plot and dialogue and taken a nation's heart by storm.

The process started slowly, although by its second week *Welcome Back, Kotter* had already improved its rating, climbing to twenty-fifth in the week's Nielsen ratings. Still, the first that many people knew of the show's sudden transformation from the creaking vehicle for a stand-up comic to the launching pad for a new teen idol was when Travolta himself realized that his own fashion sense was being hijacked for the high street.

"I'd taken a publicity picture wearing a shirt with mismatching buttons on the cuffs," he smirked. "Now my agent's niece says all her friends in junior high are wearing mismatching buttons on their shirts. If the girls can't go out with Vinnie Barbarino, they want their boyfriends to look like him," he reasoned. "Vinnie's the sex symbol of his school, even though he's dumb."

Soon the *Welcome Back, Kotter* gang realized that their audience was perceiving the show much differently than they had anticipated. The sudden demand for John to appear in television commercials confirmed it. He had always made a comfortable enough living from commercials—Marilu Henner still remembers the day he burst into her room waving a check for $181, residuals from one advertisement or another, and demanded she help him spend it all at once. But it had never been like this. Back in New York, commercials paid the rent, and a little more besides. Now, he was being offered crazy money, anything up to $50,000, simply for a few thirty second spots. John turned them down.

"They actually did offer me that much money, but they wanted me to do a whole account, which wasn't optimum for me because it would have overexposed me to an extent that could hurt," he reasoned. He couldn't necessarily afford to turn that kind of money down, he clarified, "but I had to in order to keep my integrity as an actor."

But as his personal fame soared, singlehandedly dragging *Welcome Back, Kotter* up the weekly ratings, that integrity was surely already at a premium. Knowing they were onto a winner, ABC commenced merchandising the Kotter name as though there were no tomorrow—let alone another season! *Kotter* trading cards, action figures, a board game, a Kotter's classroom play set . . . beyond the realms of science fiction programming, never before had a TV show inspired such a wealth of toys and gimmickry.

The onslaught caught everybody off guard, John in particular. "I didn't quite expect the show to be the hit it is," he admitted, dazed, at the time. "I didn't think it could get to be this big. It's crazy!" *Welcome Back, Kotter* was still marching triumphantly through its first season when the ABC studios had to ban girls aged eighteen and under from the tapings. "Their screaming interfered with it," Travolta laughed. "Now they have to have IDs showing they're eighteen or over. Personally, I think the girls over eighteen do the screaming."

He was equally amazed by the impact *Welcome Back, Kotter* seemed to have on the real-life equivalents of the high school kids it portrayed. The show, he saw, "gives hope to people. Teachers have written to me to say they use Kotter's techniques to help kids express themselves. After watching the show, whether it's because they want to act like us or what, kids write that they *want* to go to school."

Modestly, John would insist that the show's success was down to a combination of factors, the strength of the whole team paramount among them. Outside of ABC's democratically-minded ranks (and pay scale), however, few people doubted that without John, *Welcome Back, Kotter* would have been lucky to survive until Christmas. Like so many fledgling shows, it had taken a while for *Welcome Back, Kotter* to find its feet; with the additional handicapping of its so-called controversial nature, an entire season's worth of story ideas had needed revamping—and that took time. Vinnie Barbarino bought that time.

Indeed, by Christmas, the most testing time for new network series, *Welcome Back, Kotter* was standing so firmly on its own two feet that ABC had no compunction whatsoever about moving it to a tougher time slot. Its regular place after *Happy Days* had, in any event, been earmarked for the show's first spin-off, *Laverne and Shirley*; *Welcome Back, Kotter* moved to Thursdays at 8:00 P.M., head to head with that everyday tale of simple, pious, country folk, *The Waltons*.

The Sweathogs didn't even blanch, and when the 1975-76 season's ratings were compiled at the end of April, their confidence was justified. *Welcome Back, Kotter* was firmly entrenched in eighteenth place, with a 22.1 share of the market. *The Waltons* was ranked a mere .8 share higher.

John's sudden pre-eminence was the combination of many factors. His looks and the air of apparent vulnerability that permeated his character Vinnie Barbarino's "tough kid" exterior marked him instantly appealing to the teenage pin-up magazines, but those qualifications in themselves suffice only if there is room for more teenybait in the first place. Fortunately, in 1975 America, there was.

The mid-1970s was a good time for teen idols. A decade on from the wave of Beatlemania that had so dramatically washed away all before it, it suddenly seemed as though one could not turn on the television without encountering another good-looking young man with an easy smile and an overworked mailman.

Indeed, although music was the medium in which the most lasting battles were fought, in a scream-agers' iconography that stretched from the Monkees to the Jackson Five, from the *Partridge Family* to the *Brady Bunch*, and that would swiftly envelop *Kotter* as well, only one principal act, the all-singing, all-dancing, all-Mormon Osmond Brothers, had journeyed to glory without the benefit of their own prime-time TV show. They just appeared on everybody else's.

In every instance, it was plain what the attraction was. Lee Black Childers, a photographer at *16* magazine around this time, remembers most of his assignments involved "standing pop stars up against a wall, making sure their cigarettes didn't show, and rearranging the bulge in their trousers so it wouldn't scare the eight-year-olds."

The likes of David Cassidy, Donny Osmond, and Michael Jackson, the founding fathers of this new generation of teen idols, posed no such problems. Even if they had, they'd have been forgiven, for the teenybop idol was never anything so mundane as a simple star. The following at his command was almost religious in its intensity, the idol himself a shimmering godlike being whose messages might have been received by every girl on the planet but were really directed only at *you*.

There was nothing insincere about them, nothing unpredictable or dangerous. The Beatles would have been okay to date, but you would never have wanted to actually settle down with one. Donny, David, and Michael, on the other hand, were sensitive and loving, safe and predictable.

"How to fall in love with Donny . . . And make Donny fall in love with you" was a theme neither publisher nor public ever tired of. And if you didn't like Donny, next week they'd tell you how to fall in love with David, with Michael, with anyone you could possibly want to fall in love with. Even little Jimmy Osmond, the youngest, fattest, and most precocious child star of the age, was not spared.

Indeed, it was the teenybop press—in America *16* and *Tiger Beat*, in Britain *Popswop* and *Music Star*—that did the most to propagate the artists in the first place, keeping their names alive when the idols were out of sight and saturating the news stands with them when they weren't. Glossy color photos and the stars' true confessions were only part of it; a subscription to *Tiger Beat* was like having a superstar pen pal.

Not that Donny, David, and Michael had it all their own way. Spinning out of the massive popularity of the movie *American Graffiti* and the stageshow *Grease*, *Happy Days* offered a new spin on the teen idol theme: the suburban, middle-class, fundamentally '50s Cunningham family, meets the darker-than-Donny Fonz, a street-wise, leather-clad, rocker with a heart of gold.

The King of Cool, Fonzie appealed on every level—from the tough kids who could ape his imperious arrogance, to the young girls who fell for his depreciating modesty. And for the parents, there were the nostalgia-tinged anachronisms of the Fonz's life and times, the ritual importance of the soda shop, the fin-bedecked cars, and the ponytailed girls.

Vinnie Barbarino was never intended to be an update of the Fonz, just as *Welcome Back, Kotter* was not immediately targeted at the Fonz's audience. But the similarities, surburban versus urban, middle versus working class, cannot be overlooked.

Like the Fonz, Vinnie remained an anti-authoritarian figure, forever questioning both Kotter and the vice principal, Mr. Woodman, from behind the security of his leadership of the Sweathogs. Like the Fonz, his every mannerism was translated into the playground lexicon.

And like the Fonz, the actor who portrayed him was now completely divorced from anything even remotely resembling a normal life.

Since his return to Hollywood, John had been living in a small garden apartment at the Larrabee Apartments in West Hollywood, between Santa Monica and Sunset. From the outside, it was completely (and necessarily) anonymous; no name on the mailbox or on the bell, and a full-time doorman who knew exactly who could and couldn't enter. John reported, "My phone calls are screened. I never register my name or room number in a hotel I'm staying in. I have an unlisted phone. And if I go to a movie, I call up ahead and the manager sneaks me in ahead of the crowd."

Even with all this protection, however, "I still get the nuts." One morning—one of the few when he didn't have to be up at 6:00 a.m.— he was awakened by an eighteen-year-old fan hammering on the door of his apartment and refusing to leave even after he threatened to call the police. So that's what he did.

Although its security was neither ideal nor foolproof, his apartment did offer some sanctuary, and John, leaving Vinnie Barbarino's impeccable fashion sense at the door, made the most of it.

Jerry Wurms roomed with him, and he admitted, "We're kind of like the *Odd Couple*. I'm the neat one, John's the slob. He leaves his socks where they fall on the floor, and he never puts his dishes in the sink."

Hidden by a hedgerow and overlooking a small courtyard, the apartment itself was casually scattered with what a visiting *Time* reporter described as "Spanish-style furniture [that] looks as if it had been borrowed from a Holiday Inn. The walls are a nondescript orange and brown, the carpet is forgettable green. A psychiatrist would have a hard start if he tried to analyze John Travolta from the way he has decorated his apartment."

John had the entire place refurbished after reading that, although in truth, the apartment simply reflected the kind of things John cared most deeply about at the time.

Parked outside were the 1955 Thunderbird and black motorcycle bought with the proceeds of his immediate fame. And in an unused bedroom, a pinball table was piled high with model airplanes, the vintage airliners that had inspired John's other great childhood dreams. His only regret was that there wasn't room to keep his other prize posses-sion, the single-engine two-seater Aircoupe aircraft he'd just picked up for five thousand dollars.

The only other thing one noticed about his apartment was the massive amount of mail he received, an average, ABC announced, of ten thousand letters a week. Even the Fonz didn't get that much.

"It's mostly from girls between the ages of thirteen and eighteen," John explained. "They write a great deal about love, some even offer marriage proposals. But I don't want to go into it any deeper than that and get myself into trouble. You can use your imagination." Before long, he had to hire a company to handle his fan mail. "I don't have enough money to answer 10,000 letters a week myself—think what the stamps would cost!"

Most of John's fan mail was addressed to him personally; it was odd, he mused, but adults were the worst at confusing his fictional character with the real thing. Deferring to the importance of the teen press in his rise, he acknowledged, "The kids are more familiar with John, and the adults will call me Barbarino, which is sort of strange. You'd think it would be the opposite way around. But the teenagers care more about who the performer is. They want to know, 'who is that guy playing Barbarino?' At least, it seems that way."

John would have plenty of opportunity to test that theory as *Kotter*'s first season marched on.

4

◇◇◇

Making Records

K*otter*'s schedule was light: "I could do it in my sleep," John once remarked, only half-joking. "I work about three or four hours a day, then do a dress rehearsal on Monday and tape the show on Tuesday." Two decades later, too, he would remark, "It was the easiest job in the world. You get two full hard days during the week and the other three are spent playing with your friends and reading scripts you want to mess around with. It's kind of like the *Saturday Night Live* group. It's a great gig, especially when you're starting out."

Around such a workload, it was easy for Bob LeMond and his growing coterie of assistants to organize a series of increasingly lucrative promotional tours for John—so many that within two years, even before *Saturday Night Fever*, *Time* magazine estimated John's annual income to be in the region of half a million dollars. Kaplan did much the same, taking his portrayal of Mr. Kotter to a string of stand-up shows in Las Vegas, Lake Tahoe, and Atlantic City. But he played to adults who wanted a laugh. John's audience and its demands were very different.

"Before *Kotter*," one of those newly recruited aides, Lois Zetter, observed, "John was merely lovable, someone you wanted to hug. After *Kotter*, he suddenly became gorgeous and sexy"—and very, very marketable.

Zetter was employed to handle a surprising, but perhaps

inevitable, dimension of John's career—music. Although he had proven his vocal prowess in both *Grease* and *Over Here*, John had never shown, or even felt, any inclination to add Professional Musician to his resumé. Nevertheless, shortly after his singing voice was heard for the first time on the *Over Here* soundtrack, John went into the studio with producers Bob Reno and John Davis to record a handful of songs.

The results were not especially spectacular. John's voice rarely gelled with the distinctly middle-of-the-road material and arrangements he was offered, and the resulting tapes had been languishing on the shelf ever since. Not only that, but John had tuned his tonsils in public only once since, turning in a brief chorus of the Beach Boys' evergreen "Barbara Ann" in an episode of *Kotter*—suitably amending the lyrics, of course, to "Barbar-ino."

Paralleling John's rise, producer Bob Reno's fortunes had also sky-rocketed. His record label, Midland International, was picked up for distribution by the giant RCA group, and in late 1974 a Brooklyn singer whom Reno had been working with, Carol Douglas, hit the charts with a song called "Doctor's Orders."

Next, the German dance band Silver Convention slammed to number one with the infectious "Fly, Robin Fly" and came close to repeating the feat when their follow-up single, "Get Up and Boogie," made number two. Midland International was on a roll, and in February 1976, Lois Zetter announced that they had contracted John to record his first solo record.

It was a no-lose situation. *Welcome Back, Kotter* proved that John was capable of instilling wild delight in the hearts of a nation's youth; the commercial success of the *Kotter* spin-off novelties demonstrated how that delight could be translated into dollars.

Critically, too, John's musical pedigree was unimpeachable. Despite being so suddenly launched onto precisely the same campaign trail as David "Keith Partridge" Cassidy before him and David "Starsky and Hutch" Soul shortly after, it was clear that John was no overnight sensation sticking a less-talented oar into unfamiliar waters as was so often the case with singing actors—and acting singers.

Grease and *Over Here* had proven that John was a vocal star long before he hit television fame. As far as Bob Reno was concerned, John represented one of the healthiest investments he had made in a long time. All he needed now was the right kind of material—and it was already sitting on the shelf.

Blending the 1974 sessions with newer material, the *John Travolta* album emerged in March 1976 as a warm-hearted collection of light-weight ballads and mock-rockers: Eric Carmen's "Never Gonna Fall in Love Again," Neil Sedaka's "I Don't Know What I Like about You, Baby," George Benson's "Let Her In," and so on. In a way, that was its downfall—as a listening experience if not as a marketable item. The record sold like hotcakes, but the charts only tell you how many people took it home. They don't mention how often the record was played once they got it there.

John Travolta was pure easy listening. Although John, like so many TV teen idols, doubtless made the album with the best intentions and highest hopes, the overall impression was of a certain facelessness. The *John Travolta* album said a lot about what John's producer and record company wanted him to sound like, but it didn't say much about how John himself wanted to sound.

John admitted as much when, although his favorite singer was Barbra Streisand and Joe Cocker's "You Are So Beautiful" was his favorite hit the previous year, he confessed, "I don't like contemporary music that well." He conceded that country and western was some-times "interesting," and he professed a fondness for the Latino sounds of Sergio Mendes. But, he said, "My taste is not a set thing. Whatever appeals to me at the time."

Despite his own apparent uncertainty and the album's own general mundanity, *John Travolta* cracked the American Top 40 in May 1976 just as his first single, "Let Her In," commenced its rise into the Top 10. Both rode on the same wave of adulation that simultaneously pro-pelled *Kotter's* theme music, John Sebastian's "Welcome Back," to number one. Resplendent in a neat crimson sweater, John celebrated with an appearance on *American Bandstand*, the first of two appearances he would make on the show.

May 1976 also saw *Welcome Back, Kotter* wrestle back some of its young star's spotlight when it was nominated for an Emmy in the Outstanding Comedy Series category. It lost out, perhaps inevitably, to the all-conquering *Mary Tyler Moore Show*, but there was no shame in losing.

Indeed, in the face of such success, John was positively deluged by suggestions of how he should spend his summer vacation, everything from a nonstop publicity tour for the album to another wagonload of advertising contracts. Strange, then, that he should choose instead to tour New England with the play *Bus Stop*, appearing alongside actress Anita Gillete and sisters Ann and Ellen.

At least, that's what the money men reckoned. Bob Reno at Midland International was especially displeased. "When the record albums came out," the increasingly reluctant singing sensation admitted, "I was really pressured to do personal appearance tours, promoting them." The money was fabulous as well—up in the region of $25,000 per appearance. Finally, John relented, agreeing to a handful of carefully orchestrated personal appearances.

The results were predictably chaotic. In Cleveland, more than five thousand fans mobbed him. In Schaumburg, Illinois, visiting what was then the world's biggest shopping mall, an estimated thirty thousand people turned out to catch a glimpse of their idol. When he visited a mall in New Jersey, two thousand copies of the album were sold in an hour. Another appearance in a Long Island department store drew a crowd of ten thousand and became so chaotic that John had to be whisked away disguised as a policeman. In June, Midland International took out a full-page advertisement in *Billboard* magazine, simply to trumpet these triumphs to the world.

"New York's been sold! L.A.'s been sold! The Travolta phenomenon has taken the nation by storm! In Chicago, over 25,000 cheering fans packed parking lots just to catch a glimpse of their newfound hero." The ad claimed sales of more than 100,000 copies for the album in just two weeks, with the single "Let Her In" selling even stronger.

All John had to do was sit there and sign autographs.

In the wake of the hysteria, John's urge to return to the basics of his craft was even stronger. With that in mind, *Bus Stop* was really a shrewd decision, one that would keep him in the public eye (which, as the predominantly juvenile audiences indicated, was also *his* public's eye) at the same time reaffirming his own serious acting credentials.

Although it might be better-known today for Marilyn Monroe's 1956 movie version, William Inge's play is something of a sacred cow in American theater lore, and John's performance was to come under intense scrutiny for any signs of either irreverence or, even worse, Vinnie Barbarino-like irrelevance. He passed the test with flying colors.

"I wanted to act and the guy in this play is a real naive cowboy. It was a chance to fight that [typecasting] thing, play a western dude instead of all these urban types."

The downside to the tour was that John was virtually a prisoner in his dressing room. The one time he did try to get out, taking a girl-friend to a disco, the place was literally overrun by fans anxious to catch a glimpse of him.

Time magazine caught *Bus Stop*'s matinee performance at the Lakewood, Maine, summer theater. The audience was composed of "mainly thick-thighed teenagers with braces on their teeth," who spent the first twenty minutes of the play, until John arrived onstage, "clutch-ing each other, ecstatic with anticipation.

"Then the star of the show loped onstage, wearing skintight jeans and a white sombrero. 'My name is Bo Decker and I'm twenty-one years old. Everywhere I go, I got all the women.'

"The audience squealed." And kept on squealing until long after John left the theater.

"I can't believe the reaction!" John said with amazement. "The only thing I can compare it to, and I never thought I'd be saying this, is the reception for the Beatles, because those girls went bananas! Girls are fainting when I make a public appearance. It's bizarre!"

It was even more bizarre when that madness hit Ridgefield, a few miles down the road from John's home town, Englewood. Brother Sam now lived there, and that summer he arranged a fundraiser for the local Little League. Joey Travolta had already been booked to emcee; nobody expected that the third Travolta brother would also fly in for a surprise guest appearance. Their mother Helen later compared the results to sheer "Fourth of July madness."

With John's popularity, of course, there came problems. He had auditioned for a part in Terrence Malik's *Days of Heaven*, in a role he described as "James Dean's *East of Eden* and Warren Beatty's *Splendour in the Grass*" combined. But no sooner was he informed that he had won the part than ABC informed him that shooting conflicted day-for-day with the Sweathogs' Christmas special.

"It's a mess," John complained. But if *Days of Heaven* fell through—which it did—he swore he wouldn't fret. "When your bat-ting average is as good as mine," he told *Time*, playing up the Vinnie Barbarino swagger, "there's nothing to be really nervous about!"

Indeed there wasn't. Barely had John so reluctantly turned down *Days of Heaven*, than ABC made amends by casting him in the made-for-TV movie, *The Boy in the Plastic Bubble*. He would play the boy.

The Boy in the Plastic Bubble is the story of Todd, a young man born with such severe immunity deficiencies that he is forced to live his life in a specially controlled bubble environment, praying for the day when his body might finally develop the immunities it lacked.

It was an interesting role, though not, perhaps, for the reasons one might immediately assume. Despite his disability, the character was not really that different from Vinnie Barbarino—a bit smarter, maybe, and certainly a lot less savvy. But deep down inside, Todd was just as anarchic.

Attending school via closed-circuit television, he gleefully mocks the teacher and lets his friends crib his test answers by writing them on a chalkboard and holding them up to the camera. He could have run Barbarino close in the braggadocio stakes as well. No soon-er have Todd's doctors provided him with a special suit that will enable him to leave his bubble than he is challenging another boy to a push-up competition.

And yet, despite his apparent confidence and the knowledge he was America's favorite pin-up at the time, John walked onto the set a mass of insecure nerves. His mother, Helen, recalled, "it was his first serious film, and he was so eager for acceptance that when the wardrobe mistress said he was doing a good job, he waited for her every morning to praise her for the clothes she'd chosen." Even though he spent most of the movie in nothing more than a T-shirt and shorts and the rest walking round in a fetching orange space suit, John was grate-ful. "He felt that every compliment had to be returned."

Sparkling in a cast headlined by Robert (Mike Brady) Reed and Diana Hyland, John could have spent a lifetime repaying the myriad compliments he received after *The Boy in the Plastic Bubble* aired, with-in ABC's *Friday Night Movie* series November 12, 1976. Personally, however, there were but two true highlights to the production—meet-ing astronaut Buzz Aldrin, who gave him a signed photograph ("To

John, enjoyed our ball in the bubble"), and Diana Hyland, the tiny blond actress who played his screen mother.

Onlookers watching the interaction between the forty-year-old Diana and her twenty-two-year-old screen son could not mistake the chemistry that sparked between them; they would spend hours huddled together, quietly talking. Not until the wrap party did the couple admit, even to one another, that there was more than friendship involved.

"On the first meeting, I was just incredibly attracted to this woman," John sighed. "I saw the whole picture in her first ten words—depth, intelligence, beauty, perceptiveness. She had gone through a rough marriage, a lot of career ups and downs, and had come out at peace with herself. It was very sexy. The most important things were the relationships in her life. She really savored the people around her."

Now, as the *Bubble* cast party petered out, the couple "sort of kissed," as John delicately puts it, then waved good-bye. And just as he had after he first met Bob LeMond, he spent the next month wondering whether he should call her.

By his own confession, at the time he met Diana John had been seriously doubting whether he would ever have a successful relationship with another person. His drive and his ambition were his best friends in his career but his worst enemies in love. He admits, "I had almost decided to quit looking for anyone special. Then she came along and was so dynamic, I knew I had to spend time with her."

Diana, recently divorced with a three-year-old son, Zachary, understood how he felt. "She told me that she, too, had thought the same thing. Then, bam. I have never been more in love with anyone in my life. I thought I was in love before, but I wasn't."

Even when Diana told him that she was suffering from cancer and had already lost a breast to the malignancy, John knew that it wasn't important. Besides, the illness itself was in remission. She might never be ill again. The doubts John was having were all his own.

He called sister Ellen to tell her about Diana, sounding her out on the subject before admitting, "if I go into this relationship, I'm going in all the way. I'm just so scared. I don't want to be hurt again." The memories of Denise Wurms, Marilu Henner, and Joan Prather still haunted him.

Ellen simply asked him what his heart said.

"Diana broke my heart from the start, but it took a month before I decided to be with her," John later reflected. What convinced him, he explained, was "when she said it didn't matter whether or not we were together romantically—that she could have me either way, sexually or just as a friend. That was the deciding point, when I realized she appreciated me as a person, rather than just as a young stud. Then I said 'Alright, I can do this.'"

Ellen herself was overjoyed. "Diana was so classy, so dynamic, so good! She was everything Johnny ever dreamed a lady could be. No one ever loved him the way she did." Ellen and Diana, in fact, would become close friends in their own right. Ellen would also be the one to reassure her parents about John's choice of ladyfriend. The seventeen-year age gap was not something they could overlook in a hurry, but "Ellen told us how wonderful Diana was," Sal recalled, and he believed her. "'And don't forget,' she concluded, 'Johnny's been a very lonesome boy. This woman is making him happy.'"

John still cannot fully express that happiness. "There was something about her—a quality I can't define even now—that I found so appealing. It exceeded anything physical. She had every color I've ever imagined in a person."

Like John, Diana's career began while she was still at high school, although she credited it to chance more than anything else. She was fifteen when a photograph of her attending a baseball game appeared in her local, Cleveland Heights, newspaper.

"Two film companies saw the photograph," Diana later explained, "and invited me to New York for interviews."

She was not signed by either, but her interest was piqued. After high school graduation, she joined the Rabbit Run Theater in Madison, Ohio, following up with lessons at Lee Strasbourg's famed drama studio. She made her television debut in an episode of the long-running dramatic anthology *Robert Montgomery Presents*, and later landed a part in the fondly remembered medical series, *Young Dr. Malone.*

Swiftly proving herself equally at home on small and silver screen, Diana first hit national prominence in 1963, when she received an Emmy nomination for her performance in the drama,

The Voice of Charlie Pont. Later in the decade, she enjoyed a season in the seminal *Peyton Place*, playing Susan Winter, wife of Tom, the philandering minister.

Seldom settling in any role for long, Diana would divide the next near-decade between television, movies, and stage. By the time *The Boy in the Plastic Bubble* was broadcast, she had made a firm commitment to a full-length series, ABC's *Eight Is Enough*, the story of a married couple with eight headstrong children. Filming would begin in the new year. In the meantime, she watched as John's career continued to rocket upward, beginning with the return of *Welcome Back, Kotter*, in September 1976.

Welcome Back, Kotter opened its second season much as it had closed its first. Debralee Scott, who played the effervescently "easy" Rosalie Totzi, had moved on to *Mary Hartman, Mary Hartman*, but apart from that, little had changed. The Sweathogs were still the toughest, funniest, hippest kids in James Buchanan High, Mr. Kotter was still the only teacher who could match them thrust for thrust, and Mr. Woodman was still the New York Board of Education's answer to the Wicked Witch of the West.

If there was any change in format, it was to accommodate John's increasing fame and fortune. Regardless of any stipulations he may have made (and people connected with the show insist that he made few demands for special treatment), the producers could not help but be aware of his importance to the show's popularity if not to its plotlines.

The best lines, though Vinnie's character demanded that they be short and preferably monosyllabic, began falling his way, and that, in turn, required a re-evaluation of the show's style.

Conscious that John could not reasonably usurp Kaplan's role as the show's primary funny man, the team of writers who worked to keep *Kotter* on course turned their attention more and more toward real-life crises and events. They were preparing the way, after a fashion, for the real world that the show's high school audience would have to face before the series got much older. Jealousy, ambition, violence, and vice would all raise their heads during this second season, and although both the presentation and the resolution seldom deviated from standard sitcom fodder, there was a rough edge to the show that at least removed it from the cuddly confines of its debut year.

John reciprocated by broadening his own take on Vinnie. "In the beginning, I was a one-dimensional character, a sort of young playboy. Vinnie has grown since the show began. Now I play across a whole range of feelings."

Indeed, there was to be a broadening of character across the Sweathogs dimension, most notably in the portrayal of the ever-wearisome and whiny Arnold Horshack.

Emboldened by the runaway success of the *Happy Days* spin-off *Laverne and Shirley*, ABC had already been exploring the possibility of a *Kotter* spin-off for some time when writers Jerry and Jewel Jaffe Rannow approached them with the idea of a series based around the Horshack family.

Hints dropped throughout previous episodes had already presented the Horshacks as a remarkably diverse, if not demented, bunch. Now, across a two-part episode in which Horshack disappears from rehearsals for the school play, a storyline developed out of the death of the boy's stepfather, his mother's fifth husband. Arnold left school, it transpired, so that he could become the man of the house.

Anxious, of course, not to divorce this new series from the goose that had already laid so many golden eggs, ABC offered the role of Mrs. Horshack to John's sister, Ellen. Though she had long since retired to raise a family of her own, her experiences on the road with John in *Bus Stop* had been enough to reawaken her ambition. Her kids, John's oldest nephews, were ten and thirteen now, and although Ellen initially returned to the stage simply on a lark, she soon found she had the bug once again.

Unfortunately, the new show was not to be. Although the episode itself worked well, the expansion plans did not. But the studio retained Ellen. Not only had she proven herself to be a great comic actress, but the studio heads were convinced you could never have too many Travoltas on hand.

Coinciding with the return of *Welcome Back, Kotter*, Midland International released John's second single, "Whenever I'm Away from You." It would not prove as big a hit as its predecessor, clambering no higher up the chart than number thirty-eight, but still John had made a sufficient enough impression for both *Billboard* and *Record World &*

Music Retail magazines to award him the title of New Pop Male Vocalist of the Year.

John tends now to dismiss his flirtation with rock 'n' roll stardom, reflecting, "I was a Broadway performer and I know how to sing and I've done recordings. But my primary career is in acting. I love singing. I'll always love singing. I sing for myself all the time outside the shower. I'm very proud of the successes I've had as a singer. But they were usually, other than one or two, songs correlated to a movie that I was in. So I never took my singing on the same level as acting, because I felt it was a by-product more than it was the product."

And the product was doing very well for itself. November 1976 brought not only the premiere of *The Boy in the Plastic Bubble* but also the release of John's second movie, a starring role in Brian DePalma's adaptation of horror wunderkind Stephen King's first major novel, *Carrie*.

Shot back to back with *The Boy in the Plastic Bubble*, *Carrie* is the story, as author King himself put it, of the "browbeaten" teenaged daughter (well-played in the movie by Sissy Spacek) of a religious fanatic mother, whose "mild telekinetic ability intensifies after her first menstrual period." Her newfound powers have lethal results for the schoolkids who have mocked and bullied her for as long as she can remember. John plays Billy Nolan, the wisecracking, dumb-bell, thug boyfriend of *Carrie*'s chief antagonist, Chris (Nancy Allen).

It was a strangely muted role for an actor so hot; although the celluloid Billy Nolan remains as pivotal as the original novel required, he nevertheless remains largely undeveloped; King himself remarked that Nolan, "a major—and frightening—character in the book," is reduced to nothing more than "a semi-supporting role in the movie." The observation suggests that whatever motives Brian DePalma may have had in casting such a high-profile young actor in his film, they had little to do with his acting abilities.

Throughout *Carrie*'s 100 minutes, John is on screen for little more than twenty, including his demise in a fiery car wreck. Indeed, his greatest moment comes when he breaks into a local pig farm to batter one of its inmates on the head with a sledgehammer. "You won't have to worry about the bomb anymore," he assures his victim as he strikes the first blow.

Where John's performance in *Carrie* is essential to an examination of his subsequent career is in its crystallization of the high school jock character that would follow him through the next two years. *Carrie* gave John the confidence to shake off some of Vinnie Barbarino's inane goofiness and replace it with a more realistic sense of street-smarts; while John's Danny Zuko, the star of the movie version of *Grease*, could well have been Billy Nolan's big brother. And of course, any one of those boys could have grown up to be Jack Teri, Scott Barnes, Vincent Vega, or Chili Palmer.

Enclitic as the punk image became, John still insists, "It isn't me, never was. But it fascinates me in others. The seduction of dangerous charm. People that can hurt you and maybe burn you, and you know you ought to steer clear but somehow, you keep falling in." Journalist Nik Cohn later called this fascination "an affinity of darkness," but Billy Nolan was darker than most.

John reasoned, "The guy is a punk, but I wanted to work with Brian DePalma. I knew the picture itself would be interesting, attract a lot of attention. And it was a small part, I didn't think I'd get much attention. And I didn't."

Actually, he did. Off camera, for example, it was widely rumored that John and Nancy Allen were enjoying as steamy a relationship as they did when they were on. The pair lived just blocks from one another at the time and frequently arrived at the studio together early in the morning. Their protests that they were simply carpooling cut little ice with the gossips, which makes it all the more ironic that John had already paired his costar off with somebody else—even if neither she nor her prospective paramour, director DePalma, were aware of it at the time.

"I was insecure and a little intimidated by Brian," Nancy said of the man who would become her husband. "But John would always pump me up and say, 'You were terrific in that scene. People are really going to be surprised when they see you,'" and always in DePalma's hearing. She remembers how she and John would go out of their way to entertain him during filming, and John reflected later, "Even though we had smaller parts, I think Brian liked us best." One evening, DePalma joined the pair for dinner; once he'd gone home, John told Nancy, "He likes you. He *really* likes you." Three months after *Carrie* wrapped, Brian and Nancy started dating. They were married in 1979.

On release in November 1976, *Carrie* received an "R" rating, which meant that for much of John's core *Kotter* audience, both the film and the sight of their hero receiving a very talkative blow job from Ms. Allen were technically out-of-bounds. In a sense, this proved helpful, since it ensured that John's cinematic past would remain something of a secret from his biggest fans until he was ready to leap fully formed onto the silver screen.

And that jump was not far off.

He had just turned down an offer to appear in *Midnight Express*, Alan Parker and Oliver Stone's sensational study of a young American jailed in Turkey for drug smuggling, when toward the end of 1976 it was announced that John had signed a million-dollar contract to make three movies for the Robert Stigwood Organization (RSO)—he would be starring in all three.

It was precisely what John and Bob LeMond had been working toward—the end result of all those auditions, all those hours hanging around cold sets waiting for the camera, all those weeks spent being Vinnie Barbarino and Billy Nolan. It was almost crushingly perverse, then, that it was not John's acting abilities that had attracted Stigwood's attention in the first place. It was "Let Her In."

"If I hadn't done that record, my career would have been much different," John laughed years later. He had recently been written up in *Time* magazine, a portrait of the young man with the number-three song in the country and the number-one comedy show. Stigwood and his partner, Allan Carr, read the article, and the rest became history.

Over the previous decade, Australian-born Robert Stigwood had established himself among the most successful and influential men in show business. His RSO empire encompassed everything from theater and concerts to management and music publishing. In the rock music field, where he was still best-known, Stigwood first came to prominence as a record producer before joining Beatles manager Brian Epstein at the helm of Epstein's NEMS Enterprises. After Epstein died in the summer of 1967, Stigwood struck out on his own, managing such internationally renowned acts as the Bee Gees and Cream—whose guitarist, Eric Clapton, Stigwood would subsequently steer to even greater success as a solo artist.

Stigwood moved into theater in 1968, when he staged the American rock musical *Hair* in London. He followed it with the production of *Jesus Christ, Superstar*, for which an unknown John Travolta had been unceremoniously passed over, and the controversial *Oh! Calcutta*, historically remembered as the first nude musical to play Broadway.

RSO moved into movies in 1973, when Stigwood became coproducer of Norman Jewison's film version of *Jesus Christ, Superstar*. Two years later, Stigwood's production of the Who's rock opera, *Tommy*, ran out among the year's highest-grossing films—at a time when cinema audiences were best drawn by such monster-budget extravaganzas as *Jaws* and *The Towering Inferno*. Clearly he had the Midas touch, and the word around Hollywood was that if Stigwood was contemplating gearing an entire sequence of movies around one barely-tried young actor, it was obvious that the actor must be something special. Stigwood was not renowned for patronizing losers.

5

◇◇◇

Tragedy Strikes and
the Fever Builds

When English journalist Nik Cohn began to document the disco culture that he had seen spread like spilt beer across Brooklyn's danceclub floors, he could never have dreamed what it would eventually become. Certainly "Tribal Rites of the New Saturday Night," the resulting essay, had nothing in common with the dream that had taken him into Robert Stigwood's office six months before.

According to Stigwood, Cohn had dropped by to talk to him about the possibility of writing a movie.

"I said, 'OK, if you have an idea, come and see me again and we'll talk about it.' Six months later I picked up *New York* magazine and saw this cover story and Nik's name, so I immediately read it. And I thought, 'this is a wonderful film subject.'" No sooner had he put down the article than he was raging on the phone to Cohn.

"You're crazy! You come to me about writing a story for a picture. This is it!" Then he called Cohn's agent about acquiring the film rights to the story. Within twenty-four hours, the deal was done.

"Tribal Rights of the New Saturday Night," the essay from which *Saturday Night Fever* would eventually emerge, was a strong theme for a film, although it needed a mind like Stigwood's, forever alert to the incidentals others might easily overlook, to spot its potential. Cohn's style of writing is journalism at its best: fast, but

never rushed; easy, but never lazy; informative, but never schoolmas-
terly. At his best—the rock 'n' roll history *Pop from the Beginning*
and the New York City travel guide *Heart of the City*—Cohn brings
an almost fictional feel to the facts at hand, transforming the driest
tidbit into fascinating anecdote, creating images that linger long
after the page is turned.

So it was with "Tribal Rights of the New Saturday Night." Cohn
is the observer, but the reader is in the room watching the blue-collar
Brooklynites hop and hustle across the floor, living out a fantasy of
their own creation that's nevertheless as real as the paychecks they collected that week—and that they'll probably blow that night.

Cohn wrote a preliminary script based on this original article that
laid the foundations of the world into which screenwriter Norman
Wexler would introduce Tony Manero. Wexler's character is an Italian-
American who whiles away his days in the paint store where he works
and his nights in a bedroom decorated with posters of Rocky, Al
Pacino, and Farrah Fawcett-Majors. He runs with a gang, he fights with
his parents, and exactly like the lost souls who populated Cohn's essay,
he lives for just one thing: the disco every Saturday night.

Robert Stigwood was as certain that John Travolta was the man
for the role as he was that the role was right for the cinema. He remembered John from the *Superstar* auditions, "and I was intrigued a few
years later to see him pop up on *Welcome Back, Kotter*. I could see the
potential building in him, so I offered him a firm three-picture deal,
pay or play, guarantee of a million dollars." At the press conference
Stigwood staged to announce John's recruitment, the actor made a quip
that has remained with Stigwood ever since. "I auditioned for him five
years ago, and I just heard back."

Of more interest to the media, of course, was that million-dollar
deal. Broken down across three movies, it evened out at a mere
$333,000 per film, a pittance compared to what some Hollywood stars
commanded. Still, John was forced to deal with persistent rumors that
he was now a millionaire. He denied it, but he did admit that he
"could" be one in a couple of years. "In the meantime, I love the publicity that makes me out to be one now. It's fun to see your future
spread out in front of you."

He earned a lot of money, John confessed, but not as much as people thought. "Last year I was living in a one bedroom apartment. For the amount of money that was coming in, I was no better off than I was seven years ago in New York. By the time I get my paycheck, there's not much left. If you take the gross figures, you'd think I was rolling in money. But the breakdown would astound you. I pay fifty percent of my income to managers, business managers, lawyers, agents, secretaries, and staff. Of the remaining fifty percent, I'm in a fifty percent tax bracket. That leaves me with nothing."

Well, not quite. Besides, what money he did get, he was very careful with. "A couple of my friends who had money for generations said that you should target yourself to live off your interest," John explained. "So I sat down and had a long talk with myself. I said, 'Hell John, you're allowed to change with your success. Your fans want you to change. If not, what are you working so hard for? So, instead of a house, I bought an airplane."

Actually, he bought an airliner, a commercial DC-3. The workhorse of the world's airline companies ever since its introduction in 1935, the DC-3, John reminisced, was "the first true airliner. It depended just on people who wanted to pick up and go someplace."

It promptly became another expense. "I go to get the plane fixed and they charge me four times the amount that was on my estimate. I know it's because of my name." On another occasion, John took his classic Thunderbird in for repair, "and they kept it nine months. When they see me coming, the price of parts goes up. They're not even subtle about it. They just rip me off overtly. Success turned the things I really love into nightmares. I had a potential lawsuit on my plane. I couldn't get my T-Bird out of the shop!"

He acknowledged, "The average person will probably read this and think, 'Oh, I wish I had such problems,' right? But when you're in whatever reality you're in, those are the problems."

The script for *Saturday Night Fever* was still being written when John signed up for the role. He took the job on the strength of Cohn's essay alone, and he admits that when a finished script finally reached him he wondered what he had gotten himself into.

"I was in the middle of the TV show, I was too close to Barbarino, and all Tony looked like to me was an extension of him." He read late into the night with a frown so deeply etched into his face that Diana could finally stand it no longer. "Give it to me," she demanded. "I'll let you know if it's any good."

An hour later, she burst back into the room. "Baby, you are going to be great in this! This Tony, he's got all the colors. First he's angry about something, he hates the trap that Brooklyn and his dumb job are. There's a whole glamorous world out there waiting that he feels only when he dances. And he grows, he gets out of Brooklyn."

John smiled at the recollection. "She went on like that for a long time. 'He's miles from what you've played, and what isn't in the script, you're going to put there.'" And when John brought up the fact that Manero was the king of disco, "and I'm not that good a dancer," she simply snapped back, "Baby, you're going to learn." The next day, John began taking lessons with the disco dance troupe Dancing Machine.

Concentrating on what Diana told him, John put his own mind deep inside Tony's head. He realized that Tony's just a guy "who wants something more out of life than his surroundings offer him. He knows he has the potential to go ahead, but he doesn't know how. He has a fear that his life is crumbling." The disco is the only place where he can face that fear—and vanquish it.

Two years later, writer Albert Goldman said, "The Travolta hero is that archetypal modern figure, the half-conscious but instinctively attuned narcissist. His ancestors stem not so much from the silver screen as the silver mike: the extravagantly exhibitionistic and charismatic heroes of the rock age.

"Like the classic rocker, commencing with Elvis Presley and leading onto the Who's *Tommy*, the new hero [is] struggling to assert himself not so much in the world of real power and danger, but at one step from reality in the world of performance. The fact that the performance is through the mute language of dance, rather than through a jazz horn or a rock song is simply indicative of where a big part of our youth culture stands at the present moment." Or in other words, two years before it became trendy to plaster your car with "Disco Sucks" bumper stickers, disco already ruled.

The story of disco is essentially the story of a youth rebellion, but one fought without reliance on the weapons such wars were normally fought with. That was what made disco different: its easy rejection of the hackneyed representation of music as a force that could change the world. It acknowledged instead that at the end of the day it was good for just one thing—dancing to.

More than that, disco completely re-evaluated the nature of the pop music industry. Disco was the ultimate level playing surface. It abandoned the cult of the artist and the need for those artists to make lofty statements in their "art." It led by example. Disco did not, for example, go to the Rolling Stones; the Stones went to it, scoring their biggest hit of the decade with "Miss You." Likewise Rod Stewart and "Do Ya Think I'm Sexy"; likewise Blondie, whose biggest hit record actually started life under the anonymous title "Disco Song," long before the group spotted the latest Werner Herzog movie playing a few theaters down the road from *Saturday Night Fever*. It was called *Heart of Glass*. The song got a new title, and Blondie got their biggest hit.

Disco had no ego. It didn't matter who wrote the song or sang it or produced it. Nothing mattered except what could be felt on the floor. Disco had no boundaries, so it didn't recognize any. Its creators, anonymous studio wizards mainly, plundered rock, soul, jazz, even the classics, in search of simple tunes that could be fitted to its insidious beat.

As Robert Stigwood prepared *Saturday Night Fever*, or more pertinently, the soundtrack for *Saturday Night Fever*, all of these ingredients came into play. Another bumper sticker going the rounds at the time read simply, "Fuck Art, Let's Boogie." Disco was the soundtrack to a night on the town. End of story.

Still a reliable top seller today, almost twenty years after it commenced its nearly unprecedented six-month residence at the top of the U.S. chart, the two-record set that comprised the *Saturday Night Fever* album remains the ultimate soundtrack to the disco era.

Walter Murphy's dance-track take on Beethoven's Fifth Symphony, punningly titled "A Fifth of Beethoven," was a hit single more than a year before *Fever* was released. Ten minutes of The Trammps' "Disco Inferno" remain as exhausting a prospect today as they were back then. Ralph McDonald's "Calypso Breakdown" and David Shire's "Salsation" highlighted the upstart musical genre's cross-cultural plundering. And Kool & The Gang's Arabian Nights-flavored "Open Sesame" introduced some hard-nosed rhythm to the proceedings. Bat-eared listeners are still able to recall the first time they deciphered amid the din, the battle-cry of the new revolution, "I Am the Genie of Funk!"

The stars of the *Saturday Night Fever* soundtrack, however, were the Bee Gees. The group's music remains so exquisitely entwined with the movie and its star that the two are inseparable even today.

Yet only a year before *Saturday Night Fever* commenced shooting, the Bee Gees were little more than a footnote in rock history, a blast from the past whose old records—hits like "Massachusetts," "To Love Somebody," and "New York Mining Disaster, 1941"—were infinitely more likely to be played on the radio than their more recent efforts. It was with fearless tenacity that the brothers Maurice, Robin, and Barry Gibb actually survived the first half of the 1970s, a time when even Robert Stigwood's magic touch appeared to have deserted them.

All of that changed in May 1975.

Aware that the Bee Gees were no longer considered hip by a music industry sated on meaningful songs and serious messages, Stigwood's RSO record label decided to adopt the same marketing ploy they had used to promote the group's 1967 album to promote their latest single.

Copies were dispatched to America's FM radio stations, whose disdain for the Bee Gees was almost legendary, in plain sleeves with plain white labels. An accompanying note asked only that the record be played and judged by its contents. If you played it and liked it, you'd be told who it was. If you didn't, then it didn't matter, did it? By the time the artist's identity became common knowledge, "Jive Talking" was already on its way to number one.

"Jive Talking" and its album, *Main Course*, showcased a whole new direction for the Bee Gees. Working in the studio with the legendary R&B producer Arif Mardin, the trio had abandoned the sweet sounding pop of their past for an earthy, dance-inflected sound that, *Rolling Stone* remarked, "approached disco without straying too far from established pop conventions." *Main Course*, the Bee Gees' first Top Twenty album in six years, was followed by the Top Ten hit, *Children of the World*, and another chart-topping single, "You Should Be Dancing," in July 1976.

The Bee Gees were in France, recording at the semi-legendary

Chateau d'Heureville on the outskirts of Paris when Stigwood contacted them about the *Saturday Night Fever* soundtrack.

According to Barry Gibb, his message was vague at best. "We want four songs for this film." They asked him what it was about. "A bunch of guys that live in New York," he replied.

Later, of course, he expanded, even mentioning that it was a disco-based movie, but the band never once saw a script.

Maurice Gibb explained, "Robert has this funny way of giving us a challenge. Using his outline, we wrote all the songs in a very short time. It wasn't all that different from recording an album, yet at the same time we did have to keep in mind the characters and the basic plot we'd been given."

The first songs to be completed were "If I Can't Have You," a ballad they would ultimately give to singer Yvonne Elliman, and "Saturday Night, Saturday Night," an older number that would eventually metamorphose into "Staying Alive."

"There are so many bloody records out called 'Saturday Night,'" Maurice apologized when Stigwood complained that he preferred the original name. "It's corny. It's a terrible title." And if the impresario didn't like the change, Maurice added, the band would keep the song for themselves. Stigwood liked the change.

Three further songs were completed and delivered to Stigwood as rough demos; those demos were used throughout the actual filming of *Saturday Night Fever.*

Leaving Diana behind in Los Angeles, John flew to New York the fall of 1976. He was moving into an apartment building on Central Park West, taking over the lease from singers James Taylor and Carly Simon. Prior to them, John proudly related, the place had been rented by Mick Jagger—and before him, the Beatles' John Lennon.

A couple of days before he was due to move in, John dropped by the apartment. Taylor and Simon were simply moving upstairs; it seemed a neighborly thing to do. Besides, he laughingly admits, at the time James Taylor was one of his all-time heroes.

"Carly was in the hospital having a baby, and James answered the door. He said, 'I love your TV show so much, I can recite the last soliloquy of *Welcome Back, Kotter.*' I tested him and he did it. I was impressed."

Taking over occupancy of the apartment, with Taylor and Simon ever-solicitously dropping by on occasion to make sure he hadn't yet worked himself to death, John threw himself into a rigorous training regime for the film—mental as well as physical.

Disguising the face that beamed out of TV sets every week, wrapping shades round his eyes and planting big hats on his head, John joined writer Norman Wexler in making regular pilgrimages to the 2001 Oddyssey, a disco in Brooklyn where much of the filming would take place. The club owner would let them in through a side door, and John would simply lurk in the shadows, observing the dancers.

"I concentrated on every detail of their behavior I could." He quickly picked up on one essential clue: "Their whole way of dancing, moving, conversing, relating to their girls, was ritualistic. It had its set rules." It was just as Nik Cohn said it would be in his essay.

He had learned all he could from behind his sunglasses. Now John dropped the disguises. He needed to see how the discogoers would relate to him. Tony Manero, after all, would become a star in the film; John was a star already.

It usually took an hour before the first shouts of "Hey! It's fucking Travolta!" began filtering across the room. Slowly, a few guys would wander over. This was what he had come for, and this was where he learned even more.

"It was the way they'd treat their girlfriends," that John found the most illuminating. He would be talking with whoever came over, but when a girl wandered too close, their boyfriends turned on them. "They'd say, 'Hey, stay away from him, don't bug Travolta. Don't bother me, I'm talking to The Man.' And they'd actually push the girls away. Tony Manero's whole male-chauvinist thing, I got from watching those guys in the disco."

As Travolta became more familiar with the working-class club scene, he realized that class was the essence of both the movie and the disco sensation. Later commentators who missed that point clearly had no understanding of the phenomenon or what created it. In the mid to late 1970s, working-class kids were basically funneled into vocational education. There was little chance of college for them, and economic constrictions meant they wouldn't move up the social ladder. Disco gave them an outlet and made them feel important and special, unlike the nine-to-five drudgery of their everyday jobs—assuming they could find them.

Once filming began, several of these original guinea pigs were recruited as extras, and John remained alert around them. Occasionally, he was invited back to someone's house to meet his family and have a meal. He made mental notes there as well, building the nightmarish scenario of Manero's own home life from what he observed in these Brooklyn homes. The pious mother, the out-of-work father, the brother who left home to become a priest—all these characters were based on real people.

Mentally prepared, John now needed to become physically ready. "I went into training for five months, dancing three hours a day and running two miles a day. I hired the boxer who trained Sylvester Stallone for *Rocky*." He ended up shedding twenty-five pounds for the filming.

"When I started I couldn't even do one of the knee bends I do in the film. By the end of five months I had a whole new body. I don't have a high energy level, but when I read the script, I said, 'If he's supposed to be the best disco dancer, I want to be the best disco dancer.' I knew how to dance, but I wasn't that good. I really had to work to push my energy level.

"Also, I knew that a lot was riding on me. This movie is probably the most important step in my career." Three months into his training, John entered a disco dancing contest, just to find out if he was as good as he now believed. Unfortunately, he was recognized. He was roped into judging the contest instead. Still, he could compare his moves with the contestants, and he now knew for sure that he really wasn't bad.

"I worked like hell. For twelve weeks, I was up every morning at five, and didn't get home until ten at night. Then on weekends I was rehearsing the dance numbers. I needed stamina I didn't have. It was grueling."

It was also painstaking. One of the most memorable scenes in the finished movie would be the dance competition. The Bee Gees had specifically written the pounding "Night Fever" for the sequence. It was a song whose lyric encapsulated the soul of Tony Manero: you really could tell by the way he used his walk what kind of man he was. John, however, had other ideas. He had just spent five months practicing to the strains of "You Should Be Dancing." He was damned if he was going to try and adapt his routine to a completely different song.

His stance could have led to problems, but in keeping with the casual attitude with which *Saturday Night Fever* was being shot, both the Bee Gees and Stigwood agreed to John's demands. "You Should Be Dancing," after all, was an old hit of theirs, and John's routine made the whole song come alive again.

Casting continued around John's training regime, with the key role of Tony Manero's girlfriend going to Karen Lynn Gorney. Nine years John's senior, Karen was an accomplished actress, if not dancer; she had played Tara in the daytime soap *All My Children*. More importantly, she was currently dating the film's director, John Badham.

John was not initially impressed with his costar. He had been hoping Marilu Henner would land the part, going as far as to haul a supply of Marilu's photos around with him to drop into Badham's casting file whenever he got the chance. Finally, Badham agreed to let her interview, but Marilu herself believes the gesture was nothing more than a courtesy to John. "The story I heard was that I never had a shot."

Still, John fought on. At Gorney's first call, he turned to Badham and sighed, "I guess we're going to get Jessica Lange." Badham promptly sent Karen off for a new hairdo, then asked her to join him at John's apartment to go through the script. "And that's all it took for John," Badham insisted afterward. When he left to go home, Karen and John were still deep in conversation.

Other roles were less fraught. John's sister Ann was given a brief speaking appearance at the start of the film. When she asks Tony how many pizzas he wants, he has two—stylishly demolishing both slices simultaneously.

John's mother Helen had a cameo as well—an impatient customer in the paint store who Tony mollifies with a dollar discount on her purchase. The Travolta clan might not quite have become the Barrymores of Bergen County, but many a journalist would be forgiven for thinking they were. Outside the central *Fever* circus, brother Joey was even on a $50,000 a year contract with Paramount, without having to do anything except not sign with anybody else!

On January 29, 1977, Freddie Prinze, Chico in the sitcom *Chico and the Man*, committed suicide. Beset with drug and legal problems, he blew his own head off. The tragedy hit John hard. Back on the set of *Welcome Back, Kotter*, John and his fellow Sweathogs Robert Hegyes and Ron Palillo solemnly vowed an antisuicide pact. Whatever they were doing, wherever they might be, the three swore that they would drop everything and rush to be with the other if things ever got that bad.

"I can still remember the tragedy of the moment and the obvious feelings of self-preservation that permeated the room on the *Kotter* set," Palillo recalled. "There was a great deal of tension, a great deal of nervousness. Bobby and I were sitting around a table with John, and we all vowed that we wouldn't let something like that happen to us. We pledged to call one another if we ever got so depressed that we might be on the point of suicide. We all recognized that what happened to Freddie could happen to any one of us."

Little did any of them know how true those words would prove. And how soon.

As 1977 picked up speed, John scored his third, albeit minor, hit single. "All Strung Out on You," which made number thirty-four in February, had been recorded late in 1976 during a series of sessions with producer Jeff Barry, an easy-listening veteran best known for his work with cartoon hit-makers The Archies at the end of the 1960s.

Can't Let You Go, an album bringing together another eight of Barry's productions, followed. Another unadventurous collection of ballads, it was most notable for John's reading of Peter Allen's "Back Doors Crying." The song meant a lot to him during those long, dark months before he embraced Scientology, when a succession of shrinks held his emotions in check and his checkbook in thrall.

"I was very impressionable at that time. I was proud of my neurosis." Stumbling along, he explained, in the belief that you can only create art if you suffer for it first, and being encouraged in that notion by the therapists he visited, "it was like whoever's darkest or more neurotic was the most talented." He ran, too, with a pack of friends who agreed with him, who carried their failures like soldiers wear scars and blamed every rejection upon a world that could not understand them.

When he discovered Scientology, at last there was something he knew he could believe in, something that taught him finally to ask "What the fuck does that mean? I decided to drop it all, and started to do well."

But the smokey melancholy of "Back Doors Crying," with its line, "Thought I was happy only when I was sad," nailed his former state of mind with almost painful accuracy. Recording the song was John's way of permanently celebrating his victory.

Can't Let You Go rose no higher than number sixty-six on the chart; like the accompanying single, it would certainly have done a lot better had John been available to promote it. Unfortunately, March 1977 was also the month when John's entire world came tumbling down.

Shortly after John left for New York, Diana's health had taken a serious turn for the worst. The cancer, which the couple had convinced themselves was in remission, had resurfaced. Doctors gave her eighteen months to live.

John was devastated, but there was nothing he could do. He was committed to the movie, and although every fiber of his being cried out for him to stay in L.A., Diana herself begged him not to throw his career away. There was nothing he could do that he wasn't already doing, she told him. Besides, she would be spending so much time in and out of the hospital that he might as well be in New York for all the time they'd have together. And he would be flying back regularly to work on *Welcome Back, Kotter.*

Unwillingly, but with his heart truly believing the doctors' eighteen-month estimate, he left for Brooklyn. Diana alone knew that she would be lucky to survive another eighteen weeks.

Since *The Boy in the Plastic Bubble*, Diana's workload had increased, even as her strength declined. *Eight Is Enough* had been slipped into ABC's Tuesday night schedule, into the 9–10:00 P.M. slot vacated by the immensely popular *Rich Man, Poor Man—Book II*, and Diana had completed four one-hour episodes when she became ill for the last time.

Late in February, John received the call he'd been dreading. Diana was back in the hospital, and she wasn't getting better. Ellen, who'd been visiting Diana daily, accompanying her to the treatment rooms where her frail body was bombarded with the radiation that might hold the cancer at bay, gave John the news.

So far, John had kept the true nature of Diana's illness to himself. Friends and associates were told that she was merely suffering from back trouble; sometimes, John's mother recollected, he even managed to convince himself of that. Now he revealed the truth and accepted it. Filming was suspended, and John flew straight back to L.A.

Despite the hopelessness of Diana's prognosis, John wanted to get married. Diana turned him down; he was too young to be a widower, too young to spend his life mourning a wife he would barely know. But John remained adamant, and when events moved even faster than he had expected, he was truly devastated.

Sitting up late into the night with Ellen shortly before the end, he told her, "You go into marriage assuming it will last forever, but how many marriages do? Many couples spend a lifetime together, and don't have the love Diana and I have for each other. We'll just have to live for each moment."

In order to savor their last moments together, Diana insisted that she be released from the hospital. Her doctor gave her the go-ahead. He could do nothing more for her.

Two decades later, John remembered, "As Diana was dying of cancer . . . I had sympathy pain. I felt my scalp and I said to her, 'Oh, what if this is a tumor? What if I have cancer too?' And she said, 'Well honey, if you do, you're going to have to deal with it.'

"I looked at her and I thought, 'This woman is dealing with it every single minute, death is right in her face, and if she can do that, I can.' From then on, there was hardly anything that I couldn't look at without thinking, 'Okay, deal with it.' That statement was like a gift, and she didn't even know she gave it to me."

Eight Is Enough debuted to warm reviews on March 15, 1977. John and Diana watched it together, both knowing that she had a hit on her hands (the series did, in fact, run until 1981); neither was able to believe she would not live to film another episode. She would be lucky, she reminded him one night, to live even to see another one. It became a way of marking time, counting down the days until the next installment of Diana's show, then counting them down until the one after that. She didn't make it.

The evening of March 28 seemed much the same as any other. John and Diana talked, watched television, then tried to decide what they wanted for dinner. Japanese sounded good, and leaving Diana at home, John drove out to pick it up. He returned forty minutes later to find her lying unconscious. She died in his arms.

"Her last words were 'I'm going now,'" John remembers with sadness. "Then I felt the breath go out of her." That moment would haunt his dreams for years to come.

"Diana was seventeen years older than I was, but we never knew the difference. We talked all day and all night about everything. I have never been so fulfilled in my life, and when she died I felt like I lost my center. I haven't found anyone like her since."

John found solace in his work. "The Man," as the crew now called him, was back on the *Saturday Night Fever* set less than twenty-four hours after Diana passed on, flying across country on the same flight as artist Andy Warhol. "He caught me crying," John smiled sadly. "I couldn't control it. I'm thinking, 'I don't want to be watched when this is happening,' and it was an empty plane, and he's peering over. A strange scene." In his own diary, Warhol simply acknowledged that John spent a lot of time in the bathroom and looked very sad. It wasn't until later that he learned the reason.

Back in New York, acknowledging his colleagues' sympathy but keeping his own counsel, John ploughed back into his work with renewed passion. John Badham even went on record marveling, "Some of the best scenes in the movie were shot during that period. He put his attention to the work and overcame his emotional feelings."

Carly Simon and James Taylor, John's upstairs neighbors and now among his closest friends in the city, took him under their wing immediately. "I went up and visited with them," John remembers, "and [they] sang to me in their kitchen, a duet they were putting on an album. Then James wrote me a little song called 'My Name Is Barbarino but My Good Friends Call Me John.' And because I was having trouble sleeping, Carly wrote me a lullaby and put it on tape, to put me to sleep."

Looking back twenty years later, he admitted, "If someone had said, 'What's your ultimate dream?' in the seventies, it would have been to be befriended by those two people, to be sung to by them, and to have songs written for me by them. I could have died, joined Diana, and it would have been just fine."

John even kept his head and his humor when a group of fans, bored of simply waiting outside his trailer, started rocking it back and forth in hopes of luring him out. Indeed, whenever the crew or his fellow cast members asked how he coped with the adulation, he'd simply shrug. It came with the turf. He was also the first to comfort his mother after she witnessed him being mobbed by four thousand screaming fans. That came with the turf as well.

"The first thing I did when I got to New York to promote *Saturday Night Fever* was walk down Fifth Avenue. Every fifth person would recognize me and yell, 'Hey, there's John Travolta!' It was great. I got off on it. When it's least appealing is when you're eating and somebody comes up in a restaurant and takes the fork out of your hand.

"I used to think, 'Well, all this noise is temporary and they'll get tired of me and go on to somebody else.' But it hasn't happened. So now I know it isn't going to happen unless I change my face. I might as well live with it. I feel good enough about myself to go out and have a good time and ignore the mobs.

"Here's the way I look at it. If it all ends for me tomorrow, they'll still remember my face. So I've decided not to stop my life or hide from the public. I'm handling it pretty well."

What he really meant, although it would be years before he realized it, was that he hadn't even begun to handle it. Right now, all he was doing was accepting his fame, and living his life around it. Things were simply moving too quickly for anything more than that.

His parents, still living in the same house John grew up in, faced their son's success with similar equanimity; indeed, Sal's greatest regret was that it didn't all happen sooner "so I could have looked forward to enjoying Johnny's success longer." Fans lay virtual siege to the house, waiting outside for hours, even days on end, and few of them were ever content with the glossy photographs Helen and Sal kept on hand for such occasions.

Some nights, Sal sighed, fans would actually "nibble" at the house, "as if it were made of gingerbread!" Masonry was chipped away, shingles pried loose, the garden stripped bare: if it could be moved, it would be removed. And all he and Helen could do was follow their son's lead and do what anyone would do in the face of a hurricane— batten down the hatches and hope it blew over quickly.

As the summer of 1977 drew closer, however, it seemed as though that might never happen.

When *Welcome Back, Kotter* fell apart due to cast in-fighting after four successful seasons, John tried to remain above it all by keeping his weekly dinner dates with Marcia Strassman and making his occasional movie excursions with Gabe Kaplan.

Throughout the years, Travolta has always been the King of Cool.

YORAM KAHANA/SHOOTING STAR

TRI-STAR PICTURES

Whether as Vinnie Barbarino, Tony Manero, or himself, Travolta embodied the spirit of '70s hip.
SYLVIA NORRIS/GLOBE PHOTOS

Since they met while costarring in the national touring production of *Grease* in December 1972, John and Marilu Henner have been roommates, lovers, and above all, friends.
YORAM KAHANA/SHOOTING STAR

With smooth moves, loud music, and even louder clothes (shown here with costar
Karen Lynn Gorney), Travolta became the ultimate disco icon in *Saturday Night Fever*.

To prepare for his role in *Saturday Night Fever*, Travolta frequented Brooklyn discos; he even went home with some of the patrons to study their family dynamics.

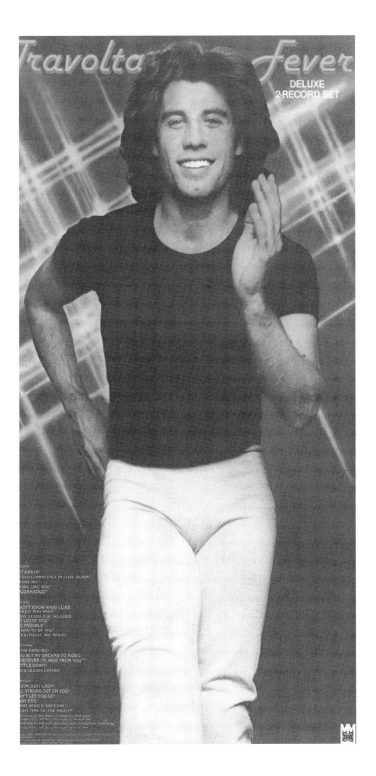

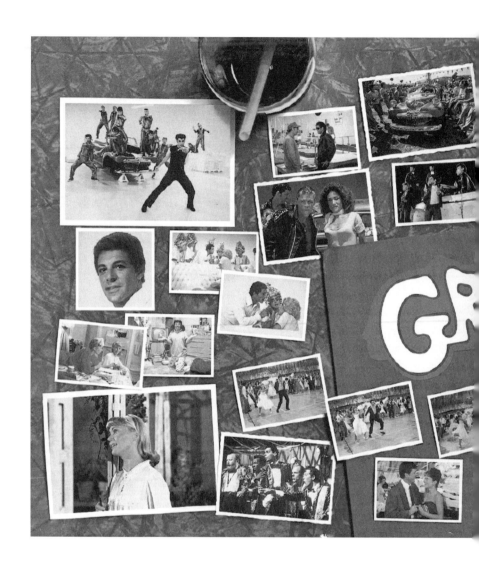

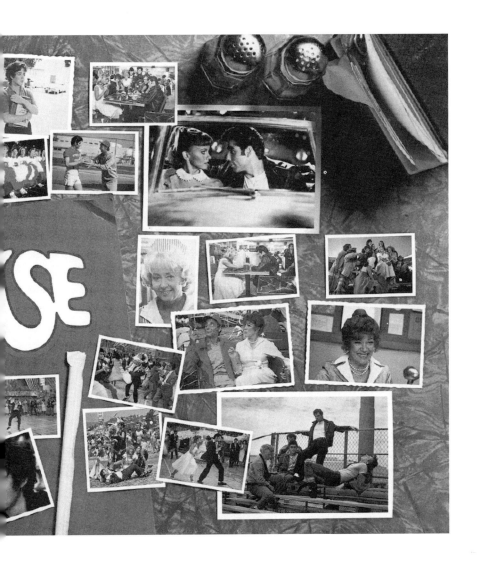

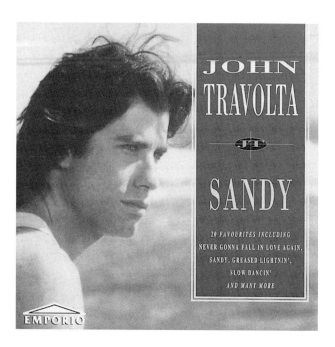

Even Lily Tomlin and Travolta couldn't save *Moment by Moment* from box-office failure.
UNIVERSAL CITY STUDIOS

Travolta appeared at The Kennedy Center Honors in December 1980.
CBS TELEVISION NETWORK

Following the disastrous debut of *Moment by Moment*, John went into *Urban Cowboy* slightly apprehensive. Still, he quickly eased into the role.
M. SENNET/SHOOTING STAR

Debra Winger starred in *Urban Cowboy* as John's girlfriend, Sissy.
LEONELLI/KAHANA/GLOBE PHOTOS

When *Urban Cowboy* coproducer Robert Evans wanted Travolta to shave off his beard, he simply wrote it into the script.
PARAMOUNT PICTURES

URBAN COWBOY
ORIGINAL MOTION PICTURE SOUNDTRACK

JIMMY BUFFETT	ANNE MURRAY
CHARLIE DANIELS BAND	BONNIE RAITT
EAGLES	LINDA RONSTADT/ J. D. SOUTHER
DAN FOGELBERG	KENNY ROGERS
MICKEY GILLEY	BOZ SCAGGS
GILLEY'S "URBAN COWBOY" BAND	BOB SEGER AND THE SILVER BULLET BAND
JOHNNY LEE	JOE WALSH

Although *Blow Out* is one of Travolta's lesser-known films, it earned him much critical acclaim.
FILMWAYS PICTURES

Although director Brian De Palma, who also directed Travolta in *Carrie*, didn't create John's role in *Blow Out* with him in mind, John convinced him he was right for the part.
COLUMBIA PICTURES

The role Travolta turned down in *An Officer and a Gentleman* was snatched up by Richard Gere, who also replaced him when he backed out of *American Gigolo.*

After turning down several roles in other Paramount pictures, Travolta had no choice but to appear in the *Saturday Night Fever* sequel, *Staying Alive,* to fulfill his three-picture contract with the company.

PARAMOUNT PICTURES

To get in top form for his role in *Staying Alive*, Travolta added ballet lessons to his already strenuous training schedule.

Travolta saw *Rocky III* while on vacation in Hawaii and knew immediately that Sylvester Stallone was the perfect director for *Staying Alive*.

Executives at 20th Century
Fox were convinced all they
needed to make a hit was
two great names, but
Travolta and Olivia
Newton-John proved them
wrong with *Two of a Kind*.
20TH CENTURY FOX

Although John and Olivia sparkled
together in *Grease*, rumors of an
off-the-set romance were unfounded.
MICHAEL FERGUSON/GLOBE PHOTOS

6

◇ ◇ ◇

Grease Is the Word

When John was first offered the
role of Danny Zuko in Robert Stigwood's film version of *Grease*, his
immediate reaction was one of total disdain. "I'd decided not to do the
part," John admitted candidly. "But then I reconsidered. I thought,
'What's wrong with doing a light musical? Brando did it [*Guys And
Dolls*]." With filming complete, he admitted, "It was fun. Nowhere
near as complicated as *Saturday Night Fever*."

The filming of *Grease* ran back to back with *Saturday Night Fever*,
crammed into the summer break between seasons of *Welcome Back,
Kotter*. Indeed, John first met the Bee Gees at the *Grease* wrap party,
when cast and crew were treated to a special premiere of *Saturday Night
Fever* that still had the Bee Gees' rough, original demos on the soundtrack. Before that movie had even enjoyed its public premiere, the press
was already discussing *Grease*, building up a head of delirium that
would only grow.

Understandably, *Grease*, the movie, would borrow a great deal
from its Broadway predecessor, including members of its cast. Joining
John from past productions were Michael Tucci; Jamie Donnelly,
reprising her theatrical role of Jan; Jeff Conaway, switching from the
part of Danny to Kenickie; Barry Pearl, who moved from Sonny into
John's old Doodie shoes. Marilu Henner only missed out on a part

because she was filming her own movie debut, *Bloodbrothers*, with Richard Gere.

The youngest of the T-Birds, Putzie, was played by another Pat Birch discovery, Kelly Ward. He had moved from Birch's *Truck Load* musical to a small part in *The Boy in the Plastic Bubble*, where he and John met director Randall Kleiser. John's sister Ellen even landed a tiny part as a waitress in the T-Birds' favorite diner; indeed, the only principle figure who did not seem to have a Travolta connection was John's costar, Olivia Newton-John.

Seven years older than John, the English-born but Australian-raised Olivia Newton-John went into *Grease* already ranked among the most successful pop performers ever. Discovered by John Farrar, once a member of singer Cliff Richard's backing group, but now a proven producer and arranger in his own right, "Livvy" arrived on the set of *Grease* with her walls already groaning beneath the weight of her success: three Grammy awards, eight American Music Awards, and a houseful of gold and platinum discs.

But if hits like "If Not for You," "Let Me Be There," and "Have You Never Been Mellow" had long since established her singing talent, she was virtually untried as an actress. Her resumé amounted to nothing more spectacular than a few comedy sketches on Cliff Richard's English television series and a role in an abortive science fiction musical called *Toomorrow* that few people had seen. If it were not for one simple coincidence, she would never even have been considered for *Grease*.

It was Robert Stigwood's partner, Allan Carr, who brought Olivia on board after meeting her at a small dinner party being thrown by Helen Reddy and her husband, Jeff Wald.

"I'd never seen her in person before, and I couldn't resist telling her that she really should be doing movies. She's just adorable, and yet she has a very special sophistication about her too. I knew if we could just capture that on film, we would have our Sandy."

Olivia was about to set out on a major world tour, but she was sufficiently intrigued by the prospect of a movie to ask Carr for a copy of the script.

Reading it while she played and replayed the original Broadway cast album, however, she began to have second thoughts. She was not worried as much about *Grease* as a whole as she was about that one crucial moment when the sweet and demure Sandy is transformed into a leather-clad, gum-chewing, biker chick. Was it believable? And if not, could she make it so?

"I didn't want to go into something I couldn't handle," Olivia explained. Just hours before she was due to go onstage at New York's Metropolitan Opera House, Olivia placed a call to John, still in town working on *Saturday Night Fever*, to ask his opinion. He told her she was crazy to worry and reassured by his kindness, she agreed to screen test.

That, too, proved to be nerve-wracking, especially because she wasn't exactly thrilled with her performance. Everybody else seemed quite happy about it, she said, but "I kept thinking, 'Here I am, a singer wanting to be an actress, working with an actor who sings.' I was very mixed up and frightened." She came through with flying colors, and with her concert commitments finally over, she settled down to study Sandy in depth.

"I first saw the show in London about five years earlier," Olivia remarked of *Grease*, "but I never thought I would ever be playing Sandy. I loved the show, but actually I think the fact that the role has been changed so the girl has moved from Australia to the United States has helped make Sandy more interesting. It explains why she is so different from everyone else, and it makes her innocence more believable. I remember when I first came [to America]. Although I wasn't as naive as Sandy by then, I can identify with why she finds it all so strange."

It also helped that she and John hit it off so well. On the dance floor, the crew nicknamed the pair of them "Fred and Ginger" even before the same nicknames were written into the movie's big dance scene. John smiled at the comparison. According to his mother, Fred Astaire had already seen *Saturday Night Fever* three times and was now describing John as the best dancer to come along since. . . Fred Astaire.

John returned to Los Angeles immediately after the *Grease* wrap party to start work on *Welcome Back, Kotter's* third season. It would prove to be his last. Although he pledged during preproduction on *Saturday Night Fever* that he would remain with the show "for as long as they need me" (translated: "until my contract expires"), he was also well aware that "someday we're all going to outgrow our parts. How long can you play a sixteen-year-old?"

Indeed, he was soon prophesying that *Welcome Back, Kotter* probably had only a couple more seasons in it, and when the possibility was raised of trying once more to launch a spin-off series, this time highlighting Vinnie, he politely declined. *Welcome Back, Kotter*, he was adamant, was "my first and last TV series."

The third season opened with a double bang. Julie's pregnancy, a summer-long cliffhanger, climaxed with the birth of twins, Rachel and Robin, while for the Sweathogs, a new school year meant promotion to a new grade, the eleventh. At least, that's what it meant for three of them. Vinnie Barbarino was left behind, and the biggest laughs in the three-part season opener came from his increasingly desperate attempts to persuade Kotter to help him out at a time when Kotter, faced with the joys of parenthood-times-two, was in desperate need of help himself.

The storyline, of course, served a secondary purpose, excusing John from the show while he wrapped up *Grease*. The Sweathogs' internal balance was maintained with the continued promotion of Arnold Horshack. Most notably, Horshack featured in the early-season episode in which he is ensnared by a cult. If John, who was also involved with what some people saw as a mind-control scam, felt at all uncomfortable with the premise, he didn't show it.

Indeed, this season would see him turn in some of his most inspired Barbarino performances yet. Perhaps most memorable was his delivery of a couple of inside jokes that remained hilarious long after the laughs had left Mr. Kotter's lines. At least, one assumes they were inside jokes. If they weren't, Dame Coincidence was truly working overtime that year.

Strangely, both were directed toward the Bee Gees. The first, in the season opener, was delivered when Julie engages Vinnie in a discussion of potential names for her babies. She runs through a handful that he rejects with a sniff, then asks, "What about Maurice?"

Vinnie sneers. "Yeah, Maurice is good. If you want him to get beaten up for the rest of his life." The relevant Gibb brother's response remains sadly unrecorded.

A few weeks later, John was at it again, this time as the leader of the Three Do's and a Don't, the distinctly awry impersonation of a doowop group that the Sweathogs have entered for a school talent contest.

Straight-faced but tight-trousered, Vinnie astounds everybody with a pitch-perfect falsetto, surely lifted directly from the Bee Gees' vocal arsenal. Even in reruns two decades later, it's a classic moment. Again, the Bee Gees' response has not been recorded, but "Jeepers Creepers, Where Did You Get Those Peepers" remains conspicuously absent from their repertoire.

Immersed as he was in his work, John continued to cope with Diana's death. On September 11, 1977, John accompanied her parents, Mr. and Mrs. John Gentner, to the presentation of the 1976–'77 season Emmy Awards. Diana was nominated in the Best Supporting Actress in a Comedy or Drama Special category for her role as Todd's mother in *The Boy in the Plastic Bubble*. The nomination could hardly be described as a sympathy vote, as is so often the case with posthumous honors. Diana had been genuinely moving in the film. When it was announced that she had won, even the hardest cynic had to blink back a tear.

What happened next, however, eclipsed even the announcement in terms of emotional impact. As Diana's parents had requested, John took the stage to accept the statuette. For a moment he looked lost. Then, he raised it above his head, and leaping up as though he was really trying to pass it to Diana, he clicked his heels and shouted, "I love you, baby!"

John might also have been on the receiving end of an Emmy that year, if not for what amounted to a civil war raging within the heart of the awards' sponsors, the National Academy of Television Arts and Sciences (NATAS). The ceremony had been all set to take place in its traditional mid-May slot when the Hollywood chapter of NATAS, believing that its members deserved more control over awards that went, after all, to shows they were largely responsible for, organized a boycott of the ceremony.

The squabble was eventually solved with the formation of a new, Hollywood-based organization, the Academy of Television Arts and Sciences (ATAS), that would take full responsibility for prime-time awards, leaving NATAS to celebrate news, sports, documentary, and daytime television.

Nevertheless, the original ceremony had to be abandoned because of the delay. While for the viewing public the arrival of another acronym was but a minor distinction, for the cast and crew of the shows nominated in the aborted May ceremony, there was a world of difference—particularly in the category for Best Comedy Series. *Welcome Back, Kotter* was among the four May nominees that were completely overlooked in September.

John, however, probably didn't even notice. *Saturday Night Fever* was scheduled to open in less than three months and already the antici-pation had justified at least one third of the movie's title. But even "fever" seemed inadequate when compared to what was really going on.

Controlling both the movie and its soundtrack, Robert Stigwood worked hard to ensure that *Saturday Night Fever* would get as much advance promotion as possible, a plan that would lead to the virtual saturation of the marketplace during the three months before the movie premiered.

The Bee Gees' gentle "How Deep Is Your Love" fired the first shot when it romped to the top of the charts in September 1977. It had been a year since the release of any new Bee Gees material, with noth-ing more than a nostalgia-heavy live album arriving to plug the gap between. Pushing the *Saturday Night Fever* soundtrack as a de facto Bee Gees album immediately broadened the movie's potential audience to include everyone who'd been waiting for something new from the brothers Gibb.

"How Deep Is Your Love" was still climbing the chart when its follow-up, "Staying Alive," was unleashed. The timing was exquisite. The movie opened the same week "Staying Alive" hit the charts on its way to becoming the second number one from the album. "Staying Alive" would remain at the top for the next month.

A slew of *Kotter* luminaries were present at the party thrown for the Los Angeles opening of *Saturday Night Fever* in December 1977. John attended with singer Carly Simon, provoking the ever-watchful tabloid press to immediately link the man they were calling Holly-wood's hottest young star to the woman whose own career had just received a welcome boost after she contributed the theme to the latest James Bond movie.

The fact that Simon was already married to James Taylor and would hardly be likely to flaunt an extramarital affair quite so promi-nently did nothing to deter the gossip-mongers. Far more pertinent was the fact that, at nine years John's senior, she was an ideal mate for an actor who had already made his preference for older women plain.

John let the speculation drift by him, saying, "The truth is, I haven't been able to meet anyone since Diana." When Karen Lynn Gorney went public with her own emotional commitment to John— "I did love him, I do love him—the way it is in the film is the way it is"—John responded with nothing more than a sad smile. "Where do people get these stories?" Still, once bitten, twice shy. When *Saturday Night Fever* opened in London and Paris, John attended the premiere with his parents.

Saturday Night Fever was never destined to be anything but a hit. What nobody ever realized was just how big a hit. Within eleven days of release, the film had grossed over eleven million dollars in North America alone; within four months, it had passed eighty-one million, eleven times its break-even target. By the end of 1978, *Saturday Night Fever* was firmly rooted among the decade's most successful movies.

Saturday Night Fever's success, Bee Gee Maurice Gibb believes, was down to the simple combination of "John Travolta and the music. That made the film. Everyone was dying to see John's first full-length motion picture, and for the part he played, he was perfect. The music made the film, and he made the film. The public went to see this guy John Travolta, and the music he danced to was good. They loved the music and went and bought the album. It was a triangle of Robert Stigwood making the film to start with, having John as the lead, which was a damned good choice, and us writing the music."

And that music continued to be inescapable.

The deal with Robert Stigwood's RSO organization guaranteed John more than one million dollars for three movies, plus a percentage of the profits, including those from the soundtrack albums. It was a shrewd arrangement. With *Saturday Night Fever*'s soundtrack having already spawned two number ones for the Bee Gees, the album had sold 700,000 copies before the movie even hit the theaters. Once that happened, all hell would break loose.

In January 1978, as *Saturday Night Fever* commenced its record-breaking residency at the top of the charts, the Bee Gees' "Night Fever" became the third chart-topper for the brothers. Their supremacy was only emphasized by the fact that the only records that could knock them off the top were others with which they were indelibly associated: Yvonne Elliman's "If I Can't Have You," which they wrote; Player's "Baby Come Back," which shared both their label and their sound; and younger brother Andy's "(Love Is) Thicker Than Water."

Indeed, Andy, too, would chalk up consecutive number ones with three successive singles; even more incredibly, the Bee Gees' next three singles would also be chart-toppers, adding up to a dominance that rivaled even the Beatles' achievements. Sales of *Saturday Night Fever* itself, meanwhile, would not be bettered until Michael Jackson's genre-busting *Thriller* finally toppled it in 1984. Still, it would sell over twenty-five million copies, establishing it as the best-selling soundtrack album of all time, with sales of 1996's remastered compact disc edition improving on that figure all the time.

And bound up with it all, at the white-hot heart of the phenomenon, there still stands a solitary figure, a man in white polyester and polished platform shoes—a human timepiece that history has stopped at four o'clock.

In the popular memory of today, the most famous frozen frame of the movie, the Four O'Clock Man, straddles the seventies like a bell-bottomed behemoth. No literate examination of the cultural legacy of the decade could be considered complete without him—preferably in color on the cover; no celluloid vision of life under Carter can fail to bring him into the picture.

Long after the pet rocks have turned back to sand and the mood rings have faded to gray, Mr. Four O'Clock will be forever framed in the pantheon of seventies arcana, up there with macramé and smiley faces. His was the image that stared out from twenty-five million record jackets, and that gazed down from glossy posters on as many bedroom walls. He was parroted in discos across the western world and brilliantly parodied in George Hamilton's *Love at First Bite*. He was larger than life.

The white polyester suit with vest, the open-neck shiny black shirt, the black flamenco-style ankle boots, the gold neck chains— John Travolta wore the clothes but the look became a uniform. Although they did so with tongues firmly in cheek, authors Jane and Michael Stern hit the nail on the head when they mourned the deathly disco phenomenon that followed and wondered what to blame for it: "the celebrity-sucking freak-show scene at the clubs? Or John Travolta's suit?"

Writing in their *Encyclopedia of Bad Taste*, the ultimate guide to Americana in all its tacky glory, the Sterns lasciviously detail how John singlehandedly "inspired millions of men without movie-star physiques to wear tight white suits, style their hair in a borough pouf, sulk like Tony Manero sulked, and strut like he strutted." And presto! "A new, truly odious macho style was created."

It was not only in America where the image raised critical hackles. East Germany's government-run youth newspaper, *Junge Welt*, reacted to what western observers had already noted to be a rising and distinctly un-Communist tide of Travolta fever behind the Iron Curtain by criticizing John's perceived attempts "to make capitalist daily life seem harmless." Their condemnation made little difference. The *Saturday Night Fever* soundtrack remained a popular attraction in East German discotheques, and western magazines bearing his picture continued to pour in through the black market. Tony Manero quite conceivably did not even know what an Iron Curtain was, but he had breached it nevertheless.

Yet *Saturday Night Fever* was not merely a chance phenomenon that happened to catch on. Tom Moore, John's director in the theatrical productions of both *Grease* and *Over Here*, was not surprised by John's success. "He had a vision of where he wanted to be," Moore said five years later. "I have a crazy theory: I think John created a vacuum, then stepped into it. He willed his success." He may have willed it, but he was then magnanimous enough to let everybody else try and grab a piece of it.

There were at least two attempts to duplicate *Saturday Night Fever* on the small screen, NBC's short-lived *Joe and Valerie*—a program that *Rolling Stone* pronounced was such "a flagrant rip-off you wonder that Robert Stigwood doesn't sue"; and ABC's more adventurous (and Stigwood-endorsed) *Makin' It*, a show that even reunited the Travolta name (albeit John's sister, Ellen) with a Bee Gees-fired soundtrack.

Premiering in February 1979, *Makin' It* revolved around a college student, Billy Manucci, who is torn between his academic studies and the bright lights of the disco scene that his brother Tony (it had to be Tony!) had conquered before him. Unfortunately, although Billy (actor

David Naughton) took the show's title song into the Top Five in March that year, chalking up yet another hit for the still omnipresent RSO label, any hopes of creating a new disco dynasty were dashed when the show was canned after just six episodes. The final ignominy came when "Makin' It" was simultaneously borrowed for the *Meatballs* soundtrack and sold the majority of copies under that movie's aegis.

Elsewhere, however, the Disco Frankenstein was unstoppable. According to *Life* magazine, within a year of *Saturday Night Fever*'s opening, there were more than ten thousand discotheques in the United States, with new ones opening at a rate of twenty a week. The Hilton Hotel chain was converting its unfashionable bars into trendy new discos. Vidal Sassoon created a twenty-five dollar Travolta-style haircut—sideburns optional. Halston launched a new line of disco wear in loose and clingy styles. Zeidler and Zeidler in Los Angeles complained they couldn't even keep black shirts and Cuban heels in stock anymore. In Brooklyn, Abraham & Strauss announced plans to open a Night Fever menswear boutique. There was even a proposal that airports attach discos to their passenger terminals for the benefit of travelers with a few hours to kill between flights.

The seediest bars converted themselves into discos through the simple expedient of installing a mirror ball and a couple of turntables. Entire communities found themselves caught up in regional dance competitions as a veritable army of little Tony Maneros, ably assisted by as many little Stephanies, vied for such lofty titles as Groton Disco Dancing Champion. Washington, D.C. promoter Jack Alix reported that his Travolta lookalike contests drew lines two blocks long. One lucky winner, a Virginia autoparts salesman named Roger Blaha, promptly moved into television himself, making commercials at one hundred dollars an hour.

In the eye of such a storm—commercial and critical, on screen and on vinyl—John threw himself wholeheartedly into his work, for only there could he live within even the vaguest constraints of normalcy. Even so, his time was at a premium.

A well-meaning pledge to host *Saturday Night Live*, for instance, fell by the wayside, although in this case it was not only the weight of John's workload that made his promise impossible to follow up on. There was also the whisper, within John's entourage and without, that an appearance on what was then still the *enfant terrible* of American television comedy would be equal to turning down an Oscar nomination. As the countdown to the ceremony drew closer, few people doubted that John's name would be among the nominees.

Lorne Michaels, *Saturday Night Live*'s long-suffering producer, took the disappointment stoically, still finding time to rave. "John is the perfect star for the '70s. He has this strange, androgynous quality, this all-pervasive sexuality. Men don't find him terribly threatening. And women, well. . ." But still it would be another sixteen years before John got a second shot at the show.

Not that *Saturday Night Live* was alone in its quandary. "I have six scripts at home from people I really admire, and I don't have enough hours awake to read them all, get my work done, and go to meetings," John complained. Once again, he thanked Scientology for helping him through the rigors, crediting it with instilling him with "a kind of casual knowingness.

"I used to get caught up in a lot of bad thoughts that people could pick up on, could invalidate me with. And invalidation can make you wither, can turn you into a cynic. I used to be very vulnerable and open to everyone, and I kept feeling the blows to my deepest self, whenever anyone did something covert."

He still worried, but his fears were under control now. He was concerned, for instance, that he had made the character of Tony Manero "too full of pain, too naked." Conversely, he worried that his own life appeared shallow in comparison with the characters he played on screen. It was the classic conflict, and ironically, it was only exacerbated by his peers' response to his performance.

Francois Truffaut, the legendary French director, sang John's praises loudly; Pauline Kael contributed a *New Yorker* review that John himself later described as "an actor's dream." Everywhere he turned, he was greeted by a virtual conspiracy of admirers, all going out of their way to lift John bodily out of the teenybop phenomenon category into the realm of serious artistry. And the plaudits continued to mount.

Most notably, he was indeed nominated for an Oscar. John was "high" on his Oscar nomination for weeks. Later he confessed that it didn't matter if he won, he simply valued it for "the recognition of work that it is—just the nomination." That was sufficient for him.

Besides, he wanted Richard Burton to win for his part in *Equus*—the same Richard Burton who ran into John backstage at the awards ceremony and told him, "If you take it from me, big boy, I'll bust your beautiful chops." Then he laughed a sonorous Welsh-accented laugh. John wanted him to win even more after that.

In any event, neither man won. Instead, the award went to Richard Dreyfuss for *The Goodbye Girl.* If John was disappointed, he didn't let it show. Indeed, he spent most of the five-hour ceremony massaging his mother's numb knees and trying to persuade her they should leave early.

Afterward John remembered, "I heard her say to my dad, 'I'm glad Johnny didn't win.' At first I didn't understand. I asked my father why she'd said that. 'She said she wanted you to have something to look forward to,' he said. She didn't need the gratification. She wanted me to be more than a one-movie star."   Her concern was understandable but scarcely likely to come to fruition. Even as John wrapped up his turn on *Saturday Night Fever*'s promo-go-round—the whirlwind of interviews and television appearances that accompanied the movie's early spring opening across Britain and Europe—he prepared to step onto another as the opening of *Grease* slid closer.

Echoing the strategy that had worked so well for *Saturday Night Fever*, RSO began leaking the *Grease* soundtrack several months ahead of the movie. And once again, the results were incredible.

Much of the soundtrack simply revamped songs already familiar from the stage show. The recruitment of *Grease*'s original musical director, Louis St. Louis, ensured that the arrangements would not deviate too far from the familiar ones.

That said, several of the movie's most notable songs, commercially at least, were those specially commissioned for the movie, beginning with Barry Gibb's joyous title theme, performed by a chronologically mismatched but otherwise ideal Frankie Valli.

Olivia Newton-John's long-time mentor, John Farrar, also contributed a couple of compositions: Sandy's plaintive "Hopelessly Devoted to You," and the effervescent "You're the One that I Want," the song that signals Sandy's transformation into the kind of girl Danny can feel comfortable around—just as Danny himself changes into the kind of boy he thought Sandy most wanted.

Accompanied by the relevant clip from the still unseen movie, "You're the One That I Want" was released as a single at the beginning of April 1978. Little more than eight weeks later, it was firmly embedded at number one on both sides of the Atlantic, a tenacious little ditty that simply would not budge. Topping the U.S. charts for a month, it dominated the British listings for nine, establishing itself as the second longest chart-topper in British pop history.

The soundtrack album followed in May, promptly racking up twelve weeks at the top in America and thirteen in England. Once again, the phenomenon was unstoppable.

"Summer Nights," another duet, topped the U.K. chart for seven weeks. Olivia's solo "Hopelessly Devoted to You," John's "Sandy" and "Greased Lightning," Frankie Valli's title theme—each was as massive as the last. For two weeks in November 1978, excerpts from the *Grease* soundtrack occupied three of the top four places on the British chart as "Summer Nights," "Sandy," and "Hopelessly Devoted to You" all jockeyed for position.

Of them all, "Summer Nights" remains the key to the entire movie, just as it was in the original stageshow. Against the backdrop of an audience of Danny and Sandy's personal peers (one batch grunting, the other lot chirruping, their chorus of "wella wella wella ugh, tell me more"), the couple give their wildly varying accounts of their romance on the beach.

For Danny, it was little short of a Bacchanalian orgy, and on the bleachers by the sports field, he lasciviously delves into "all the horny details." For Sandy over lunch at the picnic tables, it was incorruptible innocence incarnate, and Rizzo is right to send her sprawling with a kick. She says they walked along, holding hands; he says she "got friendly down in the sand." It is a scene that's played out in every school playground every day of the year—without the musical backing, of course.

As the song nears its end, their stories dovetail together, and as they do, "Summer Nights" provides Hollywood with a moment, a classic sound byte that was either the most romantic groan in the world (if you fancied John), or the most painful (if you didn't).

Gaynor Clarke, recollecting *Grease* in the British magazine *Loaded*, in March 1996, placed herself firmly in the former camp.

"His hips had a mind of their own, and his every move had me transfixed. A peculiar smirk was creeping across my face."

John's was undergoing an even wilder transformation. "Summer dreams, ripped at the seams, bu-uut . . . uoouuggh . . . "

Again? Uoouuggh. He would repeat the sound later, after the first chorus of "Sandy," but the impact wasn't so strong the second time. Uoouuggh.

For writer Gaynor Clarke, "it was the 'uoouuggh' bit that made me forget any dreams I once had of owning a pony. I wanted John Travolta."

Clarke and several million others.

With the movie's opening now only weeks away, the publicity machine stepped up another gear. John and Olivia stared out from more magazine covers than most people knew existed. The radio drenched the airwaves with the soundtrack. And on May 31, John joined the Bee Gees for the first episode of celebrity interviewer David Frost's high-profile new series, *Headliners with David Frost*, filming his segment aboard his now-luxuriously outfitted DC-3.

It was not the best interview John had ever given, a failing only exacerbated by the network's insistence on screening it over two shows, a cynical ploy *The New York Times* was quick to pick up on. "Travolta was exploited shamelessly for audience grabbing, but the sessions . . . were painfully dull and tedious, relieved only by the occasional batting of the star's eyelashes."

A sample question—"Did you feel the fates were cruel, in a way, when [Diana Hyland] was taken from you?"—perhaps summed up what might best be regarded as a breathtakingly prescient foretelling of the television magazine format that would come to dominate American TV. Most observers breathed a heavy sigh of relief when *Grease* finally arrived and John could again be viewed within more sympathetic surroundings.

Released in June 1978, *Grease* ranks among the most eagerly awaited movies of all time. Certainly its box-office business wiped the floor with every other movie luckless enough to be given a similar release date. It was the beginning of summer vacation period and school was over, but the pupils had barely registered their freedom before they stormed the cinemas to see *Grease*. Even Amy, President

Carter's daughter, was enamored, and John was duly invited to the White House to meet her.

Indeed, when the Hollywood hits of the decade were tabulated, only Spielberg's *Close Encounters of the Third Kind* had done better business, a statistic that *The New York Times'* Vincent Canby both predicted and explained when he compared *Grease's* "multi-million dollar evocation of the B-Movie quickies that Sam Katzman used to turn out in the '50s," with *Close Encounters'* "elegant and . . . benign" obeisance to the science fiction of the same era.

The analogy was not lost on John, who was himself already well aware both of how "innocent" that long-ago era now seemed, and how comforting it was for people to be able to return to it.

"Even though it's a musical and looks simple," he revealed of *Grease*, "I had to think a lot about how a guy's behavior would have differed twenty-five years ago or so. Movement had to be different. There hadn't been the drugs thing, or the awareness of blacks, so none of those styles of moving or talking had happened yet.

"Behavior, even for guys like Danny Zuko, had to have been much more foursquare. Posture was different, it was better. Also, there wasn't the urbane sense of style or behavior that kids everywhere get from TV today. There had to be an innocence that nobody was really aware of, because they didn't have the sophistication to compare it with."

He was justifiably proud of how convincingly he pulled that transition off; indeed, a decade and a half later, John was still able to rave, "I love the movie of *Grease*. I see a little boy in it. I'm thrilled that a four-year-old can go up to me and his favorite movies are *Look Who's Talking* and *Grease*. I don't want anyone to deny my connections to those films, and I want them to live forever. That's part of the fun of movies.

"*Grease*," he continued, "was something that gave me hope and inspiration before I was ever famous. . . . *Grease* is something I'll always cherish. Harvey Keitel told me once that he was in a funk years ago, and that the only thing that would bring him out of it was watching *Grease* or *Welcome Back, Kotter*. Even if I made the movie or the series for him, it was worth it. I don't want it to go away." Still a regular on cable television, it probably never will.

John could barely appear in public without seriously risking life and limb. Olivia Newton-John reported, "We went to the opening in this open-top, white '50s car. We nearly got dragged out of the car. We never knew we were putting ourselves at such risk. After that, we used to go in a hard top."

Even more seriously, John's visit to the London premiere nearly ended in tragedy. His bodyguards proved almost powerless to prevent him from being crushed by an adoring crowd. Indeed, there were so many near-crushes, so many near-riots, that after a time, they didn't even make the news anymore. The feeling was, "So, John Travolta almost became a human pancake once again. Didn't he do that last week?"

7

◇◇◇

A Momentary Lapse

As his promotional duties finally wound down, John was almost looking forward to going back to *Welcome Back, Kotter*, if only for the chance of a respite from the madness. Unfortunately, there would not be one.

Kotter's fourth season was troubled even before shooting commenced. Rumors had long circulated that Marcia Strassman was even more tired of her role than John was of his; a brilliant actress, she was utterly wasted in a role whose sole function appeared to revolve around smiling at Kotter's interminable uncle jokes (nobody, after all, actually laughed at them).

Friends had long talked of her dissatisfaction. Her *Kotter* schedule had already forced her to turn down two Hollywood movie roles, and it had played its part in shattering a couple of romances as well. The arrival of her on-screen twins the previous season hardly boded well for any further development of her *Kotter* character.

The summer of 1978, Strassman's frustrations finally exploded into the open when she appeared at a preseason press conference and announced that she had been struggling to get out of her contract for the last eighteen months.

"I hate the series. I pray every day for a cancellation. If this is what success means, maybe I should get married and have babies."

Her greatest problem was Kaplan. "It's always been hard to act

119

with him, especially in intimate scenes," she accused. "Gabe runs hot and cold, one day your best friend, the next day not speaking." Even blatant hostility, she concluded, would be easier for her to deal with than the emotional roller coaster he apparently delighted in making her ride.

Strassman's words had a galvanizing effect on the rest of the *Kotter* cast. She recalled, "When I came back to the set, the other guys on the show stood in a circle around me to protect me from Gabe. We joked that I should be wearing a bulletproof vest. But the man never said a word. Not a word." Kaplan did finally break his silence to *People* magazine. "I was shocked that she had such hostility."

With their nominal elders so harshly divided, the Sweathogs' loyalties, too, were divided. After-hours relationships soured; according to *People*, "Lawrence-Hilton Jacobs continues to hang out with Kaplan but no longer meets Strassman after hours. Robert Hegyes is on the Kaplan side, but he's stopped seeing him socially. Marcia's main ally, Ron Palillo, barely talks to Gabe and sees none of the others outside work. The one vestigial source of *Kotter* cast unity is that virtually nobody can stand executive producer James Komack." The family was falling apart.

John tried to remain above the in-fighting; his weekly dinner dates with Marcia continued, and he and Kaplan still made the regular trips to the cinema that had long since become tradition. Even without taking sides, however, he was perceived as having done so; his old basketball buddy, Robert Hegyes, was scarcely on speaking terms with him.

John responded by essentially withdrawing from the show and making public his own dissatisfaction, artistic if not personal.

"TV makes you an instant celebrity, but it eats your time like a crocodile." After three seasons in *Kotter*, Travolta was ready to move on. "I've given them three good years, but I wouldn't play a character on Broadway that long. I've nothing left to prove on that show. It's glorious what happened, and I'm proud of what I created with Vinnie Barbarino, but I want to do other things that turn me on.

"I've completed my cycle with Vinnie Barbarino," he continued. "I want to move on. Whether I had become a movie star or not, this year I would have been ready to leave *Kotter*."

Unfortunately, it was not as easy as that. "After nine months on Broadway in two shows, I was ready to leave. But then it was easier to say 'I've finished.' Now it's so hard, because there's more PR involved. If it wasn't so public, then you could be normal in your feelings towards a project."

And that was what those with longer memories at ABC were afraid of.

Six years before, David Cassidy—the John Travolta of an earlier age—had "retired" from the *Partridge Family* at the end of the show's second season. Only a substantial payrise persuaded him to return; that, and the sheer volume of public dismay that greeted his announcement.

Indeed, even Ruth Aarons, the manager who guided Cassidy through his years of greatest success, confessed to being shocked at the magnitude of that dismay. "I got letters from fans asking if I'd stopped loving them," an incredulous Cassidy gasped. "They thought I was giving up the *Partridge* show because I'd stopped loving my fans."

Even though John's contract—like Strassman's—remained watertight, the network chiefs knew that a reluctant star could be almost as troublesome as having no star at all. Around the bargaining table, the parties involved sought and reached a compromise. In return for a reduction in his *Welcome Back, Kotter* schedule, John agreed to star in an ABC television variety show when his own work schedule finally allowed.

ABC appears to be still waiting for that moment.

John continued to appear throughout the 1978–79 season but attempts to compensate for his increasingly regular absences and return the foursquare balance of the Sweathogs were less than successful. Vinnie's "replacement," Beau De Labarre (Stephen Shortridge), simply did not catch on with either the audiences or, in their still-splintered state, the Sweathogs.

Any success *Welcome Back, Kotter* had maintained in the wake of John's rise to fame had been achieved by the natural chemistry between the four actors. Thrusting a newcomer into an already established team is a risky proposition at best. Hurling one into a team already on the brink of self-destruction was tantamount to suicide.

That was hardly the show's only difficulty. Toward the end of the third season, the quality of the show itself had begun to decline abysmally, but ABC did not seem prepared to remedy the situation. When the cast reconvened for the 1978–79 season, the sole substantial plot change was Kotter's promotion to vice principal, a device that enabled him, too, to gradually fade from the scene.

Of the first twelve episodes shot that season, Kotter appeared in a scant three of them. "He's like a little daddy, sitting back and watching his kids take over," Lawrence-Hilton Jacobs quipped. He wasn't too far off the mark. *Welcome Back, Kotter* had outgrown its title, just as it had been outgrown by its brightest star.

John could only regret *Kotter*'s decline, even as he continued to distance himself from it. "I enjoyed playing Vinnie," he admitted. "I think he'd be a ball to know, because I think he's fun and has a sense of humor. His point of view is hysterical, much more funny than my own personal view on life."

At the same time, he was glad to be finally shaking it off. ABC, he would curse later, "treated us all like dumb kids. And the more famous we got, and the more valuable we became to the moneymen, the more like kids they treated us. People are so desperate to be in control—to be powerful—that they want to conquer you."

And John was having a hard enough time holding his ground as it was. The third and final movie in John's RSO deal, matching him alongside comedienne Lily Tomlin, was scheduled for release during the week before Christmas 1978. *Moment by Moment* promised to be a total departure from past Travolta movies; there would be no singing, no dancing, no pretty young costar. Instead, as John himself confidently envisioned, *Moment by Moment* would mark the start of his growing up process.

"In the overall scheme of things, the teenybopper following means nothing. You have to please yourself in this life. For a long time, I played all the games and acted out whatever people wanted from me because I was ambitious. Now I want to do more adult roles. If that means taking a chance on losing some of my followers, it's a gamble I'm willing to face."

He knew all the counter arguments as well—how no star is ever bigger than his audience and how even though he might be able to control the studio, a star could never forget that the public controls him. He knew all that, and he chose to ignore it.

"All I can do is the best work I know how to do as a serious actor. I'll never satisfy everyone, but if I try to satisfy only the audience who wants me to go through life as Vinnie Barbarino, I'll end up in the toilet. I never denied the characters I was playing, the way Henry Winkler kept denying The Fonz in print, and that made it easier for me to play other parts. You can't tell people what you want to be, you have to show them. The way I look at it, if I can please an adult audience, then the kids will grow up, too."

Such words echoed the fears of the advisers John, it now seemed, had employed simply for the pleasure of ignoring their advice. But they had seen this particular movie before: the one in which the hero decides it is time to cast off all the baggage he has carried, only to find that it's the weight of that baggage that has kept him upright for so long. John had decided to grow up overnight. Would his audience want to grow up alongside him? As *Moment by Moment* slowly came together, that question loomed larger and more threatening daily.

John himself had initiated this latest project after catching Lily Tomlin's one-woman show in New York.

"I told Robert Stigwood that I wanted to get a project with her because she was so incredible," John explained. "I think Lily is one of the most brilliant talents we have. Every time I see her, I'm overwhelmed."

Tomlin herself was not so keen. As far as she was concerned, John Travolta was simply the kid in *Welcome Back, Kotter*, a show whose success left her baffled. As far as Stigwood was concerned, however, what John Travolta wanted, John Travolta got. So he set about wooing Tomlin, opening with a few clips from *Saturday Night Fever*.

According to legend, he never had to think what his second move would be. Tomlin fell for John the moment he stepped onto the screen, and soon she was waxing as effusively as the youngest ingenue. The opportunity to star alongside him seemed too good to pass up.

Yet she, too, was aware of what a gamble this movie would be, for John if not for herself. A May-December love story between a parking attendant and a Beverly Hills housewife, *Moment by Moment* offered a strange premise for any young star, especially an actor like John. Tomlin was, in many ways, a strange costar as well; "In case no one else has noticed," wrote journalist Joan Juliet Buck, "I offer the observation that [she and John] look like identical twins." Other writers cited a distinct resemblance between Tomlin and Ellen Travolta, a familiar face now from her appearances in *Kotter*. Approaching *Moment by Moment* from a purely physical point of view, it could easily have passed for a study in incest—either that or the ultimate narcissistic fantasy.

Of course, that would not stop Lily Tomlin from succeeding Olivia Newton-John as John's latest tabloid-tattle consort, a viperlike rumor that Tomlin herself helped nurture by acknowledging, "The major thing is how sensual [John] is. And how sexy, too. The sensitivity and sexuality are very strong. It's as if he has every dichotomy—masculinity, feminity, refinement, crudity. You see him, you fall in love a little bit."

For his part, John did his best to head the gossip off at the pass.

"When I made *Grease* they wrote that I was romantically linked with Olivia Newton-John, which was totally ridiculous. When I make the movie with Lily, they'll probably write that I'm having a love affair with her." Instead, he suggested, people should content themselves with the relationship the two would be having on screen. That, after all, was the premise of the movie. It was ironic, then, that as *Moment by Moment* neared completion, John admitted, "I didn't feel that Lily and I had good chemistry. As people, we had incredible chemistry, but on screen it didn't work."

Indeed, for all his tough talk during the movie's gestation, once he was on set, John could sense that it was somehow doomed. Something wasn't gelling; even beyond his scenes with Lily Tomlin, the gut feeling, the sense of triumphant anticipation that had powered him through *Saturday Night Fever* and *Grease* was missing.

Those movies had been hard work, but they had seemed like fun. *Moment by Moment* was just work, and he didn't believe he was doing it particularly well. At one point he was even seriously considering walking off the set altogether—simply calling up director Jane Wagner, producer Robert Stigwood, the head of Paramount Studios himself, and announcing, "I'm out of here."

Bob LeMond talked him out of it. "He said I'd get a bad rep if I left, that it was too early in my career for me to call the shots. So I hung on in. It was torture." And the torture never stopped.

John consoled himself by talking only of the future. In interviews, even he was surprised at just how adept he was at dodging questions about *Moment by Moment*. "Lily said she'll kill me if I give the plot away," he teased journalist Rex Reed. "It's all very secret, you'll find out when you see it." He spoke instead of broadening his horizons even further, proudly indicating that his career was mapped out for the next couple of years at least.

His Stigwood contract completed, he signed next to star in *American Gigolo*, a movie, he explained, about a guy "who is obsessed with giving sexual pleasure to women; he cannot understand the concept of receiving the pleasure himself at all." There was also a projected *Godfather* movie, the third in the series, that would cast him as the son of Michael Corleone. *Godfather* creator Francis Ford Coppola's consent was still being awaited, but that was apparently little more than a formality.

He was being considered for a biopic of Elvis Presley. Barbra Streisand and Liza Minelli were both reportedly interested in working with him. He had just signed his own, newly formed production company to a two-movie, two-million-dollar deal with Orion. As a final postscript, Bob LeMond asked, "Is there any film with a male lead between fourteen and sixty where they are not discussing John Travolta?" By the end of 1978, John's profile was as high as any actor's can be.

All this meant that when *Moment by Moment* bombed, it would do so in the most public way possible.

That fall of 1978, John finally purchased a home in keeping with his new lifestyle, a vast Spanish-style ranch in California that had been built in what was then unspoiled countryside by a Spanish nobleman. One-hundred seventy-eight years later, Rancho Tajiguas was still isolated, lost within the orange groves, miles even from the highway that linked Santa Barbara and Los Angeles.

The whole place was ideal. It offered him the type of refuge that Hollywood never could. His only neighbors were members of the Brotherhood of Sun commune, whose sole concern seemed to be working their land.

Yet John denied that he bought the place because he wanted to "get away from it all." His main concern when he started searching for a new home, he insisted, was to find somewhere large enough for him to park his plane.

Rancho Tajiguas was not that place. But from the moment he saw it, he knew that he wanted it. "It was so beautiful that I forgot about the landing strip. I settled for keeping the plane fourteen miles away, instead of in my backyard."

It was not difficult to understand the attraction. The main house alone boasted four vast suites. The grounds were shaded by orange, lemon, and avocado trees, and bougainvillaea draped the garage and a gurgling fountain in the courtyard that John would pass every day on his way to the swimming pool, tennis courts, and guest house.

There was a pond that he stocked with carp, and he built his own screening house behind the tennis courts. He employed a servant. He took to smoking cigars. He laughed to his friends that it was his own personal Xanadu.

Sister Ellen found the extravagance hilarious. "He was still a baby! But he sat at the head of a long, long table with a buzzer [to summon servants] by his foot. We giggled so hard. This was not—repeat not— how we grew up in New Jersey."

That much was true, but even their parents could not have been too sorry to leave all of that far behind after John persuaded them to move to California to a new home just down from Rancho Tajiguas.

It was then that John learned that his mother was dying.

Helen Travolta had been ill for some time, ever since she and Sal accompanied John to Europe for the *Saturday Night Fever* premieres during the spring.

"It was one of the highlights of her life," Sal chuckled, recalling how he and Helen, ever cautiously spendthrift, first balked and then positively revolted against the price of the things they wanted to buy in Europe. To them, any extravagance was a terrible waste, so when Sal saw how expensive his favorite cigars were, he quietly rationed himself to just a couple a day. John responded by ordering the hotel manager to send up boxes at a time and to check in to make sure the old man was smoking them.

In another hotel, Helen was so shocked by the cost of breakfast that she would order only one, then split it with Sal. Even John's constant admonitions that she should just spoil herself, enjoy herself, and help herself to the studio's money did not sway her. Once again John had to take matters in hand. Every morning, he ordered their breakfasts himself, and then sat with his parents while they ate, just to make sure they didn't starve in the lap of such unaccustomed luxury.

"She never got used to having money in the family," John mourned. "She never believed it belonged to her by right."

When Helen broke off the European jaunt halfway through to fly home to New Jersey, John was told his mother was simply overtired, that the strain and excitement of the trip had grown too much for her.

Worried, but not overconcerned, he let her go and went back to the fourteen-hours-a-day regime of interviews and promotional work mapped out for him. He never imagined that the same disease that had snatched Diana from him was now gnawing the life from his mother.

Only as Helen's condition worsened did the family agree to tell John just how serious her illness was. By then it was too late.

The moment he knew what was happening, John took matters into his own hands. He had his mother admitted to the Valley Presbyterian Hospital. Afterward, he cursed, "My turmoil was more than just my mother's being at the fates of her life. It was really, 'Are we doing the right thing?'"

Helen's blood was not coagulating properly, he explained. "But the doctors got it to coagulate enough to cut into her anyway." Unfortunately, she had neither the healing abilities nor the stamina to recover from the operation.

"She should never have been opened up, and I feel I let them do it because the doctors made me feel it was okay." John remains unforgiving. "The doctor persuaded me to [let her] have the operation, and then, when it was over, he said 'Hey man, we're only a practice.' I said, 'Well, you didn't say that three weeks ago. Three weeks ago, it was a demand. She must have this operation. Now suddenly you say you're just a practice?' We had a big fight."

But it was useless. Just as he had been with Diana, John was at Helen's bedside when she died. While she was alive, he once admitted, he had referred to her as his "luck." Now she was gone, he was deeply afraid that his luck was gone too.

"Fate was playing with John's emotions like a yo-yo," James Komack sympathized. The two were talking one day, he recalled, when John suddenly let slip the haunting conflict that had been stalking him since Helen's death—maybe even since Diana's.

"Look, I'm supposed to be the biggest star in the world, and yet I've lost my girl, I've lost my mom, and my father's got a heart condition. What is God doing to me? I'd better stop and take a look at myself because I can't go on like this."

Sister Ellen agreed. "It was all so overwhelming. Suddenly he was one of the most famous people in the world and extraordinarily wealthy, but the people he was closest to in his personal life were gone. It was a bittersweet period for him."

Michelle Cohen, John's publicist, continued, "Just think of the events that have occurred during the past few years of his life: the death of Diana, and then his mother passed away." Yet there was no time for mourning. Once again, John had to simply swallow his pain, put on a brave face, and head back out into the spotlight. It was time to promote *Moment by Moment*—and he soon realized that *Moment by Moment* needed all the promotion it could get. Unfortunately, it wouldn't be enough.

The New York Times set the bad reviews rolling when it described the movie as "This year's California 'problem' picture; that is, a movie in which people suffer for reasons that never seem very urgent in settings that, though not particular to California, are emblematic of what we think of as the California culture."

What made matters worse was that even a kind summary of the plot could not disguise its innate lack of imagination. Lily Tomlin plays Trisha, a thirty-eight-year-old woman who falls in love with Strip (John), a dozy underachiever almost half her age. Already the parallels with John's own life—especially his apparent attraction to older women—were all too plain.

But *Moment by Moment* was no autobiography. In fact, it was scarcely even a story. Slow in starting, even slower in ending, *Moment by Moment* boasted both a script and direction that behaved as though they would prefer to be elsewhere.

Even John's best line was dull. Trisha asks Strip what his friends are like, but all he can do is complain. "All my friends are undependable," he mumbles. "Except Greg, and he's in jail." Indeed, the kindest thing most people could find to say was that John's character was once again closer to Barbarino than Lothario—and that really wasn't much of a compliment.

"I'm not afraid of typecasting," John excused those similarities. But still he insisted, "Although most of the characters I've played have been basically street kids, I'm trying to show new facets of that type." Tomlin agreed, adding, "[He's] closer to himself in this movie than to the street characters he's been playing."

And a resounding "uh-oh" shuddered through John's fan base.

The problem with *Moment by Moment* was not that it was a bad movie—although it certainly wasn't a good one. Its problem was that it was simply not the right movie for its time. John was coming down from two larger than life extravaganzas, films that exploded across the screen, alternately believable and incredible, throwing catchphrases out like fishing hooks and reeling the audience in with their nonstop exuberance.

Moment by Moment offered none of this—it didn't even have a decent soundtrack. And that, as the reviews piled in, was the principal problem. It simply didn't have what people demanded from a John Travolta movie. The audience walked into *Moment by Moment* expecting a chocolate cake with ice cream and soda. Instead they were handed cold gruel and a plain, stale cupcake.

Perhaps the most obviously recurring theme in the movie's savaging was the strained sexual tension between John and Lily Tomlin and the way Lily usually came out on top. It was one thing for her to hunt down a boy toy, but this was a soft boy toy. For the first time, one of John's strongest attributes had backfired badly upon him.

Knowingly or not, John had long traded on the peculiarly androgynous aura that past critics had picked up on—that sense of sexuality that on some level made him as attractive (or, as Lorne Michaels put it, unthreatening) to men as he was to women.

It was an attribute that had a long history in Hollywood and beyond: Rudolph Valentino, Elvis Presley, Mick Jagger—all had flirted with an effete effect, condemning themselves in the eyes of their foes to a lifetime of rumor and crude innuendo.

In the past, John, like those forebears, had employed his sensitivity sparingly: at the end of *Saturday Night Fever*, when Tony arrives unexpectedly at Stephanie's Manhattan apartment and asks if they can be friends; in *Grease*, when Danny corners Sandy at the jukebox, to apologize for the way he's behaved.

And always it had been balanced by his character's inherent toughness. Tony Manero won his scars in a gang fight with the Hispanics; Danny proved himself most famously at Thunder Road but most lastingly in the battlefield of fumbling high school crushes. When he gives Sandy his ring, and she proudly accepts it saying, "Now I know that you really respect me," he almost audibly curses his own sensitivity.

Those shades are nowhere to be seen in *Moment by Moment*. His role as a surfer dude gigolo disrupts the endearing balance found in his previous characters. The role provoked one journalist to damn John's character as "a kind of hairy-chested Jane Russell," a "him-bo" in the parlance of the mid 1990s. John Travolta, it was widely pronounced, had blown it. Or maybe just lost it. Or maybe, he hadn't even had it to begin with.

"When the movie wasn't the big hit we all thought it would be, it was a blow to him," Michelle Cohen, John's publicist, confided. But it wasn't so much that the picture had failed that hurt. "It was all the vicious attacks on John's ability."

Although according to *McCalls*, "the nicest word that anybody had for [the movie] was 'inane,'" and *Newsweek* described it politely as "feeble" and "misconceived," the impression that the vast majority of reviews seemed to give was that it wasn't *Moment by Moment* that had bombed so abysmally. It was John and, in the words of *Newsweek*, "the media, sniffing blood, responded as if it were the second Guyana massacre."

Across the western world, *Moment by Moment* was discarded with disdain; by the time news of John's distress had penetrated the Iron Curtain, the Soviets had to struggle to come up with some fresh bile. But they managed. Writing in the *Literaturnaya Gazeta*, Yuri Borovoi announced not only that the hated capitalist icon was completely washed up, but that "only one joy is left to him, the childish habit of gluing together brightly colored model airplanes."

Already hurt, confused, and utterly unable to believe what was happening, John's discomfort was further compounded when Midland International chose that same disastrous month to resurrect his musical career.

Suggestions that John might record a new album with Carly

Simon had petered out, and John's only visit to a recording studio in recent months had produced just one usable track, a version of Jennifer Warnes' recent hit, "The Right Time of the Night."

It was a lackluster performance at best, but the song was nevertheless tacked on to the nearest thing to a new album Midland could muster, a two-album repackaging of *John Travolta* and *Can't Let You Go*, released under the significantly unimaginative title, *Travolta Fever*. Released in time for Christmas 1978, it stalled at number one-hundred sixty-one.

"Every time I did an interview after *Moment by Moment*," John sighed, "writers went right to the negative things first." A flop movie, a flop album, a flop love life . . . "Why can't they ever ask about positive things?"

But it was what was printed rather than what was asked that bothered him the most.

"Things never come out the way I said them," he complained, wondering aloud why he even did interviews. "I don't have to. Robert De Niro and Al Pacino don't do them, so why should I? It isn't going to help my career anyway. If my product is good, they'll all want to do cover stories on me whether I give interviews or not. If the movie isn't good, they won't want to do anything."

And that was precisely what John felt like doing. Nothing. He had barely even finished "promoting" *Moment by Moment* when he announced that he was going back to Rancho Tajiguas. And there he was going to stay, "as elusive as Garbo," as one journalist put it, "and as difficult as Sinatra."

8

○○○

Retreating to
Ranchos Tajiguas

Johnn was due on the *American Gigolo* set in January 1979, to begin rehearsals. He had already been to Milan to pick out his Giorgio Armani wardrobe and was one day away from learning his lines.

Less than three weeks now remained before work would commence, and that, says Michelle Cohen, was when "it suddenly hit him. He couldn't start. He could have collapsed, or heavens knows what. The impact of everything left him totally exhausted. It came to the point where one morning, he couldn't go to work. It all caught up with him. So he decided to get out for a while, while he was still ahead, because in this business you can get burned out very quickly."

The awful memory of Freddie Prinze had never gone away, but that really wasn't what was topmost in John's mind. More than anything else, he was hurt, angry, and very, very, tired. *American Gigolo* was just one movie too many—and one year too soon.

In years to come, John would be able both to describe and rationalize his decision to bail out on *American Gigolo*. "I tell you honestly," he explained, "I was thinking all the time of the pizzazz of the film, of the body language. I wasn't seeing that the dialogue was stilted. Then I met the writer-director, Paul Schroeder, and he was so rigid about his words on the page, so possessive of his words. . . the more meetings I had with him, the more uncomfortable I became."

Stuck within those confines, John was right to abandon the project. He knew from long experience that he was at his best when he could relax into a role; he also knew, however, that that was only possible if the role could be relaxed around him. The perfectionist Schroeder simply couldn't comprehend that. That's when John finally realized that his role was beyond redemption.

At the time, such thoughts were little more than vague apprehensions, barely audible echoes all but lost in the cacophony of alarm bells raised by instinct alone. He didn't know why he felt this way, and frankly he didn't care. All he knew was that January wasn't simply drawing closer, it was smothering him.

John was in the kitchen of the house he had recently purchased in Santa Monica when a new feeling suddenly hit him, halting him in his tracks as he reached out for something to steady himself with.

Kay, his assistant, glanced over—was he alright? She knew what he'd been going through and how he had been feeling lately. They'd talked long and late about this new film, just as they had the last one.

"Kay?" John's steely eyes seemed fogged, just as his face was clouded. "I have a nauseous feeling in my stomach. I shouldn't be doing this, should I?"

Kay knew exactly what he was talking about and exactly what he wanted to hear. It was what she'd already been hinting at herself for several days. She answered quickly and simply. "No."

The following morning, John called Michael Eisner, the president of Paramount and invited him over to the house. John still remembers the details of that meeting.

"He said, 'What's going on?' And I said, 'Look, my mom just died. I'm not very happy about that, and I'm not very happy about this movie, *Moment by Moment*, that I just did, and I really don't want to do *American Gigolo*. I beg of you to let me out.' He said, 'You're out.'" John was replaced on set by Richard Gere.

John did not extract himself from *American Gigolo* without a price, of course. The film would have been the last under his contract with Paramount. "The next day," John conjectures, "Eisner must've thought, 'What do I get for letting him out of this movie? Because next week the cameras are rolling, and he's not gonna be there.'"

Eisner was back with Paramount's conditions that very afternoon. In return for John bailing out on Schroeder, the studio demanded not only that he complete his contract with them, but that he commit to one further film at the same rate of pay he would have received for *American Gigolo*—two million dollars.

Desperate only to retreat, John agreed. And having retreated, he became a creature of legend.

He tried, briefly, to lead a normal life. If the cameras were off, surely the spotlight would diminish as well? No chance. If anything, in fact, it intensified. Six months before, John Travolta sightings had seemed a dime a dozen. Now that they were scarcer than hen's teeth, everybody wanted to be part of the hunt.

Outside a Beverly Hills restaurant, a young photographer named Todd Wallace approached the limousine John was traveling in. The car came to a halt, the driver leaped out, and in full view of a crowded street, the UCLA student was grabbed and punched. Then two of the bodyguards without whom John never left the house moved in. Seated in the back of the car, his eyes fixed, his face impassive, John could see the entire thing. He felt the whole car shudder as Wallace was slammed against the windows, but he did not move a muscle. He did not seem to care.

Neither did he seem to care when Sal, his father, was hospitalized in the new year. His heart condition was worsening, and the entire family flocked to his bedside back at the Valley Presbyterian Hospital.

Or did they? According to Michelle Cohen, John visited the hospital every day to sit with the old man as he lay in intensive care. Contacted by the press, however, a hospital spokesman insisted, "Mr. Travolta did not visit the hospital while his father was here."

Instead, it was reported, he remained sequestered within the isolation of Rancho Tajiguas, a silent recluse, a morose, bearded shadow drifting sadly through the orange groves, untouchable, unapproachable. Servants were let go, and his phone rang unanswered for days on end.

Occasionally, he would pass a few words with the commune members working on the border of his property, but even his own office didn't really know what was happening. He might phone in to say hello, but that was about it.

When one tabloid claimed that he was contemplating retirement, John's office turned inquiries away with a terse "no comment." When another alleged he was planning his comeback, as though he'd been away twenty years instead of twenty weeks, it drew the same response. According to Michelle Cohen, even she didn't know how he felt or what he was doing. Wherever the stories about John were coming from, it wasn't from his PR office.

Bob LeMond tried desperately to quash the speculation, to buy John the time he needed to dispel all his demons. It wouldn't work, but still LeMond had to try.

"For four years," he persisted, "John was on a skyrocket. He had no time to deal with the deaths, to adjust to his change in financial status, or to accept the criticism of *Moment*. He was physically exhausted."

LeMond continued his reassuring mantra even as it became painfully obvious that John actually was everything his manager was now insisting he wasn't. "He has a great advantage over the stars of the past," LeMond promised. "He's not neurotic and he's not self-destructive." In truth, he had no advantage whatsoever. One rumor insisted he was suicidal, most of them claimed he was neurotic as well. And all of them knew he was scared. They just didn't realize how scared. Nobody did.

The family rallied to John's side, but he rejected their advances. Finally, despairingly, even the ever-loyal Joey snapped. "You can't just closet yourself away and let other people take care of things for you. You've got to run your own life. John's too introverted and not assertive."

Maybe he'd hoped that his words would cauterize the wounds John was licking. Instead, they just opened them further. Now there was nobody John could trust. Just because he was out of the limelight, it didn't mean he hadn't seen everyone else who was in it; he'd certainly noticed his older brother creeping in there.

Sunnyside, Joey's first movie, was a case in point. No matter that its reviews all concurred that the film itself was laughably bad, there was still no doubt that this hackneyed tale of a bad-to-good street kid trying to bring an end to decades of gang warfare in his neighborhood could have spun straight out of one of John's vehicles.

It didn't matter whether Joey was the instigator of all this or not. John was still getting the distinct impression that "Joey's business associates were using me to make things better for Joey's career, using my name, our physical likeness." The two were very close before John became famous; now, "I saw people around him taking advantage of my situation." The two brothers would not be truly reconciled until John attended Joey's marriage later in the year.

Safe behind his locked doors and darkened windows, John knew what people were saying about him and his situation, and it hurt. But it wasn't as simple as they seemed to think for him to re-emerge from his cocoon. It wasn't a matter of just returning to the spotlight; it was a matter of re-evaluating that spotlight as well.

"Suddenly, it's very hard for me to do just any play, or any movie. *Moment by Moment* proved that. I thought I was going to get away with doing a little art film that wouldn't cost very much, that no one would pay much attention to!" In later years he would rationalize the movie's failure by observing, "Most people didn't see it anyway. My hardcore fans didn't see it."

At the time, however, all he could do was laugh at his own naiveté and admit that the experience had soured much of his own ambition.

"It's taken the fun out of being able to get up and do anything you want." He had been idly considering a return to Broadway, but he "slowly realized, 'God, if I get this much focus on a film, I couldn't get away with doing a play somewhere.'"

It was logical thinking, but still one of John's business associates told *Life* magazine, "It's the Elvis Presley complex." Presley spent the last years of his life paralyzed behind the gates of Graceland, venturing out for concert tours, but even there remaining deep within the shelter of his bodyguards and buddies.

John, however, wasn't even that gregarious. "If Streisand could go to the supermarket," *Life*'s confidante argued, "Why can't John? He thinks he has to have armed guards at all times, and everyone tell him how great he is. When you are so cloistered, you have no perspective." And when you have no perspective, it's hard to have any friends.

"I've got this strange reputation for being a loner," John justified, "but it's not that simple." It wasn't his reputation that was crippling him. It was fear.

"I just don't want to lose the power, don't want to blow it all. That's why every decision gets harder." In print, he sounded almost megalomaniacal. Perhaps he was. But he also sounded pleading. "Right now the game's mine. I don't want it to go down the drain."

Of course, he confessed, "there are things that I can't do now, and places I would like to go that I can't. But I like everything that's happened to me. I wouldn't give up my stardom just to get to go to Disneyland." And that was the point, wasn't it? John had risen to the top, a top that—maybe Tom Moore was right—he had visualized during his ascendancy and simply created when he got there.

Having reached it, he found the cliché was true: it is lonely at the top. But it's even lonelier when you discover that what you thought was firm ground is really thin ice and that the only time you're truly safe is when you're standing perfectly still.

The failure of *Moment by Moment* had cracked the ice; John stepped out of the milieu he knew, and he had felt the surface shifting beneath him. So he withdrew not because he wanted to, not because he needed to, but because it was all he could do.

He could not freeze time around him, he understood that. But he could freeze himself within time. In doing that, he could freeze his fame too. If he never moved again, he would never do anything wrong and he would be locked forever in the history books like James Dean on the road with a gun slung over his shoulder, Marilyn Monroe with her skirt blown up over her underwear, or Tony Manero striking the hour. The game would still be his.

The problem was, legends could do that because legends are dead. John Travolta, however, was still very much alive, and when he glanced out of the windows sometimes the press corps cars parked on the far side of the fence and the news helicopters that flew over the compound every few days reminded him that the rest of the world knew he was still alive, too.

And the phone just kept on ringing. So one day, he answered it.

It was Bob LeMond, and he had just one question. Did John want to be a cowboy? An urban cowboy?

Like *Saturday Night Fever*, *Urban Cowboy* was developed from a

magazine article. Aaron Latham's *Esquire* story was about the phenomenon exploding down at Gilley's, a three-and-a-half-acre honky-
tonk in Pasadena, Texas. Young Texans—up to seven thousand at a
time—were nightly descending upon the club for a drink, a dance,
and a few back-breaking rounds on an eight-hundred-pound
mechanical bull.

In journalistic terms, Gilley's was virgin territory before Latham
dragged it into the cold light of newsprint. Like the disco scene around
the Oddyssey, it had hitherto existed simply for itself, a self-sufficient,
self-absorbed, and thoroughly self-contained universe. It made its own
laws, addressed its own morals, and dealt its own justice to anyone who
transgressed either. For a city's worth of blue-collar cowboys, it was the
ultimate role-playing game, and even the pick-up lines were part of the
fun. "You a real cowboy?" Sissy asks Bud in the movie. When he says
that he could be, she takes him home to bed.

Urban Cowboy's heart remained rooted in Latham's original examination of America's obsession with its Wild West past, as seen through
the eyes of a real-life love triangle. It is an obsession that outsiders alone
tend to notice, for to America itself, it is simply another way of life in
the melting pot of culture.

But it goes beyond that; it is not only a way of life, it's a cultural
touchstone, a remnant of a time in which nothing was not what it
seemed. The good guys always wore white hats, and the bad guys
always wore black; the lawmen all had silver stars, and if you couldn't
sort out your problems like civilized beings, you simply settled them
like men, with fists and guns—then back to the saloon.

In this world of macho make-believe (for even at its wildest,
the West was never that simple), the eternal popularity of cowboy
films is merely the first stone in a millpond, causing ripples that
extend through country and western music, Stetson hats and
embroidered boots, and finally washes ashore in places like Gilley's
honky tonk.

"It was one-hundred percent prime redneck," coproducer Robert
Evans later reflected. "The girls at Gilley's were tougher than any line-
backer for the Chicago Bears. One of them, Milly, held the record for
taking on one-hundred sixty-eight guys riding the bull in one week!"
Before the *Urban Cowboy* crew wrapped up in Texas, she had already

been dethroned by another girl. The movie's heroine, Sissy, tentatively riding the bull just to see if she can, had a long way to go before she caught up.

John paid his first visit to Gilley's on February 17, the day before his birthday. It was an operation that had been schemed with the ultimate secrecy but was almost cancelled after television's Rona Barrett leaked the news on *Good Morning America.*

Amongst Gilley's regulars, John's recruitment was viewed with considerable distaste; throughout the movie's gestation, the feeling had been that *Urban Cowboy* should be made with a cast of unknowns, with the songs attracting the audience. The movie rights had been picked up by Irving Azoff, the manager of the Eagles, for $150,000, and a tentative soundtrack featuring the Eagles, fellow Azoff clients Linda Ronstadt and Jimmy Buffet, and Waylon Jennings had originally been mooted.

By January 1979, these original plans were scrapped, and a big name star was being actively sought: Gary Busey, a native of nearby Baytown, was one possibility, but when John's name was raised the Gilleyrats, as the bar's regulars were known, had few other topics of conversation for the next month.

Bearded and slightly overweight, John arrived at Gilley's accompanied by Azoff, writer Aaron Latham, director Jim Bridges, Jerry Wurms, and a host of others. Scooped up from the airport by a fleet of limos, they reached the bar to discover that news of their arrival had gotten there before them. A crowd of regulars, accompanied by wives and daughters, awaited them, but John barely batted an eyelid. He was too busy staring at the mechanical bull. And when a local challenged him to get up and ride it, John simply smiled. "Not yet. I'll ride it eventually, but not today. I need to take one home and practice on it in my back yard."

All that day and late into the evening as he hung out at Gilley's, John's enthusiasm for *Urban Cowboy* was evident. By the time he had returned to California, however, his excitement was waning and was replaced by caution. If he succeeded in this new role, his career would be back on track. But if he failed, he might as well kiss his career goodbye. Knowing that Azoff and Bridges desperately wanted him; knowing, too, that they would be prepared to wait before he gave his decision if they believed that decision would be the one they wanted, he decided to proceed with the utmost caution. It would be mid-March before he finally confirmed his acceptance of the role, early April before the contracts had been finalized. John eventually signed on for two million dollars, plus a percentage of the gross.

Throughout John's seclusion, the press circled Rancho Tajiguas like vultures. Aside from them, the one person who seemed to come and go at all regularly was Marilu Henner, still a close friend long after the pair ended as lovers.

She made a difference. Talking John through the ghosts that haunted him, she cajoled him back to life simply by bringing her own life back into his. They had always been like children together, laughing and playing. She called him Johnny, and he called her Henner. Long ago, he'd taught her what to do when things got too heavy. "Don't throw a pity party, get out of town. Throw a new reality into the mix."

Without even giving him the chance to argue, Marilu got up one day and demanded, "Pack your cases, we're going to Chicago to stay with my folks." John was at the airport before he even knew what hit him.

They walked into the house just as the garden filled with grammar school children. Unbeknownst to Marilu, her niece was having her graduation party there. Unbeknownst to John, he was now the star guest.

Marilu remembered, "The information spread like wildfire in the neighborhood that John was in town. The party got lots bigger than we anticipated. I was worried about how he would react, but I needn't have. He went around and introduced himself to everyone. He talked to all the graduates and to their relatives. Johnny was completely and graciously the master of the situation."

The following month, John was out again, this time at his father's wedding.

It was no secret that Sal's decision to remarry so soon after Helen's death had left John confused and distraught—all the more so, perhaps, because the bride-to-be, June, had been Helen's nurse throughout her final illness and had then nursed Sal through his own more recent convalescence.

He could not fight it, though, and he would not, for deep down he understood what Sal was doing. "Look, I just absolutely want my dad to be happy. Life can go on—it must. Love is creative. His marrying again was a compliment to my mother. It was like, 'Hey! That worked for forty-eight years. I want it again.'"

John's only disappointment was that his appearance at the wedding turned a family occasion into headline news. The couple moved into the house in Woodland Hills that John had bought Sal after Helen's death, and that Thanksgiving brother Joey was the only Travolta absent from the house. Things were still rough, but they were getting better.

Stepping back out into the sunlight was the best thing that John could have done. Selecting *Urban Cowboy* for his next movie was the second best.

John had his bull installed in a newly built corral on the grounds of Rancho Tajiguas and rode it for weeks, until he really was as good as his movie character is meant to be. When he rested, he practiced his Texan accent; when he relaxed, it was in the company of the real-life urban cowboys whose own peculiar lifestyle he was about to explode into nationwide prominence. While he trained, Jim Bridges shot background footage at Gilley's and scouted locations—the Houston livestock show and rodeo, the petro-chemical plant, and so on.

He was aware of the locals' continued distrust of John but did his best to calm their fears. "I don't see any problems at all," he told *Houston Post* critic Bob Claypool. "I've got to be excited, simply because he's the best young actor in the business. Plus, he's really enthused about the project. When he visited the club, he simply fell in love with the place and everything about it. He and one of the employees, Pat Wright, traded belts, and he just had a great time talking to the people here and seeing what it was all about."

Bridges acknowledged that "there have been some difficulties in negotiating the contract, but John simply wanted to get involved in the whole project—which is very understandable. I tell you, he's one of the sweetest people I've ever met."

Shooting was scheduled to begin in April, only to be postponed when John decided to go to Tahiti instead for what his staff described as his first holiday in four years. A May start, too, was cancelled after John was bitten on the lip and cheek by his dog, leaving wounds that required plastic surgery. It was mid-June before shooting began in 1979.

It was one of the hottest, wettest summers on record, and the shoot already threatened to be miserable, sticky, sweaty, cranky, and cramped. John would shrug the discomfort away. "Yeah, it's hot. But if you think this is hot, you should see where we shot *Saturday Night Fever*. It was much worse than this."

Indeed, as John flew down with sister Ellen beside him, he was glad simply to be going to work.

Ellen remembers, "Coming from L.A. to Houston with Johnny on his jet, seeing him so dressed up and handsome in an expensive cowboy suit, I thought he looked like a four-year-old oil man, like the richest four-year-old oil man in the world."

Bob Claypool continues, "He simply eased into the club. He looked totally different now. He'd lost weight since his first visit and was now a slim and trim version of young cowboy manhood, all togged out in Western shirt and jeans, boots and hat, and with a cowboy belt that—in time-honored Gilley's tradition—sported the owner's name in back, just plain 'Bud.'" One of the Gilleyrats even reckoned John looked "exactly like one of our old shitkickers."

For other people, however, John's cowboy credentials were of secondary importance. What really mattered was the bushy black beard that still consumed half his face, but which he now reckoned disguised the dog bite. If you believed that, Robert Evans responded, you'd believe anything.

"It covered his good looks and I was not going to have it. His cleft, his smile, made him a star. Now I get him with a beard." He looked, Evans swore, "like an Italian butcher."

But when Evans ordered him to shave the beard off, John refused. "He didn't want anyone to know him. He was scared after *Moment by Moment*. It was a way of hiding." Another way of hiding.

Spending his forty-ninth birthday with Michael Eisner, Barry Diller, and Don Simpson, Evans snapped, "He shaves his beard off, or I shut the picture down today." He meant it as well, even though it sometimes seemed that he was the only one who could find fault with John's new look. Even the movie's director, James Bridges, was standing up for the star. "He likes it. So does Travolta's whole coterie." But Evans was adamant. "I'm not taking any orders from any starlet who's just become a star." John was working for him, not the other way around. That, he told Paramount chief Eisner, "is why you overpay me."

"How many scenes have you shot with Travolta?" Eisner asked.

"Too many," Evans responded. "About six." So they concocted a piece of dialogue that seemed to direct its ultimatum toward John's character in the movie but was actually a pointed mandate directed at John himself.

When John's character, Bud, applies for a job at the oil refinery, he is told that they'll take him on as a gopher but on one condition. "We don't hire guys with beards."

"The next day," Evans proudly reported, "the biggest star in the world shaved his beard off. Then, till the end of the picture, the biggest star in the world refused to talk to me."

Not that Evans was alone in that. For all the support he had shown John, director Bridges, too, found that simply communicating with the star was often infuriatingly difficult.

You couldn't just bang on the door of his trailer and ask if he had a spare minute or two. First you had to make an appointment with one of the flunkies who were always on hand—Robert Evans described John as having more advisers than the President.

You told the first one what you wanted to ask, she passed it on to the next man in line, he'd pass it on to somebody else, and by the time someone called back to "just check on one thing," you'd have forgotten what it was all about in the first place. Either that, or the scene would have already been shot.

Finally Bridges, too, laid down the law, and if he hadn't been so frustrated, he would probably have found it funny. John "couldn't be disturbed" when Bridges demanded that they talk. Instead, he had to pass his ultimatum on through the same thick layers of aides and assistants. Thankfully, it was the last time he had to do that.

"I said, 'I cannot make this movie this way. When I want to talk to John, I cannot have to go through three secretaries.'" He, too, threatened to close down the movie, and a narrow stairway to the star was constructed shortly after.

The crew and cast (including John's sister Anne in another cameo role) remained in Houston for several months, a period during which John continued his social rehabilitation.

Travolta fever hit Pasadena after John made a surprise appearance onstage with the Bee Gees at Houston's Summit Arena on June 30. Dancing on stage while the band played "You Should be Dancing," he drove an already fever-pitch audience to hysterical proportions, and from that night on, Bob Claypool later wrote, "it was obvious that all the *Urban Cowboy* rumors were true, and the groupies and hangers-on and letter-writers and phone-callers responded accordingly." What had been a trickle of curious fans come to find out whether that really was John Travolta working with the film crew became a flood.

Renting a ten-thousand-dollar-a-month mansion, which the press promptly christened "Fort Travolta," John filled the place with visitors: costar Debra Winger, briefly the subject of another speculative love affair, his family, Marilu Henner, and Diana's son Zack, with whom he had remained extraordinarily close, and who now lived with his father, Joseph Goodson. He entertained them with meals and movies; later in the shoot, he took his guests aloft in the three-hundred-thousand-dollar Cessna 414 he'd just purchased.

The set itself, however, remained closed to all but essential personnel, and word quickly got around that it was John who had demanded that the restriction be enforced with iron rigidity.

Frustrated, disgusted, wanting merely to get on with their jobs, the pressmen who gathered outside the locked gates rechristened the star "John Revolta," joking about the handful of sightings they had made. The star looked older, rougher, and paunchy. When the first promotional photographs crept out from the studio, it was even circulated that John had had his picture retouched to draw attention away from what he himself called his thunder-thighs.

Resentment turned to animosity. "Spoiled brat John Travolta is flagrantly throwing his weight around on the set of his new movie, and anxious producers have caved in to his outrageous demands," snarled the *National Enquirer*, quoting an unnamed Hollywood producer as saying, "he is worse than Streisand and Sinatra combined. Demanding a private house on location is practically unheard of. Even Sinatra stays in hotels."

The same source condemned John's ban on press contact as "unprecedented and ridiculous," while the Hollywood Women's Press Corp awarded John their Sour Apple Award for 1979 for his services to unnecessary secrecy and ill-humored grouching and a *Rolling Stone* writer was reportedly so furious at not being able to procure an interview with the star that he smashed one of John's car windows.

Even so, the lock-out was not perfect.

According to John, there were "about ten incidents" of other people either breaking onto the set or into his mansion. On one occasion, his security people even found a girl hiding in a closet. On another, a freelance photographer was evicted from the set, at the same time as another was firing off shot after shot for the *Houston Post*.

Yet the Gilleyrats had no complaints whatsoever about John and his entourage. "The only people I've seen them keep away from John are people who needed to be kept away," one said. "Even some of the extras are just crazy—they'll go up to John between scenes and want to introduce every friend they've got in the world to him. And make him sign autographs too!"

Other tales of John's friendliness and generosity crept out, including one of how he paid the hospital bill for an extra who was hurt in a car accident. And while the press gnashed their teeth and waved their empty cameras, fans had no trouble at all getting snapshots of the star; eating out, he always found time to pose with customers and staff.

With considerable relief, then, the production moved back to Los Angeles for the winter, John flying home aboard the new Cessna. But still, the shoot's problem with invaders was not solved, and John's uneasiness continued to grow with every new infraction. He finally erupted in understandable terror the evening that a Los Angeles street gang physically gatecrashed the set. In the ensuing chaos, a single gunshot rang out; John remains convinced that it was fired in his direction. Immediately he ordered the production shut down. He hired further protection and returned to the set fully flanked by his own private army. *Urban Cowboy* was completed amid a veritable sea of muscle.

Afterward, John gathered his bodyguards, sisters, and Marilu together, and flew them all to Lake Tahoe to ski. Marilu quipped, "When we were younger, we used to kid each other about having no taste in clothes. Now we'll go away for the weekend and take six suitcases with us."

From Robert Evans' point of view, *Urban Cowboy*'s problems were by no means over with the wrap party. John's contract demanded that he share with James Bridges the final say on the editing. Although Bridges later commended him for not pulling a star trip—even if he did insist on cutting the scene in which the offending beard is removed—Evans grew increasingly unhappy as work continued.

"I'm looking for *Saturday Night Fever* goes west, not *The Red Shoes*," he stormed at Bridges, when he first saw the fruits of the pair's cutting-room labors. Evans had already had a call from Michael Eisner, warning him that John was present in the editing suite every night; he warned him, too, that "if we change the name to *Urban Cowgirl*, don't blame Paramount."

Watching the finished film, Evans knew exactly what Eisner meant. "Where's the fuckin' raunch, the sweat, the dancin'? There's no heat! It's all been shot. Now I'm lookin' at a fuckin' ballet!"

Bridges, however, refused to budge. "We don't have to be exploitative. John's the biggest star in the world," and as Evans himself put it, "When director and star lock together, you can win a battle, but the war? Forget it. *Urban Cowboy's* double-album soundtrack was pure platinum. *Urban Cowboy*, the film, was sterling silver."

Bridges himself was in no doubt that *Urban Cowboy* was a great film, and that it was John who made it so. "He worked his ass off. I can't sing his praises too highly. Travolta can do anything. He's our only major star, and he's just growing into his talent."

Urban Cowboy opened in June 1980, exactly one year after shooting began. It was, many writers argued, make-or-break time for the fallen face of the 1970s, but Marilu, seemingly adopted as John's unofficial spokesperson, argued that John was in fact more carefree than she had seen him in ages.

"Johnny's been really high lately, excited by life and very much his old self again. I think it's got a lot to do with 1980; shedding the decade, leaving it behind you. Everything seems very positive right now."

John agreed. "I don't have to do anything I don't want to do." He was speaking financially—with combined sales of over nineteen million, his share in the soundtracks to *Saturday Night Fever* and *Grease* alone ensured he need never worry about money again.

But he could also have been speaking from the standpoint of someone who had seen both the heights of fame and the depths of despair. He understood that true happiness was only derived from knowing that nothing really matters unless you care passionately for it.

"*Moment by Moment* definitely left me anxiety-prone and frightened. I'm more experienced now. I know how to deal with it all a little better. Even if *Urban Cowboy* does half as well as [*Saturday Night Fever* and *Grease*], I'll probably get more pleasure out of the outcome because I've had the downfall and I'm back into some sort of reality."

But what was that reality? Still unwilling to leave the house without his band of bodyguards, John attracted headlines wherever he went. He had to abandon going out to restaurants completely, simply because of the mayhem that ensued. He even smiled sadly, "You wouldn't think so, but the classier ones are the worst." The cheaper ones were simply chaotic.

One Sunday in May 1980, while staying at his newly purchased two-bedroom house in Studio City, John decided to visit the deli down the road.

"I just decided to spend a quiet morning reading the papers," he chuckled. "I don't know why I thought I could do it." Within moments he had been chased home again by a horde of autograph hunters—and that was before his latest movie had even opened. If he had ever doubted that his star still hung in the Hollywood high, he certainly must have been reassured.

Yet when John announced that he was going to keep his future options open until he saw how *Urban Cowboy* fared with the critics and the box office, it was easy to zero in on the insecurities that still haunted him.

The days when the possible projects had cascaded from his lips seemed a long time ago. Now it was sufficient for him simply to say that he and his company had read three hundred scripts in recent months and joke, "When I get depressed, I should just look at that list of names. If I could do a movie with each one of them—what a career, no matter how the project turned out!"

In fact, a number of possible films were under discussion. Jane Fonda had apparently been courting John for a revival of *A Chorus Line*, while Francis Ford Coppola, temporarily free of the specter of a *Godfather III*, had expressed interest in shooting a musical with John.

He was also considering playing a rock star in a movie, and he flew to see Bruce Springsteen at the Philadelphia Spectrum to research the part.

Warner Brothers approached him next, first about a role as an undercover cop in *Prince of the City*, a part that eventually went to John's old *Grease* companion Treat Williams; then as a morgue attendant in *Happy Days* star Ron Howard's wonderful *Night Shift*, starring alongside Henry Winkler, the former Fonz. What a publicist's dream that would have been!

John rejected them both (a young first-timer named Michael Keaton replaced him in *Night Shift*), but the studio, not to be dissuaded, offered him the title role in *Arthur*. When John turned that down as well, the studio went for Dudley Moore, who was probably better suited to the role to begin with.

But that was not the point. John was bankable business again. Milos Forman was even putting forward the bizarre but eminently saleable notion of pairing John with another great dance legend of the age, the defecting Soviet ballet dancer Mikhail Baryshnikov.

The two dancers, after all, had already gone head-to-head in 1978, when Baryshnikov's own cinema debut, *The Turning Point*, set off in pursuit of many of the same awards as *Saturday Night Fever*. The idea of a full-blooded collaboration was distinctly fascinating.

But even this idea paled in comparison with one final project: the possibility of John portraying his old idol, James Cagney, in a film version of Cagney's younger days. Cagney and his wife even flew out to Rancho Tajiguas to discuss the project, and John, laughing for the journalists who were allowed onto the grounds for the occasion, announced loudly, "Cagney's my biggest fan, he thinks I'm great."

Cagney was not the sole visitor whose name stood out from the ranch's voluminous visitors' book. Jane Fonda, Mohammed Ali and Tom Hayden also passed through. But still Cagney was the one who made the greatest impression on John.

"It's so important for me to talk to people like Jimmy Cagney. They're giving me hope because they've gone through the same thing as I have." Cagney and his wife, John continued, were only intending to remain with him for two days; they ended up staying for four, sitting around trading stories and watching each other's movies. "Cagney loved it here. He said it was the most beautiful house he'd ever seen, and they were four of the nicest days of his life. Imagine that! I was so honored."

The veteran also handed on a piece of advice that John would never forget. "I asked him how he kept up with the pressure of the public, the studio, the press. I said I can't keep up with it. He said, 'Let me tell you, son, vaudeville was so cutthroat that after that, the films were a piece of cake.'"

Or in other words, count your blessings.

9

◇◇◇

Back in the Saddle

Urban *Cowboy* announced John's return to the movie mainstream in the most strident terms it could. It created another wave of fever that this time truly defied prediction.

Reviews were good from the outset, with Vincent Canby's write-up in *The New York Times* setting the tone for most of them. Casting *Urban Cowboy* as "the most entertaining, most perceptive, commercial American movie of the year to date," he acknowledged the inevitable parallels to *Saturday Night Fever* but did not allow them to distress him.

"Like *Saturday Night Fever*, the new movie also focuses on the particular hangout of people with names like Bud and Sissy and Wes and Pam"; like *Saturday Night Fever*, it captured them having a great deal of fun in the kind of environment most observers had barely dreamed existed. And like *Saturday Night Fever*, it made people want to share in that world.

Within weeks of *Urban Cowboy*'s opening, the manufacturers of the eight-hundred-pound mechanical bulls upon which Bud and his cronies prove their cowboy vitality were reporting record orders—from places they'd probably never heard of before let alone shipped their merchandise to. The mechanical bull came to symbolize John's return. You expect to find such things in the pseudo-frontier towns of Texas and the southwest, but *Urban Cowboy* would send them bucking into New Jersey as well.

Urban Cowboy was another phenomenon, pulling in one-hundred million dollars at the box office and although the staying power of both it and the mechanical bulls was scarcely equal to that enjoyed by Tony Manero and the disco music boom, it had less to do with the popularity of *Urban Cowboy* or its star than with the impracticalities inherent in remaining aboard a bucking bronco for anything remotely approaching an impressive time span. Within a year, most of the machines were under sheets in the backrooms of bars.

No longer running scared from the attentions of his public, John celebrated his rehabilitation by signing up for another movie almost immediately.

In many ways, however, he had taken the easiest option. Leaving the Coppolas, Fondas, and Formans at the altar, John chose instead to return to the director who had handled his big screen near-debut, *Carrie*'s Brian De Palma.

But if it was a return to the womb in terms of personnel (De Palma's wife, Nancy Allen, would be on board as well), the role itself was something else entirely, an almost defiant corollary to the lifestyle-defining characters John had played in his most successful past. And yet *Blow Out* would become both Brian De Palma's *pièce de résistance* and John's pre-*Pulp Fiction* masterpiece—an astonishing movie that succeeds on many levels.

But it could all have turned out so terribly different.

For a start, *Blow Out* was not an easy role for John to land.

"I didn't write the role for John, because I thought he was too young," De Palma confessed. Only after meeting him again for the first time in six years and realizing that "he was no longer a boy, but a grown man and quite right for it," did De Palma change his mind.

De Palma was also forced to rethink the identity of John's costar. Neither he nor Nancy Allen had even considered the possibility of her taking the role. But, Allen recalls, "When John said I should play the part [of Sally Bedina], logic went out the window and I reacted emotionally. I love John and I wanted to work with him"—even if it meant laying herself open to some of the crudest humor Hollywood gossip had yet laid claim to. There again, comparing John and Nancy's behavior in one film to the title of this latest, it was hard to resist making the same jokes oneself: from blow job to *Blow Out* indeed.

Accepting the part also demanded that Nancy overcome one of her greatest phobias: she would have to film a scene submerged in water.

"Even though it was a five-foot-deep tank at Burbank Studios, I became hysterical," she recalled. "I was afraid to ask questions because I didn't want the special effects crew to think I was stupid. Thank God for John. He asked questions for me, and taught me buddy breathing."

John, for his part, would relish the underwater scenes, even performing his own submarine stunts. In fact, he was so impressive that at the end of the shoot the crew presented him with a special reminder—a floating directors chair inscribed "Esther Travolta," a reference to Hollywood's greatest aquatic star, Esther Williams.

Even with its leading characters established, still *Blow Out* was not home free. Thrilled by *Urban Cowboy's* unprecedented success— there hadn't been a cowboy movie that huge in years!—Paramount was desperately trying to come up with a suitable vehicle for John's final contracted movie. Whether by accident or design, John was having a hard time actually accepting anything they suggested, much preferring, it seemed, simply to sit on his hands and fly around in his planes.

With neither party ever admitting it, they had arrived at an impasse. Faced with the possibility of John willfully permitting his reborn fame to dribble away through inactivity, Bob LeMond finally convinced Paramount to "loan" him to Filmways for this one feature.

Stylistically, *Blow Out* owes a considerable debt to Michaelangelo Antonioni's 1966 classic *Blow Up*. Both movies concern the freak witnessing of what may or may not have been a murder, both track the witness through his own attempts to untangle the ensuing conspiratorial skein. De Palma's movie title, of course, is an acknowledgement of this homage.

Where the two movies divide is in the style of directorship. *Blow Up* is very much a child of its times, referencing the psychedelic experience that was just then seeping from the arty underground into mainsteam consciousness and gaining notoriety with the gratuitous inclusion of both revealing nudity and loud rock' n' roll.

Blow Out eschewed the music and retained the nudity only within the context of its hero, Jack Teri's job. He is the sound engineer at a studio that specializes in soft porn movies, and it is while he is out one evening recording the noises of the evening for the studio's audio library that he witnesses and records an auto crash, a car skidding from a nearby bridge into the water.

Racing to the scene, Teri succeeds in rescuing the passenger, Sally, alone; only when he reaches the hospital does he discover the drowned driver was a prominent politician, "maybe the next President of the United States." He is informed, too, that the presence of a passenger is to remain a closely guarded secret. It was bad enough, he was told, that the senator was dead. Why make things worse by throwing a prostitute into the soup?

When Jack replays his tape of the accident and discerns a sound he hadn't noticed before—a gunshot immediately before the noise of the car's tire exploding—the storyline takes its first savage twist. Echoes of America's greatest real life political intrigues—Chappaquidick, Watergate, the death of JFK—abound and rebound. The viewer's own notions of what "really" happened there alternately clarify and obscure Jack's attempts to uncover the truth.

"The excitement of the film," *Rolling Stone's* Michael Sragow would write, "comes in watching [Jack] strip away his own insulation and commit himself to exposing the truth." The *New Yorker's* Pauline Kael, the critic who did so much for *Saturday Night Fever*, went even further, comparing John to a "very young Brando," as she cites his "willingness to go emotionally naked, [with] the control to do it on camera."

Less reliable, however, was *The New York Times* review that described Jack Terri as "the only thoroughly decent character in the film." Until the final scene, the viewer would agree. But Teri's dedication to uncovering the conspiracy, it turns out, is no greater than his commitment to fulfilling the task his studio boss gave him at the beginning of the movie—to find the perfect scream for a *Psycho*-like shower scene.

The most telling reviews, though, were those that remarked that if *Blow Out* had been made by Paramount or any of the major studios, it would have been one of 1981's biggest hits. Instead, it was a box-office flop, not because it was not a great movie but because, as John himself put it, "It was Filmways' last hurrah. They didn't even have enough money to promote it. The company was already going under. It would have taken *Jurassic Park* to save that company."

Despite *Blow Out*'s failure, John remained buoyant. "I never expected it to be [a hit]. It's a success to me. I thought it was a clever movie with a good role, directed by Brian De Palma, who I love." Indeed, in any examination of the so-called Dark Ages that consumed John's career between *Urban Cowboy* (some might even say *Grease*) and *Pulp Fiction*, *Blow Out* remains a beacon, a thunderous performance in a marvelous movie offering incontrovertible evidence that whatever other failings John might have exhibited as his career lurched from flop movie to worse, the erosion of his talent was not among them.

John himself indicated his own appreciation of the break *Blow Out* provided him by admitting De Palma and Allen into his closely guarded inner sanctum of friends.

"There was always an affinity there, but now we're closer than ever," he exclaimed, "and I know the friendship will last for a long time. They're loyal people to their friends. They support you totally. I feel so relaxed with them, like I could say or do anything. There's no strain at all. It's almost like a family. Sometimes I think of Brian and Nancy as my parents." And particularly indulgent parents at that. "We're into heavy eating when we're together."

All the same, their association with such a well-known figure did cause the couple some qualms. "Just going out with John can be frustrating and imposing at times," Allen complained. "Twenty people queue up for his autograph while you're trying to have a conversation."

John maintained his ready acceptance of such trials. He had overcome his devils; now, he said, "I feel that people like me." Completely reversing his self-proclaimed reputation, he continued, "That's why I like to go out in public a lot, to a public restaurant rather than be in seclusion. It confirms their affinity for me. It gives you the confidence that people love you. I need that. If I ever got the feeling that the public didn't like me anymore, that would really hurt."

Indeed, John threw himself back into the limelight with such determination that he even succumbed to what could only be described as the gratification of a publicity agent's wildest dream. He started stepping out, publicly and sensationally, with Brooke Shields, the fifteen-year-old ingenue who had already been entrancing a nation for almost a decade.

It was an unconventional relationship in the eyes of the media. At twenty-seven he may not have been old enough to be his paramour's father, but it was nevertheless a romance made in tabloid heaven. John and Brooke loved it; the gossip columnists loved it; even Shields' mother loved it. Indeed, Teri Shields herself set the ball rolling in the first place, deliberately arranging for the pair to meet at photographer Patrick Demarcheller's Los Angeles studio. She told the press it was her daughter's "first summer love."

Indeed, while it lasted, the relationship was as traditional as any liaison between a twenty-seven-year-old man and a fifteen-year-old girl could be. For their first date, they went out for a Chinese meal, then John dropped her home at 7:30 so she'd be able to finish her homework.

He bought her a Rolex for her sixteenth birthday in May, and the following month, when Brooke returned to L.A. for the opening of her latest movie, *Endless Love*, she accompanied him to see *Superman II*. The following week, the couple were in New York, attending another Bruce Springsteen concert.

"The things John says are so sweet," Brooke gushed; "Brooke exudes goodness," John replied. Overseeing it all, Teri Shields would say things like, "I'd like to have him as a son."

Yet amid such public billing and cooing, a degree of cynicism was inevitable. Both *Blow Out* and *Endless Love* were being handled by the same publicity company, and when the press campaigns ended, it seemed, so did the relationship. By the time John had another movie to promote almost two years later, Brooke wasn't even a penciled notation in the diligent interviewer's notepad.

"We had something of a romance," John conceded elusively. "It depends on the degree you want to get involved."

Immediately following *Blow Out* and the tireless promotional routine both John and De Palma threw themselves into, the director began piecing together his next project, a remake of the 1931 gangster classic, *Scarface*. Al Pacino already promised savage brilliance in his reprise of Paul Muni's title role. And this time, John figured prominently in De Palma's plans from the outset.

Unfortunately, it was not to be. "Things got too complicated," John blithely explained. What he really meant was that neither his pleading nor Bob LeMond's negotiating skills were sufficient to persuade Paramount to loan him out again. They refused even to listen. In so doing, they ensured that John's career arc would finally commence the downward plunge that *Blow Out* had done its best to ward off.

Following *Blow Out*, Martin Amis wrote more than a decade later, "there was a general expectation that [John] would soon fall under the sway of such directors as Francis Coppola and Martin Scorcese. Instead, he fell under the sway of Sylvester Stallone."

As John re-emerged following *Blow Out*, Paramount had offered him the lead role in *An Officer and a Gentleman*, the sweeping military romance that also starred Louis Gossett Jr. and John's *Urban Cowboy* sidekick, Debra Winger.

John rejected it, believing—correctly as it turned out—that "the girl had the best part." Besides, he had only just finished *Blow Out*; "I wasn't ready to go back to work." Instead, he intended to go to pilot school to earn his jet pilot's license. Nothing, not even a potentially monstrous movie, was going to sway him.

Just as he had with *American Gigolo*, Richard Gere stepped into John's shoes, and the movie of course went on to become one of 1982's biggest box office hits. But John had no regrets.

After the movie came out, John discussed career moves with his old *Bonnie and Clyde*-era hero, Warren Beatty.

"Do you think I should have done *An Officer and a Gentleman*?"

Beatty looked puzzled. "Why?"

Now it was John's turn to look puzzled. "Because it was a commercial success, of course."

Beatty shrugged. "John. You have two of the biggest movies in movie history. Why do you need another? Just do good movies."

John took Beatty's advice to heart. Unfortunately, what works in theory does not necessarily always work in practice, particularly when one has a studio breathing down one's neck. And Paramount's breathing was getting heavy.

The studio took John's refusal to make *An Officer and a Gentleman* remarkably well—maybe too well, Bob LeMond figured. There was an old expression that kept coming to mind—"give 'em enough rope." Paramount had all but bent over backwards to give John an easy and potentially very successful way out of his contract, and John had thrown it all back in their faces. That was an awful lot of rope. And when LeMond learned that Robert Stigwood and Norman Wexler, the sequel-starved producer and writer of *Saturday Night Fever*, was spending a lot of time lately on the phone with Michael Eisner, he had a pretty shrewd idea what was going to become of it.

Furious, he called John and begged him to reconsider his decision about *An Officer and a Gentleman*. At that point, there was still time.

John refused, even after LeMond outlined his fears. Paramount was owed a movie, and sooner or later, they were going to demand it. They could already have had him up for breach of contract over *American Gigolo*, LeMond carried on. The fact that they hadn't meant one of two things. Either they really were the indulgent pushovers John seemed to believe they were—which he himself doubted very much—or they had something up their sleeve that John really wouldn't like. And by the way, whatever did happen to Tony Manero?

John flipped. "Oh no. Oh no they don't."

Robert Stigwood had been dreaming of a sequel to *Saturday Night Fever* ever since 1978. John, for his part, had been dodging it for just as long.

His objections to the scripts Stigwood proffered were simple; they had been encapsulated in his response to the first treatment Stigwood ever showed him, just weeks after the first movie opened.

"I didn't like it because the character was antidance. He wanted to go to block parties in Manhattan, and social counseling, getting the neighborhoods together." That simply wasn't Manero's style. Neither were other ideas that simply attempted to relaunch John's career as the king of the discotheque.

He didn't change his mind back then, and he wasn't going to change it now. He didn't know what had happened to Tony Manero, and quite frankly, he didn't particularly care. "Ah, it's nothing to worry about," he laughed to LeMond. "If they try to pull that one, I'll just turn it down."

LeMond sighed. "Yeah. And I bet they'll listen as well."

Just weeks later, Paramount called him up.

Looking back on this tangled web from a decade's distance, John could see that he had walked into precisely the trap LeMond had anticipated.

"What Michael Eisner was saying was, 'If he's not going to do *An Officer and a Gentleman*, then we're going to have him do a sequel to *Saturday Night Fever*,'" John explains. Even he cannot excuse his own arrogance. He can, however, account for it. He had walked out on *American Gigolo*, he had gotten his own way with *Blow Out*. Who was to say he wouldn't make it three in a row with this latest scheme?

This time, however, Paramount was sticking to its guns. "Nine months went by and I couldn't do a movie at another studio because I was under contract to Paramount," John recalls. "And Paramount wouldn't let me do anything except the sequel to *Saturday Night Fever*."

Frustrated and furious, John took the studio's attitude out on LeMond. Again hindsight plays a great role in explaining what happened next; at the time, it was enough that after more than a decade of working together, John dismissed LeMond as his manager.

"I was the one who was saying no and then wanting him to fix it," John regrets. "There came a point when he called me and said, 'There's nothing I can do. [Eisner] won't let you out of doing the sequel.'"

John responded angrily, without thinking. "I said, 'Well, if you can't fix this, why am I paying you fifteen percent? This is something I need you to fix.' He said, 'Sorry, I can't do it.' And I got really mad, didn't think, and let him go."

At the time John reasoned, "Bob and I were in a rut. I just felt that I knew what to do if something came up. There were no more discoveries. It was time for independence."

Today, however, he admits, "If I had that to do over again, I wouldn't have. It wasn't fair, because I made every move to get myself in that predicament."

When LeMond fell ill a few years later with the malady that would end his life, John admits, "I felt so bad. He had given me twelve of the best years of his life as a mentor and manager. I felt guilty. I wanted at least to end it with words of appreciation and care." He never did admit to LeMond that he knew it was he who had screwed things up so badly, "but I think by my presence, I kind of admitted it."

So would the subsequent meanderings of his career. Already dangerously directionless, John was now rudderless as well.

In August 1981, Robert Stigwood invited John aboard his yacht to try to thrash out an acceptable plot for the now upcoming sequel. With original screenwriter Norman Wexler joining them on the team, a new script came together over the next few months. It featured Manero finally achieving the dream that had closed the first movie by moving into Manhattan to work as a dance teacher and supplementing his income as a bartender.

The next step was to assemble a cast, a director, a budget—and some reasonable excuses for the inevitable media questioning.

It was not long in coming. Interviewing John for *Rolling Stone*, Nancy Collins remarked outright that after *Saturday Night Fever*, "You said you had nothing more to say about the Tony Manero character. What changed your mind?"

"I grew up and so did he," John answered simply. "That's all." The movie would be best served, he figured, if he kept the real machinations to himself.

Unlike *Saturday Night Fever*, when he was gratefully involved in the most minute details, John sat out this new movie's gestation, whiling away his time instead in the kind of pursuits he had always dreamed of indulging in. He devoted himself to learning: violin lessons, French lessons, flying lessons. He took his understanding of Scientology into what he considered to be the upper echelons of his own spiritual development—to the point where he could actually audit himself.

While he was amusing himself in whichever way he fancied, John also sorted out the greatest problem haunting the still moribund sequel project—the absence of a director.

He was on vacation in Hawaii at the time, watching the latest in Sylvester Stallone's self-directed stream of hyper-heroic pugilist movies, *Rocky III*. Suddenly, John found himself mulling over the possibility of roping Stallone himself into the fray. The man, after all, seemed to have a way with sequels. But more than that, his own background wasn't really that different from Tony Manero's, the archetypal tough street kid made good.

"*Rocky III*!" John exclaimed. "Stallone made a sequel better than any I've seen in my life. And I said, 'If only he could give me half the excitement, it would be tremendous.'"

Immediately, John was on the phone to his new agent, Michael Ovitz, at the high-powered, high-profile Creative Artists Agency. He knew that Stallone was numbered among Ovitz's other clients, and with Paramount's grateful blessing, a meeting was set up, star to star. It was a success.

"We got on," John recalled, then added mysteriously, "our viewpoint was similar about the movie." When Stallone suggested that the script needed a rewrite, John agreed; "I trusted that it would turn out well, and boy, did it turn out well. If I had the ability to write, and I was as good as Stallone is at it, this is what I would have done." Stallone was brought on board as director and coproducer for a million-dollar fee.

Stallone was indeed the right man for the job. The first time they met, he told John, "There's nothing in the world you have to worry about except the acting. Everything else, I want to know about." And he was true to his word. "I was there for him twenty-four hours a day," Stallone boasted. "It's the way I always wanted to be treated, so I gave him that license to concentrate."

He described the final script for what was now being called *Stayin' Alive*, out of deference to the Bee Gees' best-known *Fever*-era hit, as "somewhat biographical—Tony's life, John's life, and my life all fused together. I've seen the faces of rejection, I know what it's like to be on the losing end." If he were younger, he sighed, he would have liked the lead role for himself. "I probably don't have John's talent to pull it off, but in my fantasy, that's the kind of thing I would have liked to have done. I guess I just did it in boxing, and he's doing it in dance."

The problem now was John, a super-sexy dancing star who was by his own admission both "out of shape and overweight." John pledged to do something about it—and promptly returned to a medium that, two or three years before, he had despaired of ever being able to experience again. For twelve nights in July 1982, John appeared on stage at Colorado's Snowmass festival, playing a young seminarian alongside veteran actor Charles Durning in a production of *Mass Appeal*.

Director William Shorr had no doubts of the play's appeal to

John: low pressure, less media coverage, and no restrictions. "To get actors like this, we must offer an environment in which they can stretch artistically, where they are free to fall," Shorr explained. And although John gave just four interviews to a handful of local newspapers throughout his time in the Rocky Mountain resort, still the two-hun-dred-ninety-seat auditorium was sold out for all twelve nights of the play's run.

During his stint in Snowmass, John stumbled across the answer to Stallone's weight-watching prayers. Nearby Aspen was hosting the acclaimed dance company Ballet West, and John occasionally dropped by to watch them work. Finally, he contacted the company's Sharee Lane to ask if she would be willing to give him ballet lessons three times a week.

Coupling that with a daily workout at a local gymnasium, John felt himself returning to his fighting fitness. He was so pleased with the results that "after three weeks, I told Sharee I'd like to steal her away from Ballet West and take her to California to work every day with me.

"She got the Company's permission, and the day after Labor Day, we started three-hour classes, six days a week." He continued working out, too, "lifting weights and all that, to get my body symmetrical and in shape. So I did six hours a day, six days a week, of physical activity."

On top of this, Stallone assigned a trainer, Dan Isaacson, to work with John on what the director himself described as "a very tough regimen. A lot of people wouldn't have stuck it out, but John had total dedication."

A typical day now began at 7:30, a frightful hour for someone who didn't normally go to bed before four. After a small chicken breakfast and an hour of relaxation, it was time for work. Stallone designed the backbreaking regimen after spending hours poring over photographs of dancers to see which muscle groups he needed to accentuate. From nine until one, it was aerobics and dance; after a lunch of broccoli and more chicken came two or three hours of weight training. John would then wind down with a mile or two of running, a small dinner, and bed, with the whole routine fortified by a heavy program of minerals and vitamins. "It's not a program I would recommend to anyone else," Isaacson admitted. "We moni-tored him constantly."

John emerged with a body that left even Stallone feeling envious. His weight had dropped from 180 pounds to 168; his chest had increased an inch and a half to forty; his waist decreased from thirty-three and one-half inches to thirty.

"People like Sly can look at a body like clay and mold it," John exclaimed. "I never thought of designing a body. I just thought, 'Diet, run, lose it, and you'll look good. I didn't think of shaping the shoulder, the triceps, the waist." Stallone reciprocated by joking, "If John keeps it up, I'll have to fight him in *Rocky IV*." He then outlined what was wrong with the star when they first started talking: "His legs were too thin, his waist too thick, his chest too scrawny and he had no strength in his arms."

Now, "at twenty-nine, he looks like a Greek god." Now, he was everything Stallone dreamed he could be. On one occasion, John realized to his horror that he was in danger of becoming something more than that as well.

He was eating out with a friend when he noticed one of the other customers staring at him. Finally, John had had enough. "That guy keeps looking at me," John snarled to his friend. "I'm going to deck him."

"You're going to do what?"

"I'm going to deck him."

The friend shot back a look of absolute amazement. "John, you're not going to deck him. You're not going to deck anybody. The word 'deck' isn't even in your vocabulary. You've never decked anybody in your whole life. What are you talking about?"

On the set, John was paired with choreographer Dennon Rawls and a dancing cast that included Finola Hughes, the original White Cat in Andrew Lloyd Weber's *Cats*, and *Flashdance*'s Cynthia Rhodes; for all concerned, Stallone's vision of *Staying Alive* as an extravaganza veering from Broadway to jazz to ballet was a challenge, but it was one that John, in particular, rose most impressively toward.

"Quite frankly, he's the most spiritual dancer I've ever danced with," the British-born Hughes said enthusiastically. "I guess it's because he's so much of an actor too. He acts it all out when he's dancing."

Rhodes was similarly effusive. "He's very strong. Strong energy, and strong physically and mentally. He looks incredible when he dances. It's like he's been dancing all his life."

Yet despite the enthusiasm going into *Staying Alive*, no one doubted the immensity of the task before them. "Being in a sequel is much scarier than being in the original," Stallone admitted. "You're playing catch-up. It's like going up against your older brother. It's intimidating."

10

◇◇◇

Lost in the Eighties

By the summer of 1983, John had
been Auditing himself for close to eighteen months, hooking himself
up to the E-Meter and working through his problem and pains alone.
It was a process that, in Scientological jargon, qualified him as an
Operating Thetan, or OT. There are eight levels of OT: only the highest can successfully Audit themselves—a target that no more than
50,000 other people are believed to have achieved. Acknowledging a
worldwide population of Scientologists that runs into the millions (the
Church currently boasts more than seven hundred centers in at least
sixty-five countries), that is a remarkable achievement.

So it came as a surprise when, in the August 18 issue of *Rolling
Stone*, John responded to a fairly routine question about his continued
membership in the Church by confessing, "I haven't had any Auditing
for about a year and a half." Then, when journalist Nancy Collins ques-
tioned him about the strength of his faith, he responded with what
appeared to be considerable doubt.

At a time when Scientology's funding was coming under increasing media scrutiny, John acknowledged that he had ploughed a considerable sum into it himself. "Ten thousand dollars?" asked Collins.
"Twenty thousand?" John thought for a moment. "Maybe in that ball-
park, yeah."

But now, though he continued to believe Scientology was "pretty brilliant," he also admitted, "I try to separate the material and the organization, because I don't agree with the way the organization is being run. I believe that the material is more worthy than the individuals who are handling it. I wish I could defend Scientology better, but I don't think it even deserves to be defended, in a sense."

His disillusionment caught the industry—and the Church—completely by surprise. Although John had never been one for preaching his beliefs, he had always remained steadfast in his devotion to his creed.

The Celebrity Center immediately went on full alert. Yet according to Ken Rose, the caseworker who claims to have been involved with John when the actor first joined the Church, John's disenchantment was nothing new.

"He's been very disaffected at times, and it took a great deal of work to get him back in." On this occasion, however, "It was rumored that J.T. was gone, was no longer a Scientologist and had made public statements." Something needed to be done.

Rose is glib in his recollection of what happened. "A bunch of people went and held his hand, and evidently he was gotten back in." However, *Time* magazine's May 6, 1991, "special report" on Scientology placed a sinister spin on the story. In fact, the article resulted in the Church suing the magazine for $416 million in libel damages.

Author Richard Behar wrote, "High-level defectors claim that Travolta has long feared that if he defected, details of his sexual life would be made public. 'He felt pretty intimidated about this getting out and told me so,' recalls William Franks, the church's former chairman of the board. 'There were no outright threats made, but it was implicit. If you leave, they immediately start digging up everything.'" Specifically, the allegation continued, the Church would reveal information offered up in Auditing sessions.

Behar also noted that Franks himself was "driven out" of the Church in 1981 after attempting to reform the organization. The article continued with Richard Aznaran, a former head of security, recalling David Miscavige, the leader of the Church, "repeatedly joking to staffers about Travolta's allegedly promiscuous homosexual behavior."

The rumor that John was gay was not new, even in the early

Travolta received his star on Hollywood
Boulevard in June 1985.
RALPH DOMINGUEZ/GLOBE PHOTOS

Broadway veterans Travolta and Liza
Minelli appear together at an awards
ceremony.
GLOBE PHOTOS

Travolta escorted Eva (Mrs. Kenny)
Loggins to a gala honoring designer
Valentino in 1988.

Jamie Lee Curtis and Travolta's attempt to capture the health club craze of the 1980s in the film *Perfect* failed to live up to its name.
PAUL JASMIN/COLUMBIA PICTURES

Director Robert Altman enticed John out of hiding to appear in his 1987 television adaptation of Harold Pinter's *The Dumbwaiter*.

Travolta met his future wife, Kelly Preston, on the Vancouver set of the forgettable film *The Experts* in 1987.

Look Who's Talking Too may have been panned by the critics, but it was still a box-office success, grossing almost fifty million dollars.
TRI-STAR PICTURES

Friend, neighbor, fellow Scientologist, and *Look Who's Talking* costar Kirstie Alley (shown here on the set with John and director Amy Heckerling) played an instrumental role in Travolta's courtship with Kelly Preston.
TRI-STAR PICTURES

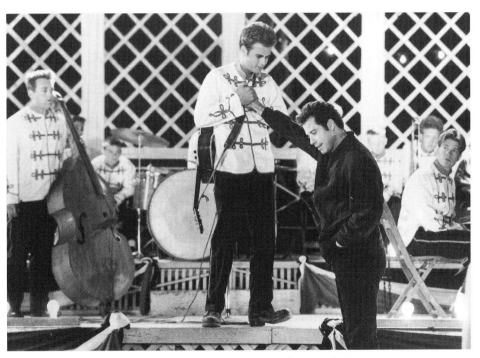

Shout, the tired story of a hip teacher bringing rock 'n' roll to a small Texas town, costarred Jamie Walters, now a member of the *90210* gang.

Although Miramax executives needed convincing that Travolta was the right choice for the role of Vincent Vega in *Pulp Fiction*, Quentin Tarantino never doubted it for an instant.
LINDA R. CHEN/MIRAMAX

Travolta, shown here with costars Samuel L. Jackson and Harvey Keitel, saw Vincent Vega as a grown-up Tony Manero.
LINDA R. CHEN/MIRAMAX

Travolta and Preston at home in 1992 with their new son, Jett.
THEO WESTENBERGER

Travolta met Jack Lemmon at the 1995 L.A. Film Critics' Awards, where John won the Best Actor Award.
LISA O'CONNOR/SHOOTING STAR

Actress Anne Archer (*Fatal Attraction, Patriot Games*) and Travolta at The Church of Scientology.
RON DAVIS/SHOOTING STAR

Mark Fuhrman's gay connection • Nigel Hawthorne gets real

THE

Advocate

THE NATIONAL GAY & LESBIAN NEWSMAGAZINE   SINCE 1967

APRIL 4, 1995

John Travolta

Jodie Foster

RUMORS

Why gossip about an actor's alleged homosexuality can't stall a successful career

$3.95 USA • $4.95 CAN • £2.95 UK

ISSUE 678

The 'New' Hollywood

GQ

OCTOBER $3.00

HOW HOLLYWOOD WOULD DRESS...IF IT HAD TASTE

John Travolta Throws His Weight Around

By Tom Junod

Made Men
Who Make
Movies
Abel Ferrara's
Thug Life
Will Michael
Eisner Eat
Hollywood?
Tarantino's
Early Years

San Antonio Express-News

PARADE

"I've lost lots of
people that I love.
But I guess that I've finally
learned that when it comes to
loving people, you don't
really have a choice. If you want
to feel alive and experience
something wonderful, you have
to risk great loss."

AN INTERVIEW WITH

John Travolta

BY DOTSON RADER

INSIDE: Simply Delicious Apples And Pears...By Sheila Lukins

Travolta agreed to play Chili Palmer in *Get Shorty*, which he originally turned down, only after Danny DeVito and Quentin Tarantino convinced him to read the book.

White Man's Burden was a risky decision for Travolta; although it wasn't a box-office sensation, he remains proud of the film and pleased with his decision to appear in it.

Travolta and Preston married in a Paris hotel in 1991; when they returned to the U.S. they renewed their vows in a civil ceremony just to make sure everything was legal.

When Travolta met Quentin Tarantino at his Hollywood apartment, he was stunned to discover that it was the same apartment he had lived in more than a decade earlier during the *Welcome Back, Kotter* years.

Travolta and Preston are joined by Tom Hanks and his wife at a 1995 Academy Awards luncheon.

Steven Spielberg takes a moment to chat with John and Kelly at the 1995 American Film Institute Honors.

Co-Golden Globe Award winners Nicole Kidman and Travolta pose for the press.

Travolta proudly accepts a 1996 Golden Globe Award for his performance in
Get Shorty.

As shooting wrapped on John Woo's *Broken Arrow*, the director and Travolta were already discussing teaming up for another project.

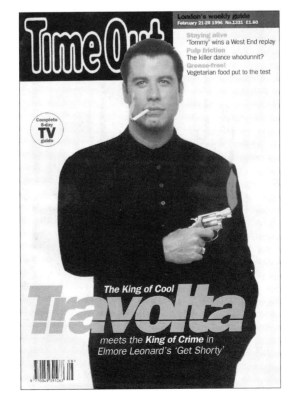

Travolta took on an unusual role in 1996's *Phenomenon*, which costarred Robert Duvall, Kyra Sedgwick, and Forest Whitaker.

1980s. Indeed, the first stirrings began around the time of *Moment by Moment*, a knee-jerk reaction, John's journalistic supporters insisted, to the deliberate sexual ambiguity of the roles he had specialized in—products of bewildered machoism reacting to the almost painstaking sensuality with which Travolta seemed blessed; maybe even a backdated allusion to the at least partially convincing cleaning-lady drag John wore through one of the earliest episodes of *Welcome Back, Kotter!*

"The rumors about me were so extraordinary," John laughed. They didn't bother him, though. "The gay rumor about male stars is such a classic that it didn't surprise me to hear it about me, because I'd heard it about the others. They say that about me, Marlon Brando—every male, especially the first year you become a star. I've heard it said of just about everybody."

Pressed by *Rolling Stone*'s Nancy Collins in that same 1983 interview, John firmly refuted the suggestion that he was gay. But whereas he firmly believed that "[this rumor] wears off after a while," the gay rumor mill would continue to churn around John. Reports of his apparent break with the Scientology hierarchy simply gave it renewed circulation.

John and the Church alike have remained silent on what really happened that summer following the publication of the *Rolling Stone* story. But whatever it was, it did the trick. From here on in, John's actions and statements on behalf of Scientology would be those of the truly devoted acolyte. He demonstrated as much in May 1985 when he joined a host of other Scientology luminaries—including actress Karen Black and musicians Chick Corea, Edgar Winter, and Nicky Hopkins—to protest an Oregon court decision that awarded a former member, Julie Christofferson Titchbourne, thirty-nine million dollars in punitive damages against the Church.

John arrived at midnight aboard his private jet to hold a press conference extolling the virtues of Scientology. He was as unequivocal then as he is today about its benefits, and when asked about the so-fashionable claims that Scientology is little more than an exercise in mind control, he still snaps. "Give us a fucking break!"

As *People Weekly*'s Karen S. Schneider ran down a list of Scientology's best-known practitioners, names like Tom Cruise, Priscilla Presley and her daughter Lisa Marie, Kirstie Alley, Karen Black, and the voice of Bart Simpson (Nancy Cartwright), John simply thundered, "being the bold personalities we are, do you honestly think we'd let ourselves be controlled?"

Marilu Henner accompanied John to the premiere of *Staying Alive* in July 1983, and immediately all the doubts he had originally entertained about tangling with a sequel to *Saturday Night Fever* resurfaced—and were justified.

"Only the presence of John Travolta turns *Staying Alive* from an unqualified disaster into a qualified one," complained *The New York Times'* Janet Maslin. "[He] survives the film, but he would have been better off almost anywhere else—even *Flashdance*."

Elsewhere, England's *The Face* condemned, "while *SNF*, for all its clichéd routines, at least had some character of its own, all that's available here is a nod to the original when Tony opens his wardrobe to see his white suit and black shirt still hanging there." Not, reviewer Giovanni Dadomo continued, that they would have helped him much. The "tame and limp" dance sequences that close the movie reveal "a basic conceptual flaw" that apparently no one had considered beforehand. "Travolta—though he was adequate enough in a disco—can't actually dance."

There really was no answer to that, and John, for once, didn't even try to think of one. For the first time, he was able to ignore his reviews. Jokingly, he thanked *Moment by Moment* for giving him the thick skin he now could wear like armor. "That was the worst press attack I had ever experienced," he reflected. "Whatever else I encountered later was mild by comparison."

Besides, if everyone believed the critics, the critics would be out of a job. At the box office, *Staying Alive* more than lived up to its name. The summer hit of 1983 would ultimately gross more than sixty-five million dollars—a more than respectable tally—and John, rejuvenated once more in the eyes of Hollywood's moneymen again saw his future reaching out for him.

In interviews, he talked excitedly of his next projects. On Mike Ovitz's advice, he had turned down Ron Howard once again, this time passing on *Splash*, a movie about a mermaid. Tom Hanks grabbed it instead.

But he was excited about a proposed reunion with Olivia

Newton-John, another that would pair him once more with Brian De Palma, even a return engagement with Sylvester Stallone on a project John had now been connected with for more than half a decade, *Godfather III.*

Francis Ford Coppola, the saga's creator, remained adamant that he wanted nothing to do with such a thing; he had even remarked only half in jest that "if I were to make *Godfather Part Three*," it would be a joke, a farce, *"Abbot and Costello Meet The Godfather."* So the studio thought they could take it away from him, without considering that *The Godfather* without Coppola would be like—Abbott without Costello. They took it away and thought, "Why shouldn't Stallone have a go at it?" After all, the man did have a way with sequels.

John revelled in all this speculation. Less than three years before, he had talked wistfully of making a movie only every two years or so. Now he was dreaming of banging them out.

"The days of waiting three or four years between projects are over," he insisted. "You can't have the perfect vehicle every time." He talked excitedly of taking his lead from the matinee idols of the past, the Hollywood legends whose output was so prodigious that they could afford the occasional failure. They knew their reputation and their box-office appeal was based upon an entire body of work. Spencer Tracy made thirty-seven movies in less time than it had taken John to make seven. Gary Cooper made forty.

He wasn't worried about flooding the market, either; sometimes, in fact, he wondered what market he'd be flooding? "In the '30s and '40s, there were twenty, fifty, box-office stars. Now there are three of us—me, Richard Gere, and Stallone. I'm not forgetting Redford or Newman or Pacino or De Niro or Dustin Hoffman. There are still people out there to deal with—Burt Reynolds, Clint Eastwood. But those guys are of a different generation. I'm talking about ten years from now. Who'll be the sexy stars ten years from now? Me, Richard Gere, Stallone. That's it."

If he wanted to make a movie a year, why shouldn't he? Two movies, three movies, what did it matter? Speaking with a confidence the remainder of the decade would seem to go out of its way to belie, he concluded, "I know now that one movie isn't going to make all the difference for me. And believe me, that's settled me down a lot."

The promised reunion with Olivia Newton-John, five years after their success in *Grease*, was already underway when John let slip the possibility of a second movie together. They had, in fact, already struggled through some thirty screenplays before John finally called Olivia to rave about the sole treatment that caught his eye. It was called *Second Chance*. "If you don't like this, I don't think we'll ever find another movie to do together."

Olivia read the script and agreed with him, leaving one to wonder exactly what quality control stipulations they gave their respective agents. Because if this really was the best script they were offered, it wasn't just John and Livvy who were in trouble—it was the entire movie industry.

The project was doomed from the start, and no amount of cosmetics could change it. Even its title was ill-starred: *Second Chance* is one of the most unsuccessful movie titles in history. Five consecutive failures have been released under that name.

Correctly reading at least that one portent, 20th Century Fox quickly changed the name—and got that wrong as well. *Two of a Kind* had already been seconded for George Burns' TV movie debut, which aired in 1982, a year before its big-screen namesake made it to the theaters. One wonders how many people passed the movie house by, simply cursing, "Oh no, not that one again?" And then one wonders how many people wished that they had.

Next, there was the matter of casting. If John's standing had declined in the five years since *Grease*—and *Staying Alive* notwithstanding, there was little argument there—Olivia's had positively bombed, hitting bottom with her starring role in what ranks among the worst modern musicals ever conceived, *Xanadu*.

Her records still sold as well as they ever had, with 1982's "(Let's Get) Physical" proving one of her biggest hits ever. But all that proved was that people liked her singing voice. Besides, she had hardly been deluged by acting offers since then. If 20th Century Fox were hoping that simply reconstituting an old winning combination would surmount all such problems, they had another thing coming. Winning combinations only work when both sides of the combo are already winning.

Last but not least in the catalog of catastrophe, there were the events of the first day of filming, when Olivia, a committed and outspoken animal lover, bent to pet a passing stray dog. It bit her. If that was not an ill omen, what was?

Two of a Kind was intended as a lightweight comedy, with John and Olivia cast as a talentless thief and a luckless actress adrift in a world upon which a disappointed God is about to unleash a second Great Flood.

Man is too selfish and greedy, the Lord has decided. It's time to knock everything down and start anew. The one thing that will change his mind is if someone can show him just two people out of all the billions on the planet who would willingly sacrifice themselves for each other. Oh, and no goody-goody holy folk, either. They have to be selfish as well. Frank Capra could have had a ball with that plot.

Twentieth Century Fox sank twenty million dollars into *Two of a Kind*—fourteen million making it, and another six put away for the advertising budget.

There was a lot to advertise as well. An impressive supporting cast began with Oliver Reed, brilliantly, if somewhat troublingly, cast as the Devil; it also included Beatrice Straight and John's *Mass Appeal* costar Charles Durning, who play the one-last-chance angels; it culminates with Gene Hackman, who modestly portrays God—modestly because not only does Hackman not appear on screen but also because he doesn't appear in the movie's credits either.

The movie's other selling point was sex—and not just any old sex, either. This was John and Olivia having sex, Danny and Sandy finally consummating the five-year tease that began when their car flew away at the end of *Grease*. Although Olivia admits that she asked herself afterwards, "God, what did I just do?" John did no more than shrug. "We have a real attraction, so it just made it completely natural." Besides, as *People* magazine's Carl Arrington pointed out, John was well aware that "a heartthrob intrigue is good publicity for a movie." The sex scene passed off safely and tastefully.

Nothing was left to chance. Taking a leaf out of Robert Stigwood's book, Olivia's management began greasing the promotional wheels a month before *Two of a Kind*'s December 16, 1983, release by issuing the title song, "Twist of Fate," as a single and a well-received video. Adhering strictly to the plan, the song lost little time in breaching the Top Five, just as the film came out.

The album didn't do too badly, either, despite featuring little more than a ragbag of unremarkable easy-listening numbers, three mid-dling songs by Olivia, and—out of respect for their mutual past—one new duet between her and John. That might have made a good single as well, but John, it is rumored, stymied that stunt. Instead, "Take a Chance" simply sneaked out on a B-side. It was no "Summer Nights," after all.

A second single from the movie, Olivia's "Desperate Times," would be a hit shortly after, with a third, Patti Austin's "It's Gonna Be Special," picking up significant airplay.

But the movie itself was a bomb. "Utterly rootless," condemned *The New York Times.* "No element of reality has been allowed to intrude on the show-business superficiality of the exercise." Even more damagingly, critic Janet Maslin prophesied with unswerving accuracy that "not even the most ardent Travolta and Newton-John fans are liable to like the stars' notions of how these characters should behave." For John, coming off the critical turkey that was *Staying Alive,* his last two movies really had been two of a kind. "And a third could be calamitous."

And yet, true to his newfound but strangely desperate belief that nonstop work was the way to go, no sooner had John completed *Two of a Kind* than he was away again for *Perfect.* The drama would link him once again with Marilu Henner and director James Bridges, with Jamie Lee Curtis thrown in for box-office icing.

Perfect marked the first time John and Marilu had gotten the chance to work together since *Over Here.*

One previous attempt to pair them up on screen, in Charles Shyer's *Irreconcilable Differences,* had fallen through when John pulled out. According to Marilu, he simply "was not into moving forward on a fabulous script." The movie went ahead instead with Ryan O'Neal and Shelley Long. Whether it benefitted from the change is debatable.

But was *Perfect* any wiser a choice? It offered a complicated role but a peculiarly appropriate one for John. He played Adam Lawrence, a fictional *Rolling Stone* reporter, researching a story on what Marilu Henner gleefully describes as "the health-club-as-meat-market scene" that had exploded into the American mainstream early in the 1980s.

Aerobics classes, superstar keep-fit videos, early morning work-outs, and of course, John's own contribution to the mania's bestselling literature, 1984's *Staying Fit* guide—such things had long been bubbling beneath the surface of American suburbia. *Perfect*, however, alleged that the obsession with health was allied with a corresponding obsession with getting laid. Increasingly, evidence suggested that a lot of health clubs were little more than pick-up joints.

That was one way to look at *Perfect*. The other was to see it as a callous attempt to have lightning strike thrice and bind the nation up in another Travolta-generated craze (as if there weren't already enough fitness freaks on the streets). The twist was, instead of making the film from an already-existing investigation, which is how *Saturday Night Fever* and *Urban Cowboy* were born, *Perfect* would be about the investigation itself. There was even a place in the movie for *Rolling Stone*'s real-life founder, Jann Wenner, adding a touch of verisimilitude to the newsroom scenes.

John was certainly struck by the role of Adam Lawrence. "He's the most intellectual character I've ever played," John glowed. He acknowledged that his personal experiences with the press, *Rolling Stone* included, had done much to prepare him for the role. "I've been one of the most interviewed people in modern times. I think I know a lot about how it's done." Marilu Henner added, "For the first time, Johnny's showing a thinking man's sexuality."

He was also showing a thinking man's maturity. Director James Bridges had been understandably nervous at the prospect of working with John again after his experiences with the flunkies on the *Urban Cowboy* set. When he discovered that John was at last his own man, his excitement was boundless. "Once John got rid of all those people, he was much more comfortable. He feels secure, and some of it has to do with listening to his own voice." Although it really dated back to his recovery from the *Moment by Moment* debacle, John's newfound confidence also had a great deal to do with his sudden realization that he wasn't a kid anymore. On February 18, 1984, John turned thirty, a milestone he had initially intended to celebrate by fueling up one of his planes and simply flying from city to city, throwing a party in every one.

He changed his mind at virtually the last minute, suddenly realizing that if he wanted thirty to be followed by thirty-one, an airborne bar crawl around the continental U.S.A. was probably not the smartest thing he could do. Instead, he called his sister Margaret and her family down to Rancho Tajiguas for a much more restrained celebration.

"I have it on videotape," John laughed. "It's so weird. If you've seen photographs or film of those old-age homes where they had kids' birthday parties with hats and things—that's really what this looked like. It's really sort of pathetic."

As *Perfect* got underway, John and Marilu began dating again. Her marriage to Freddie Forest had collapsed, and John confessed, "For the two years she was married, we didn't see each other. I missed her a lot."

Now they were making up for lost time. They spent Christmas 1984 together in Jamaica, and Marilu still remembers it as "the most romantic and intimate time we had ever shared."

With Marilu by his side, John slipped into his now-established pre-movie-release disappearance, vanishing from the public eye as he built up the energy to deal with the forthcoming publicity storm.

Journalist Nancy Collins was one of the few media people who was able to track him down during this period, although it was hardly for the customary reasons or under the happiest circumstances. Collins' mother had recently been diagnosed with pancreatic cancer, and her children were, as Collins put it, trying "to fill her hours with as much life, glamor, and pizzazz as we could manufacture.

"I wanted to surprise Mama and deliver a real live movie star. But if I had one ironclad rule, it was: never ask a celebrity for a favor. Then I remembered. John Travolta's mother had died from cancer, as had his girlfriend. I'd interviewed him twice, and we'd gotten along well. He was a sweet man. Perhaps . . ."

John came through for her. "At about 9:00 P.M. at the hospital, a wild-eyed young nurse came hurrying toward me. 'Is it possible that John Travolta is calling your mother?'" When Collins spoke to him afterwards, John shrugged her thanks aside. "I've been there. I know what it's like."

Perfect was poised for release in May 1985. As John's first movie in eighteen months, it was guaranteed a certain amount of hyperbole, but John himself was gratified to see that it was his vivacious costar, Jamie Lee Curtis, who seemed to be receiving the most media attention.

Since making her debut in 1978 in two of John Carpenter's most scarifying movies, *The Fog* and *Halloween*, the daughter of Tony Curtis and Janet Leigh had slowly but successfully established herself among America's most silently successful box-office draws. Always her best roles seemed to be secondary to her costars' in billing if not in execution—she had trampled both Eddie Murphy and Dan Aykroyd in *Trading Places*, after all. Now, she was finally getting the attention she deserved. If she also absorbed some of John's share of the spotlight, he was glad to give it to her. He had other things to attend to.

As soon as they arrived in New York City, John and Marilu bolted straight for the United Nations Plaza Hotel—"not the most likely place for showbiz people," as Marilu put it. But though they should have been preparing for one of the greatest moments of their lives together—the premiere of the first movie they had ever made together—the opposite was true.

Despite their outward aura of happiness and the feeling among friends that time had simply stood still since their first flush on *Grease*, the affair was troubled. Marilu still demanded more commitment than John was willing to give; John still spent more time at his job than she was able to allow. There, at the United Nations Plaza Hotel, just days before "their" film was released, a relationship that John had long before described as "the longest marriage of all," one that had outlived any other the two had ever enjoyed, finally came to an end. Almost fifteen years had passed since they first met, but now it was time to say good-bye.

"If I can't make it work with you, then I know I can't make it work with anybody," John told her as they parted. "You're someone who deserves so much more than I'm giving you." They were due at a press party any moment, but all they could do was cry.

Although it would ultimately receive a number of warm reviews, *Perfect* quickly proved distinctly imperfect. "Too superficially knowing to be a camp classic," warned *The New York Times*, "it's an unintentionally hilarious mixture of muddled morality and all-too-contemporary self-promotion."

Even the publicity photographs of John and Jamie Lee Curtis earnestly sweating their butts off seemed discouraging, almost daring audiences to want to see the movie—a dare few people would ever take them up on. The soundtrack album looked even worse. Curtis had spent a good chunk of her early career running away from psychos and lunatics. Now it looked as if she'd become one. And if you can't beat 'em, join 'em; John looked pretty creepy as well. No matter how poorly the movie did (which was very poorly indeed, as it happened), the soundtrack was doomed to do even worse.

For John, this latest failure was less soul-destroying than an opportunity for some serious soul-searching. He was, in any case, reasonably pleased with the movie—a decade later he would insist, *"Perfect* did work on various levels. I think it's a film to be re-evaluated."

But the breakup with Marilu had left him confused and bewildered; whether it was the memory of Diana that prevented him from caring too deeply or simply a factor within his own being, close to a decade had now elapsed since he had become involved in any relationship worth more than a handful of tabloid headlines. Sometimes, he despaired of ever finding happiness, just as sometimes he despaired of ever recapturing his Hollywood crown. Close to a decade had also gone by since he had last been involved in a movie whose success could not be unfavorably compared with another.

In public, he determined not to let it bother him. "No movie has ever been that important to me," he would reflect ten years later. "You feel bad. You feel a loss. But give a guy the benefit of not being insane. Leave it at 'bummed out.' Disasters are earthquakes, plane crashes, the Titanic. I'm sorry, but a bad movie is not a disaster."

At the time, too, he reasoned, "It's been the biggest lesson of my life observing what's happened with Michael Jackson." It proved to him that he was not alone in suffering from too much adoration. Although Jackson's rise on the back of his *Thriller* album was still unhindered by his attempts to follow it up, it did not take a genius to know that when a new album did arrive—five years later in the shape of *Bad*—it wouldn't matter how good it was, it wouldn't be *Thriller.*

"The same thing happened with *Saturday Night Fever* and *Grease*; what was good became a mania. I remember saying to myself, 'How do you top this?' Even if you do, it only happens once, because you're only surprised once. You're forced to compete with yourself, and you're maxed out. So you just do good work and hope you can stay there."

Unfortunately, like Michael Jackson, John was not staying there. Before, as he had pointed out in the 1983 interview with *Rolling Stone*'s Nancy Collins, of the Top Ten grossing movies of all time, "I was the only actor the public came to see as an actor. The rest of the top grossers were all special-effects films—*ET*, *Empire Strikes Back*, *Jaws*, *Raiders of the Lost Ark*. I may be the only actor the public went to see instead of a shark."

But now he realized that the John Travolta the public had flocked to see then, was not the John Travolta he could offer now. Reminiscing over the disco fever that had swept America in emulation of Tony Manero, or the line of disco clothing he had once intended to market, he acknowledged, "[people] want to wear what I wear when I dance. After *Saturday Night Fever*, kids wore white suits and black shirts and thought they were John Travolta for a day. But even I wasn't John Travolta. I was an illusion created by a film. It was a dream."

And the dream was over. In the age of the yuppie, an age when simple personal improvement was superceded by personal greed, John's personification of the working-class-kid-made-good simply did not compute any longer. Glitzy ostentation had been replaced by secretive hoarding: the gold Rolex hidden beneath the cuff of the designer jacket, the personal computer concealed in the briefcase. And the gold chains and chest hair were securely locked away in the closet.

Even though John strived hard to escape that role, to prove that he could act alongside the best Hollywood could offer, it was obvious that's all he was doing—acting. And all the while, his audience would hold its breath in anticipation, just waiting for his features to crumble into the rubber-lipped smirk that was Vinnie Barbarino . . . Tony Manero . . . Danny Zuko.

If they're good, actors and actresses suspend reality, taking on the characteristics of the roles they are playing. In John's case, it didn't matter how good he was. In *Blow Out*, *Two of a Kind*, and *Perfect*, it was never possible to forget that you were watching John Travolta. And if you were watching John Travolta, well, like Stephanie remarked of Tony Manero, you were watching a cliché.

It wasn't that he had been typecast, nothing so simple as that. Rather, John had come to epitomize a time that most people preferred to leave unremembered. It had become old-fashioned before the fashions themselves had grown old, a hangover from a Hollywood that had itself fallen by the wayside.

Jamie Lee Curtis, his costar in *Perfect*, once remarked, "in terms of lifestyle, John's very much a movie star in the old tradition. He loves being a movie star, and he makes no bones about it." John himself continued, "If I saw a star resentful of what he has, I'd say, 'How dare he?' God, if somebody is not going to live it to the fullest, why did you want it? Growing up, if I had thought while watching *Bonnie and Clyde* that Warren Beatty and Faye Dunaway didn't jet around and dress up and have fine things, it would have killed me."

Now all stars seemed resentful, cowering from the fame, hiding from the flashbulbs, and surfacing between movies, it seemed, only to fire off another volley of complaints about the pressures of stardom. They lamented how all they really wanted was to lead a normal life away from the cameras and away from the lights. Hey! Here's a pen and paper. Write the studio and resign. Scot Haller, interviewing John for *People Weekly* best hit the nail on the head when he wrote, "In the age of angst, Travolta has proved to be an anomaly: the unapologetic movie star."

And what would it take for this unapologetic movie star to return to the scene of his earliest triumphs? Not another movie, John now realized, not even another *Grease* or *Saturday Night Fever*. It would require an entire shift in the market's demands—a return, if not to the basics that he had grown up with, then at least to an appreciation of what those basics had meant, and an understanding of stardom not as something that is distributed willy-nilly, to be shared or shattered according to whim, but as a gift to be enjoyed and to be seen enjoying. And until that time came, John was simply prepared to wait.

"I was burned out after those films," John explained as he prepared for that layoff. "It wasn't the movies so much as the publicity tours after the movies. I must have done fourteen hundred interviews." If someone had come up to him after *Perfect* and told him he would never have to work again, he revealed, "I would have said, 'Great!'"

Although he would contract a new manager, Jonathan Krane—Blake Edwards' partner on *The Man Who Loved Women*—over the next eighteen months, John established himself as the virtually forgotten man of the Hollywood Hills. As reclusive as ever he was in the painful aftermath of his mother's death and *Moment by Moment*, the difference was that this time, John would enjoy his seclusion.

Finally admitting that he was sick to death of Los Angeles, John sold Rancho Tajiguas and moved across country to Spruce Creek, near Daytona Beach, Florida.

"I feel like I'm more part of real life outside of L.A.," he reasoned. "I like the contact with people. In Florida, I live in a real neighborhood."

Well, that was one way of putting it. Some communities are built around railroads or highways; Spruce Creek was centered around a four thousand-foot landing strip. John fell in love with it to the tune of half a million dollars. That's what he paid for his new French Provincial-style home. It had four bedrooms, four bathrooms, a swimming pool, and of course, a matching airplane hanger. Jonathan Krane marvelled, "You can fly your plane into the garage and literally open a door and enter your living room."

John still lived alone. Often he let days go by without seeing anyone but his houseboy and a personal trainer. He'd go to bed, as usual, around four in the morning, sleep until three unless he had an appointment, and that was how he liked it. John was no longer "obsessed with his career."

Rather, John told *Vogue* later, he simply felt blessed to be alive, "which is pretty good going for any icon. I mean, you look at [James] Dean, Jayne Mansfield, Buddy Holly, whoever—their record for survival is not so hot. If they even made it past thirty they were ahead of the game. And here I was, zooming forty, with all my family and friends around me, my health and my hair, and lots of other good stuff besides." Plus, he didn't need to work, so he didn't.

His collection of planes and his experience flying them were the chief beneficiaries of his withdrawal. A Lockheed JetStar 731 was his current pride and joy; it seated ten, had an inflight steward, and seldom flew with less than full catering onboard. Although he'd bought it little more than one year before, he'd already clocked up two-hundred hours in it flying to England, France, Greece, and even Egypt.

He'd parted with the DC-3, but he still owned an airliner, a four-engine propeller-driven Lockheed Constellation. And for short hops, there was a Cessna Citation, a little business transport jet able to operate from shorter airfields than anything else on the market. Was it true, he was once asked, that he was considering giving up show business to become a commercial pilot?

"No," he replied. "But it's true that I wanted to become a commercial pilot, just because it would be cool to say I was one."

11

◇◇◇

Look Who's Starting
a Family

For a year and a half, John lived in virtual solitude—at least when compared with the madness he had grown so accustomed to. That was probably the biggest difference between this "retirement" and the last one. Very few people came looking for him. They simply didn't bother to bother him. Nothing came along so important that when John turned it down its backers would stay and argue.

So when a phone call came in from ABC vice president Gary Pudney late in 1986, John was more than happy to talk with him. Pudney knew John from way back. He had been an executive at ABC when John was a Sweathog, and they had remained in touch ever since.

"Every year Gary Pudney called me about doing something for television," John smirked, "and I'd be very polite and back off." He was as aware as the media critics, who scanned the listings for stories, how movie stars who faded from view only to return on TV were perceived. It meant that times were hard and the star was getting desperate. The power of television may have had the movie industry on the commercial ropes since its arrival on the scene, but when it came to artistry, the small screen still played second fiddle.

That hadn't changed between Pudney's last call and this. What was different was John's own perception of his status. "The pressure was off, that's everything in a nutshell."

Previously he had been agonizingly aware that "because of my past, I can't just be mildly successful. I have to be hellaciously successful for my work to register."

By the fall of 1986, however, eighteen months had passed since *Perfect*. "There were no high stakes, no twenty million dollars breathing down your neck." Although he admits that when Pudney invited him down to the network for a chat, "I thought to myself 'How am I going to get out of it this time?'" The temptation simply to do *something* was there. And when Pudney told him who else was involved, that was it.

Robert Altman had stayed away from television even longer than John. Twenty years had elapsed since his last work in the field, and even then he had already established himself among Hollywood's most visionary directors with credits that merely started with the original movie version of *M*A*S*H*.

Since that time, Altman's stock had increased manifold, but still he nurtured personal dreams. One in particular remained frustratingly unfulfilled. He wanted to televise a series of one-act plays by the English playwright Harold Pinter. "I had tried to sell the idea to HBO a couple of years ago," Altman lamented in 1987, "but Pinter was too esoteric for them." When Pudney finally gave him the go-ahead, Altman was amazed; by the time ABC had finalized the cast for the first of the plays, Pinter's *Dumbwaiter*, he was positively stunned.

"For years I'd been looking for something to bring John back to television," Pudney told *The New York Times*. "Originally I was thinking of something musical, but when Altman suggested *The Dumbwaiter*, I thought of John." Still, he had to admit that Altman "gave me a rather skeptical look when I mentioned his name, but I set up a lunch and they got along famously."

John met with Altman at the Russian Tea Room in Manhattan. It was an informal meeting, but John was already certain he wanted the part—so certain that he memorized great passages of the play and perfected a Cockney accent to deliver them in. Then, while Altman ate his lunch, John launched into his act.

"Frankly, I didn't know how familiar Altman was with my work before then," John explained self-effacingly. "I really think it was my performance at the Russian Tea Room that made him think I could do the part." At the end of the meal, Pudney laughs, "Altman gave that famous Hollywood line, 'Hey kid, you've got the job.'"

Playing opposite John would be Tom Conti, as legendary an actor in his own right as John and certainly the equal of Altman in terms of inspiring awe. *Merry Xmas, Mr. Lawrence*, in which Conti completely stole the show from star David Bowie, and *The Norman Conquests*, in which he held his own even against the redoubtable Penelope Keith, showed Conti at the peak of his powers. But John, as Altman knew he would, fit right in.

The Dumbwaiter is the tale of a pair of hitmen who are hiding out in a deserted English mansion after a job . . . deserted, that is, aside from whoever—or whatever—is sending them increasingly cryptic messages and commands down the dumbwaiter. It is a challenging play in that there are no more than two castmembers. In the week of rehearsals in Montreal prior to the February filming, then, it was important not only for John and Conti to gel, but also for them to be able to bounce off one another's feelings as their on-screen relationship became ever more frayed.

It worked. "He and Conti are very funny together—they're like the new odd couple," Altman laughed afterward. He admitted that he had indeed been a stranger to John's work until they met. "But I remembered seeing him play oddball characters on television, and this part in *The Dumbwaiter* is essentially a comic character. The dialogue is non-sequitur dialogue, and it's hard to learn. But John brought it off."

The hour-long *Dumbwaiter* was aired on ABC May 12, 1987; it was not a major ratings success, but as Gary Pudney explained beforehand, "We're not looking for a huge rating. Pinter is kind of obscure for the masses. Maybe Travolta's celebrity will give us a chance to reach a few more people, [but] even if only fifteen million people see it, more people will be exposed to a Pinter play than ever before. That's something to be proud of."

Successful or not, *The Dumbwaiter* did stir John out of his eighteen-month torpor, although he rejects that description of what the rest of Hollywood still refers to as his lost years.

"I traveled the world, I studied Scientology. I spent time with friends, family. I mean, it wasn't that I wasn't offered anything—it was that for various reasons, I decided not to do them. Certain movies came up and I just went, 'Naaah.'"

Freshly invigorated by the *Dumbwaiter* experience, John now seemed determined to make up for lost time. It helped that he still didn't need the work—that he was just following personal whims—because even his biggest fans would have a hard time explaining how he fell into some of the projects that came his way over the next few years. Rudderless since Bob LeMond's stormy departure, John was now hopelessly aimless as well.

Although he did enter discussions with Whoopi Goldberg about collaborating on a comedy and was passed over for a biopic of Howard Hughes, these projects fell by the wayside. John committed himself instead to *The Experts*, director Dave Thomas's tale of two out-of-work New Yorkers who believe they have been hired to open a nightclub in Nebraska but who are actually working for the KGB as raw material for rookie spies to study.

The Experts was filmed in the winter of 1987 on location in Vancouver, the Canadian city whose cheaper hotels and facilities had established it as a favorite location for American filmmakers. It was not an inspiring effort, and neither—John aside—did it boast a particularly inspiring cast: Ayre Gross, best known from parts in *Soul Man* and *House II*; Charles Martin Smith, the accountant antihero of the remade *Untouchables*; horror star James Keach; and Kelly Preston, a youthful veteran of what would in earlier times have been classed tasteless B-movies.

Preston "was one of about six women who were auditioning for the part," John remembered. But she was the only one to catch his eye; when they met at a screen test, they started dancing instinctively.

"I liked her immediately," John continued, "and I liked her even more when we started rehearsing and I found out she liked to travel and she didn't mind flying. She liked to dance. She liked to eat. It was so refreshing. I thought, 'Wow, she could be fun.'"

He also discovered that although she was not a Scientologist, Preston did have some experience with it. She and her husband were introduced to certain Scientology principles by their acting coach,

Milton Katselas. Now, just as he had been initiated into the faith by Joan Prather, John began leading Kelly further along.

"Scientology addresses you as a spirit, not as a body or an animal. That's the start point. From there on, there are limitless concepts." As he and Kelly got to know one another, she felt able to talk about her marriage, which was slowly disintegrating.

Nine years John's junior, Kelly recalls, "When we first met, I developed a bit of a crush on him. But it was actually more of a professional relationship with a little bit of a crush in there." The only downside to what John began to sense was a budding relationship was that, despite all the problems they had discussed, despite the rocks her marriage was crashing upon, Kelly was still legally wed. Although they would remain casual friends, when *The Experts* wrapped so did their relationship.

The Experts did not do well; indeed, immediately following its low-key opening in Oklahoma and Texas in January 1989, it suffered the even lower-key fate of immediate demotion to video.

However, the team of John, Dave Thomas, and Charles Martin Smith remained together for a second, very bizarre, project that same year: a live-action rendering of the adventures of Boris Badenuff and Natasha Fatale, the Pottsylvanian nemeses of Jay Ward's cartoon heroes Bullwinkle and Rocky.

Under Smith's direction, Thomas and Sally Kellerman starred, while John accepted a simple cameo role, appearing on screen for the blink of an eye as he attempts to deliver roses to supermodel Natasha. Boris slams the door in his face.

Though its heart was in the right place, *Boris and Natasha* never stood a chance of recapturing the mindless glory of the original cartoon. Executive producer Kellerman made a passable, if unlikely, Natasha, but Thomas was completely wrong for Boris.

Furthermore, a reasonable story in which the bungling spies are dispatched (by Fearless Leader, of course) to steal a time-travel microchip from its American inventor, was marred by unnecessary intricacies. Ultimately, what could have succeeded as a riotous farce was reduced to nothing more enduring (or endearing) than any other contribution to the post-*Top Secret* comedy espionage drama. Faring even worse than *The Experts*, *Boris and Natasha* never made it to the cinema.

It remained unseen until 1992, when it was premiered on the Showtime cable TV network.

John barely noticed. His planes still demanded all the spare time he could give them. He was planning another upgrade, replacing the Constellation with a beautiful Gulfstream II, and when his feet did touch the ground, Disney World was just up the road. Within a year of moving to Spruce Creek, John had visited it three times. It all seemed so idyllic that John himself acknowledged it would take a very special project to lure him away.

That project, it turned out, was just around the corner.

John already knew Kirstie Alley, the actress who exploded into prominence in the *North and South* miniseries before becoming a national heroine on *Cheers*, from their shared faith in Scientology.

So when he was offered a part in her latest movie, a bizarre look at everyday life through the eyes of a newborn baby, he took it partly out of respect for Alley and partly because of the movie's bizarre premise. How often, after all, is one offered a part in a film that kicks off with a talking sperm?

It proved to be one of his wisest moves in a long time. *Look Who's Talking* became the surprise hit of 1989; the last hit, perhaps, of a decade that had treated John badly, but that now seemed to be anxious to make amends.

Maybe it was the appearance of the Bee Gees' "Staying Alive" on the soundtrack that jogged the old memory banks; maybe it was the chance to see John simply playing an ordinary guy, doing ordinary things, even cracking his face into that familiar old grin. But suddenly, magazines whose staff were barely able to write when *Saturday Night Fever* jolted their big brothers and sisters were talking of John's comeback as if he really had been away—and not simply overlooked.

Publicly, too, *Look Who's Talking* could not be stopped. In its first seventeen days of release, *Look Who's Talking* earned forty-six million dollars; with the blessing of its leading stars, it also raised one-hundred thousand dollars for NarAnon International, a Scientology-inspired drug rehab program for which Alley was the international spokesperson.

"Look who's talking about John Travolta," *People Weekly* teased.

"Hollywood, mostly, and for a change, they're saying nice things about him."

Buffy Shutt, President of Marketing at Columbia/TriStar, *Look Who's Talking*'s distributor, continued, "You do hear his name being bandied about more. Even the more cynical people who've seen him in this movie have discovered him again. His name is back on the lists." Shutt was absolutely delighted for John; even more delighted that it had been TriStar who had helped engineer his return.

Ironic, then, that TriStar had actually gone out of its way to underplay John's involvement in the film.

"It wouldn't have been fair to the movie to sell it as a John Travolta film," Shutt excused them. "When you have an actor whose past few movies didn't do well, you have to stop and think. And we wanted to sell it as a comedy." Company President Jeff Sagansky agreed. "I didn't worry that John Travolta's name would keep people away," he remarked. "But I didn't know if it would be a huge draw."

John apparently agreed with the strategy. "He liked his work in the movie, and he didn't want the release to be blown," Shutt concluded. Print ads for the movie didn't even picture him; instead, Mikey, the wisecracking baby with a voice suspiciously like Bruce Willis's, donned a Walkman and shades, and that was the one clue would-be theatergoers were given. For many, John's involvement remained a secret until they were already sucked into the film and Mikey started trying to convince his unwed mom that John's character, James, is the one that she wants (ooh ooh ooh).

"You're never out of the business," Jonathan Krane, who produced *Look Who's Talking*, tried to explain. "It wasn't as if John was missing. He was just waiting for the right picture to come along."

But he also knew that if anybody believed that, they would believe anything, so it was almost apologetically that he mentioned that John already had two more movies lined up for release, an action-packed drug epic called *Chains of Gold* that reunited him with Marilu Henner, and another low-budget one-off called *The Tender.*

Even then he knew that few people would ever learn that those movies existed, let alone get to see them. And with John now hoping his career might be on the up again, it was probably for the best.

Co-written by John and made by Krane's own film production,

Chains of Gold featured John as Scott Barnes, a social worker and reformed alcoholic whose concern for a missing boy (Joey Lawrence) draws him into conflict with a murderous crack gang.

Chains of Gold deserved a better fate than that awaited it: beset by financial problems that eventually shut down the production company, *Chains of Gold* did not even receive a cinema opening. Instead, it was given a premiere of sorts at the Directors Guild, with proceeds going to Scientology's Ability Plus schools, followed by a nationwide airing on the Showtime cable TV network September 15, 1991. *The Tender* would not get even that far.

Look Who's Talking, however, simply wouldn't stop raking in money.

John's return to prominence aboard a movie that not even its makers dreamed would gross one-hundred-forty million dollars, stunned many people. What didn't surprise them was the speed with which the tabloid media was back on his case.

They were old sparring partners, after all, and with John back on track, it was only right that they should become reacquainted. Except the tabloids had learned some new tricks since last time; either that, or society had loosened up enough to let them take the kid gloves off the old ones.

On May 8, 1990, the *National Enquirer* ran with a Travolta comeback of its own, the resurrection of the hitherto moribund rumors of his alleged homosexuality

The magazine's source was Paul Barresi, a porn star who had appeared fleetingly alongside John in *Perfect*. He collected one-hundred thousand dollars for his claim that he and John had shared a homosexual relationship that dated back to 1982, when John picked him up at a health spa, and that ended scant months before *Perfect*'s June 1985 release.

At the time, John himself refused to comment on the claims, a stance that either proved they were not worth the newsprint they were printed on or was tantamount to an admission, depending on one's point of view. More likely, his silence only proved that he was hard at work on the sequel to *Look Who's Talking*, the imaginatively titled (but otherwise creaking) *Look Who's Talking Too*.

With baby Mikey joined now by a sister, Julie, *Look Who's Talking*

Too returned John to Vancouver for the summer of 1990. By "sheer coincidence," as John later put it, one of the first people he bumped into was Kelly Preston, also in town to shoot a movie, *Disney's Run*. Even more coincidentally, they were booked into the same hotel.

John had seen Kelly just once since *The Experts* wrapped, at a Christmas party thrown by Kirstie Alley at her home in Penobscot Bay, Maine. Now divorced, Kelly had also put behind her a relationship with another actor, *ER* star George Clooney, and was now engaged to Charlie Sheen. Alley, however, didn't believe it would last, and as she sidled past John, she whispered in his ear, "Why don't you two get together?" John laughed.

"She said, 'I don't know why you and Kelly aren't together,' and I said, 'Frankly, neither do I, but it's too late now.'"

Or maybe it wasn't. In Vancouver, John and Kelly's friendship picked up where it had left off with *The Experts*; the difference this time was that Kelly was no longer married—or engaged. She and Sheen split in April 1990, just before she left for Canada.

Looking back, John says, "It was almost destiny in a certain way. We were going to spend the summer in the same hotel together and we were not involved with anyone. I said, 'This is it. I know this is it!'"

Kelly, too, was happy to make some allowance for the workings of fate. "When I was fifteen and my family was living in Australia," she recalled, "we went to see *Grease*. Before we walked in, I saw this poster and I had this flash that I was going to be with this man, you know, in the future."

The night John asked her out for the first time, she remembered another experience with a premonition. Attending a disco class with her mother "and about two-hundred other women," the teenaged Kelly proudly informed the instructor that he might be able to dance like John Travolta, but one day she would marry him. "I didn't really remember it until [John] asked me to go out and we started dating, and then I said 'Oh God!'"

Their first date, Preston recalled, was dinner in Seattle, two-hundred miles down the road. But it was only a short hop in the reality that was suddenly building between her and the man of those long ago dreams. There John proposed a relationship that would be "ongoing, committed, with a view to marriage and children." She accepted.

The couple continued dating after their movies wrapped, and in December, following the opening of *Look Who's Talking Too*, they flew to Switzerland for a year's end get-together with about thirty friends. Suddenly, with everyone awaiting the midnight chimes in the Palace Hotel restaurant in Gstaad, John produced a six-carat diamond ring and asked Kelly to marry him. Or at least, he tried.

"Sally Kellerman was with us," John remembers. "She didn't know I was proposing, and she kept tapping me on the shoulder in the middle of my proposal. I'd say 'I have something to ask you, Kelly,' and then I'd get this tap on my shoulder every time I was about to do it. It was like an *I Love Lucy* episode. She kept on tapping me, 'John, I've been meaning to tell you how great this evening is.' She interrupted me like four times. I finally said, 'Shut up, I'm trying to propose to Kelly!'"

"I had no idea he would propose," revealed Jonathan Krane who, with his wife Sally, was sharing John and Kelly's table. Neither did Kelly, he smiled; when John proposed, she screamed.

John later admitted he hadn't been certain what was going to happen either. "Earlier that day I'd passed by a jewelry store and seen the most beautiful ring. I told myself, 'You're going to propose in six months anyway, why not just get the ring now?'" He bought it, then discovered that he couldn't wait to pop the question. "That night I shocked the heck out of everyone!"

"We've found the right partner in each other," John knew right away. "I think you have to do more work in finding the right partner than you think you do. I think as romantic as it is, it's almost as logical, as it should be. Meaning you have to ask yourself several questions, like: do you really have the same interests? Do you really have the same purposes and goals? Do you have the same hobbies, interests, profession? If you don't, are they of comparable magnitude to some degree?

"The level to which you can find these areas comparable can guarantee a certain amount of success. Kelly and I for the most part, I'll say eighty-five to ninety percent, are comparable in our goals and wishes."

The couple returned home to learn that despite the critical panning that awaited *Look Who's Talking Too*, the film had again done well at the box office and was well on its way to a forty-six-million-dollar gross. Although almost precisely one-third of the first movie's gross, it was still a respectable result. For want of anything else to do, John put his name down for the next in the series. The one with the talking dogs. *Look Who's Talking Now.*

John and Kelly continued working through the first months of their betrothment, with John's attention now directed toward a goofy little drama called *Shout.*

Set in the mid-1950s, and directed by Jeffrey Hornaday, best known as the choreographer for *Flashdance*, *Shout* set itself up as a cross between *Boys Town* and *Don't Knock the Rock.* John plays Jack Cabe, a middle-aged music teacher who imports this new-fangled rock 'n' roll into a sleepy Texas town—or more accurately, into one corner of it, the Dotheboys Hall.

It was a familiar premise, rendered even more so by the familiarity of its soundtrack, a boisterous battery of old-time devil's music. Unfortunately, the script's apparent indecision regarding Jack Cabe's true mission leaves *Shout* annoyingly unfulfilling. Does he bring rock 'n' roll to the town to give the kids some new distractions? Or because he's seen its effect on the rest of America, and he simply wants it to cause even more trouble here?

Faced with the smug sanctimony of some of the city fathers, one hopes that it was the latter. But one gloomily suspects it was really the former and wonders whether John put as much energy into his performance as he did into buying his summer house in Maine.

Probably not. He'd already spent fifteen years searching for it and would likely have spent the next fifteen as well if Kirstie Alley hadn't told him about the tower- and gable-festooned twenty-bedroom stone mansion that was up for sale just down the road. Built by a Philadelphia tycoon at the turn of the century, John bought it on the spot. "I looked up and down the East Coast for fifteen years," he explained, "for a home that could house my whole family—and when I say 'whole family,' I mean the tree." And that meant roots as well as branches. He and Kelly were going to be parents.

In September 1991, with Kelly two months pregnant, she and John flew to France to attend the Deauville Film Festival, stopping off first in Paris. Kelly described it as "the most beautiful, romantic city in the world."

They made no bones about Kelly's pregnancy. "I absolutely wanted a child," John proclaimed to the curious Parisian journalists. "Otherwise I would probably never get married. Marriage is complicated and you can do without it. But a baby has to have a real father and a real mother."

The French press was already conjuring up visions of some kind of shotgun ceremony when the news broke that it was in their fair city, in the salon of the Crillon Hotel at midnight on September 5, that the couple would fulfill the expectations building around them and wed.

Unlike the high-profile Travolta weddings of a decade previous, when both his father and brother Joey had married in the glare of a hundred flashbulbs, John kept his own nuptials so secret that even the hotel staff were unaware what was happening until a three-tiered wedding cake was ordered at four o'clock that afternoon.

The French authorities, too, were left in the dark, an oversight that apparently raised questions over the marriage's legality; to be on the safe side, John and Kelly would marry again in a civil ceremony once they returned to the United States. In their own eyes, however, and those of their Church, everything was above board—the ceremony was conducted by a French Scientologist minister.

Although it was stunned by the suddenness of the ceremony, the American press lost little time in tracking down the happy couple's relatives, even as John and Kelly set off the following morning on the two-hour drive to Deauville.

They discovered some contrasting reactions. Sal Travolta, now seventy-eight years old, was overjoyed—"Johnny is the baby, so it's fitting that he would be the last one in the family to marry and have a child. We love Kelly. She's a very nice lady."

Kelly's mother, Linda, and stepfather Lee Carlson (her father died when Kelly was three) appeared less accommodating. Tracked down at their home in Hawaii, Lee merely remarked, "We know about it, and we don't have anything to say to anybody."

Nobody had much to say about *Shout* when it opened in America the following month, either. As *The New York Times*' Caryn James put it, and John was surely already aware, the "unintentionally silly" movie had little to recommend it and even less to provoke audiences into seeing it.

"No one expects John Travolta to go on playing the disco king forever," James' review continued. "But who would have thought he'd turn into Dick Clark's evil twin?" John would chalk *Shout* up to experience; with a gross of just over three million dollars, Hollywood would chalk it up as another flop. It seemed the comeback celebrations were a little premature again. Either that, or John really was doomed to a roller-coaster career.

If so, he was back on the downward slope.

John had already admitted that he agreed to appear in *Look Who's Talking Now*, the third and most ambitiously absurd of the *Look Who's Talking* movies, simply "to keep alive in show business." It didn't matter that a sequel-sated media had already dubbed it *Look Who Won't Shut Up*; it was the only movie on offer, so he took it. Beyond it, his schedule was empty.

Look Who's Talking Now was dreadful, and everybody knew it. Even if they didn't, its box-office gross of ten million dollars would leave little room for dispute. Even the public was sick of these new-style talkies.

Ah, *Look Who's Talking Now*. "That would be the one with the talking dogs," author Martin Amis smirked. He then invited his readership to join him picturing John "in his twenty-room chateau in Penobscot Bay, Maine, or in his second home in the Spruce Creek Fly-in development, or indeed en route between them at the controls of one of his three airplanes, in actorly preparation for the dogs movie: thinking dogs. . . talking dogs."

"I try to be realistic," John sighed as though this were the first time someone had drawn such an unappetizing parallel. "You know, you can't dance without legs. I would continue to work with the best that was offered. But I did think, 'Well, it's over.'"

"Where I felt it most," John continued, "was in the very innards of the movie industry—the agents, producers, studio heads—where a temperature was placed on you, a need was placed on you, a desire was placed on you. But I never quite felt it from the public. I felt like they were, 'Hey, where ya been?' Or, 'When's the next one?' It was yesterday to them." That's what made his failures so hard to take—the fact that as far as the public was concerned, he was still John Travolta. And John Travolta was still a star. He felt he was letting the people down. Again.

The critical rebirth that attended the original *Look Who's Talking* had already fallen by the wayside, and if he wasn't back to square one again, he was damned close. It was time for another break, and with Kelly's pregnancy now approaching its end, it was welcome.

But if *Look Who's Talking Too* had introduced John to his future, its sequel, in the most bizarre fashion, would bring him face to face with both his past—and his destiny.

Over the past couple of years, Quentin Tarantino had established himself as the latest new kid on the directorial block, a savage, intense, writer-director whose work, ignored for years by even the outer limits of the Hollywood mainstream, had suddenly exploded into a cult that literally knew no bounds.

His ultraviolent debut, *Reservoir Dogs*, had already proven the art-circuit hit of the previous year; his screenplay, *Natural Born Killers*, was to be realized by Oliver Stone; now he was planning a vampire movie, *From Dusk Till Dawn*. That summer of 1993, he contacted John to offer him a part in the film.

"He is one of the very best American film actors around," Tarantino raved. *Blow Out* was one of the few movies guaranteed a place in Tarantino's constantly changing top ten movies of all time, and he freely admitted, "he was awesome in [that]. I used to watch that film over and over and wonder why other directors weren't using him."

He was less keen on John's more recent roles, of course; "As much as I like John Travolta, I couldn't bring myself to watch some fucking talking baby movie," he famously cursed to *Vanity Fair*. But still, he knew he had to work with John.

And John was interested, if not in the vampire flick, then at least in doing something with the brash young director. Finally, in January 1992, Tarantino invited him to Los Angeles to visit his apartment and just hang out for a while.

As John took down the West Hollywood address, it seemed somehow familiar. As he turned into the street, he realized what it was. Tarantino was living in John's old apartment, the one he'd rented when he first moved to Los Angeles almost twenty years before.

"When I got there, I knocked on his door and said, 'Before you say anything, let me tell you something about the apartment you live in. You have maroon and pink tile in your bathroom. Your refrigerator is on the north wall. You have an oddly-designed window in your bedroom.' I named about half a dozen things. He went nuts!"

He went even crazier when he found out how John knew so much about the place. John continues, "I told him, 'I was cast in *Carrie* and *Welcome Back, Kotter* [two more of Tarantino's favorites] in this apartment, and now you're living in it.' We couldn't get over that."

But there was more! Inside, prominent amid Tarantino's collection of Hollywood clutter, stood a veritable shrine to John Travolta—a Vinnie Barbarino doll, lunch boxes, even a few of the board games that had been thrown onto the market at the height of John's popularity in *Saturday Night Fever, Grease* and *Welcome Back, Kotter.* It doesn't matter that Tarantino insists he was never aware of his apartment's serendipitous history. If anybody ever makes a movie about the ultimate obsessive fan tracking down his idol for who knows what sort of purpose, Tarantino already has the opening gambit. It's called his life.

"I've been collecting this shit for years," Tarantino modestly remarked as the two men surveyed the collection. John smirked at the memory of the boardgames in particular. "They're very stupid games. How do you play the *Grease* game?" He didn't have a clue, and maybe he still isn't certain, but when Tarantino challenged him, John not only took the bait but also won at both *Grease* and *Kotter.* In return, Tarantino insisted he autograph both boxes, and then they got down to talking.

"It didn't look as if he had a project in mind," John remembers. "He kept talking about some horror movie, and I am not a horror movie guy. His interest in me seemed to be. . . generic. It was a very funny meeting."

But it was also a remarkably chastening one. With the boardgames and memorabilia all returned to their shelves, Tarantino suggested wandering down the road for a coffee. They talked some more, went back to the apartment, "And then Quentin let me have it. He said, 'What did you do? Don't you remember what Pauline Kael said about you? Don't you remember what Truffaut said about you? Don't you know what you mean to the American cinema? John, what did you do?'"

John flinches at the memory. "I was hurt—but moved. He was telling me I had a promise like no one else's. I went out of there with my tail between my legs. I was so devastated. I couldn't find the words. But I also thought, 'Jesus Christ, I must have been a fucking good actor.'"

And it had taken him only twenty years to realize that.

The two parted with Tarantino convinced that although *From Dusk till Dawn* probably wouldn't be happening, at least with John (it was eventually released in 1996, directed from Tarantino's script by Robert Rodriguez and starring Kelly's old flame George Clooney), he did have a role for his hero. All the hero needed to do was wait until it was written.

In the meantime John kept out of the spotlight as he prepared for the birth of their first child. "I've turned down three jobs since last New Year's"; he would reject two more in the months following the baby's birth. There again, "they were highly forgettable movies. Maybe I would have done them if I'd been bored," but he admitted there was little chance of that for a while.

The pregnancy and the delivery were both handled according to the principles of Scientology.

"We believe everything starts at conception," explained Kelly. Even before the child's birth, then, Kelly would read to him and play music. "You have to take care of women during pregnancy and during birthing," John continued. "Because everything that happens to them is a reflection of what's going to happen to our future."

The birth itself took place in almost total silence. "There's a lot of pain going on, so the idea is, you don't want to contribute to that pain by adding verbal statements because they're recorded in the mind of the baby. Later that could cause certain kinds of fears or neuroses or even psychosomatic illnesses. Even if the mother were to injure herself during the pregnancy, she should keep quiet. She should keep quiet even if she sneezes."

Jett Travolta weighed in at a healthy eight pounds, twelve ounces. "After he was born and cleaned up, I held him for hours while Kelly slept," John reflected. "When they came to take him away for various tests, I said, 'No, you can't see him today. You'll have to do it another day.' I went a little nutsy."

Still, John admits the first thing he and Kelly did with the newborn was a mistake. "We left the hospital too soon. We should have stayed a second day but we were anxious to get home."

Kelly picked up his story. "We thought, 'Oh, we've got our family now, we'll start our new life. Just be peaceful in a cozy home by ourselves.' And the first couple of days were blissful. We were like, 'Oh, three hours of sleep, isn't it wonderful? I can live like this.' And then, by the fourth day, it was like delirium had set in. We were like zombies."

"Why didn't anyone tell us?" John asked. "We could have afforded a nurse."

With the arrival of Jett, John and Kelly moved their main home up to the mansion in Maine, maintaining Spruce Creek now as their summer residence and flying the Gulfstream II back and forth as the whim caught them. On one of those flights, one of John's personal worst nightmares came horrifically close to fruition. He was shuttling Kelly and Jett between Florida and Maine when the plane lost all its power in a series of seven contagious systems failures. And there was nothing that John or his copilot could do about it.

"That was almost a disaster," John shudders. "When you fly a plane, you buy into the idea that it's dangerous fare and that you'll do the best job to have it not be. But you don't like tying others into that play. So my thought was, 'God, for the one time in my twenty-three years of flying, why does it have to be a time when my family's on board?'

"On the other hand, maybe it gave me that higher sense of survival and protectivism because of them. Man, I was cool as ice. Everyone thinks I'm cool on screen, but me in that cockpit, that was cool!"

With just three minutes of juice on the backup battery, a distress call was put through to the nearest control tower, and John began wrestling the Gulfstream in to land.

"We were at about a thousand feet, and I was looking for an airport, hoping it was Washington and not Baltimore or something, where the buildings are taller. I noticed the Washington Monument on my second turn around the area, and I knew National airport was close."

Touching down, "People came down from the offices at National to congratulate the pilot who brought that plane in safely. They had no idea it was John Travolta!" John completed his journey in his Learjet.

Back in Maine, John and Kelly spent their time designing a nursery that, as Kelly proudly boasted to one journalist, was not for Jett's benefit alone. "This is wonderland. John and I got together and figured out what all our fantasies were as kids."

Jett's bedroom was decked out like the fuselage of a plane. Above his head, a floor-to-ceiling papier-maché beanstalk wound up a beam. There was an ice cream parlor, a seesaw, a pretend school and supermarket, a Peter Pan-themed room with glow-in-the-dark stars on the ceiling, a cowboy room, and toys wherever you looked. It was a child's vision of paradise, but it was an adult's as well. And *Entertainment Weekly* journalist Jeff Gordinier was not alone when he mused, "John loves his son so much that he built him the playroom. But he loves planes so much he named his son after them."

12

◇ ◇ ◇

Welcome Back, John

The role of Vincent Vega, John knew, was one he would never have dared take in the past. Not even Ben, hiding out in a deserted mansion while the dumbwaiter creaked and whirred malevolently beside him, was like this guy, a sleazy hitman with a heroin addiction. Yet there was also something similar about him, a linear descent from all the street punks and losers he'd played in the past: from Billy Nolan, if he hadn't died, to Jack Teri, if he hadn't had a conscience; from Danny Zuko if he'd never met Sandy, to Scott Barnes if he had started doing crack instead of feeding the guy who made it to the alligators.

That, however, was the difference, the "ifs" that divided his former creations from Tarantino's.

"I had to make a decision whether or not I wanted to [play the part]," John admitted. *Chains of Gold*'s heavy-handed assault on crack culture notwithstanding, he was proud and thankful that he had avoided the drug scene throughout his career, even as he created scenes (through *Saturday Night Fever* and *Urban Cowboy*) that "some people chose to experience with drugs." But even that did not explain his concern. What it came down to was whether he could be believable in such an astonishing role.

Yes, he believed he could.

"I felt I could do a change-up in a little film that no one will see, or in a big production like this with a great cast that everyone sees. You know, if I'm gonna play someone as bold as this heroin hit man, I'd better do it in good company with a great script and a great director. Because to do it with any less than that, you're taking a big chance. I like taking chances, but not if I'm going to fail at the artistic part of it. And I think that in this case I lucked out, because Quentin, who believed in me as an actor, gave me this stellar opportunity."

John had stayed in touch with Tarantino since that strange but fateful meeting six months before, and when he received the script for *Pulp Fiction* with the order, "look at Vincent," John knew he would not be disappointed. "It was an amazing script. Beyond clever, it was alive and unique and real."

The one problem was that as much as John loved the character, as much as he wanted to play it, he instinctively believed that "there is no way in hell they're going to let me."

Tarantino laughed his fears off, but when he told his backers at TriStar that John was set to play Vega, they confirmed every one of them. They suggested Tarantino contact Daniel Day-Lewis instead. Tarantino's partner, Lawrence Bender, was not particularly enthusiastic either. "You can get anybody in the world," Bender sniffed. "Why do you want John Travolta?"

"You can't blame them," Tarantino admitted. "Movies are very expensive, and they want to hedge their bets. I imagine that if I were a producer, I'd have the same considerations." All of which, John admitted, "kind of shows how my light had died. The studio wanted an actor with. . . a higher temperature."

But Tarantino was adamant. Either he made the movie with Travolta. . . or he didn't make the movie at all. Besides, he knew, John did have one ace up his sleeve.

Interviewed by the *Los Angeles Times* recently, critic Pauline Kael had been asked how she felt now about her long-ago championing of the young Travolta. What was it she called him—the new Brando?

The doughty Kael saw the trap before it was even laid.

"She said something like 'he's so essential and valuable to the American theater that he's sorely needed,'" John smiles. "For me to hear that when the chips were down made me feel like, 'Oh my God, I better do something good. I better live up to this!' It made me feel that people were glad I was alive."

John continued to be honest about his role in *Pulp Fiction*, however. "Quentin had far more to lose than I did," he admitted, recalling the day when he himself told Tarantino, "No, I'll do *Look Who's Talking Four* instead. In which the chairs talk." Tarantino ignored him.

John revealed, "I said to myself, 'I've got to do something in this movie that not only I've never done before but maybe no one has ever done before, because it's going to be one of the few shots I have to regain a kind of significance in the industry.' I knew I was up against the wall on this one."

Tarantino, however, remained absolutely fearless. He'd made his decision, and he was sticking with it. He knew it was the right one to take.

"Reporters ask me, 'So what made you choose him? He's not really that hot anymore!' Look, I've walked down the street with some big stars, okay? I cannot walk two feet down the street with John Travolta. People stop their cars. People are clawing all over him and stuff. It's like, he's a movie star!" And next to him, the rest were just amateurs.

Even for a veteran like John, working alongside Tarantino was an absolutely new experience that completely reawakened his enthusiasm for his trade. "I'd never known anybody who was so certain in what he wants, and yet gives you the freedom to go down as many paths as you want. I liked that he's an actor as well as a writer-director, because I found myself trusting him. And he wasn't so self-absorbed with his script that he would be averse to changing things. I would say ninety percent of everything he wrote is in that movie, but there's ten percent where he allowed any actor who felt uncomfortable to alter a line or whatever, as long as it was effective.

"For instance, if I had trouble with the way a line was structured, I'd say, 'Do this line for me as an actor, the way you would do it.' And sometimes he'd say, 'You know what? You're right. It doesn't work. I'm gonna change it.' But it was a rare occasion that you'd ever want to change anything. I felt, 'Wow, I really like being a film actor again.'"

John continued to feel that way even when he realized it was actually going to cost him a lot of money to appear in *Pulp Fiction*.

"In order to have my family with me on the production, it cost me about thirty grand," he explained, balancing that against the $140,000 he was receiving. Incidentally, his *Pulp* pay stub registered $5,000 less than film critic Gene Siskel received when he sold the white *Saturday Night Fever* suit that he'd purchased for a mere $2,000.

John didn't care. "If you want to put Harvey Keitel, Bruce Willis, Uma Thurman, Rosanna Arquette, Eric Stoltz, Sam L. Jackson, and Chris Walken in a film together for eight million dollars, instead of sixty million as Quentin did, it's understood you can't afford to pay anybody anything. But that's cool, because if it turns out like *Pulp Fiction*, inevitably you get another offer that's of high quality and pays you better.

"I said to Quentin, 'You gave me my hat back as an artist.' I felt the same about doing *Dumbwaiter* with Altman. These are the movies that you make to keep your integrity as an artist. And also to know why you're doing the stupid ones." He continued, "You know, I started out with an Oscar nomination, and I proceeded to have enormous hits. But I never got another nomination. So I'd like to be in a film where there's the kind of role that would be artistically deserving of, you know, where I started."

For its cast, as much as for the thrilled audiences, *Pulp Fiction* echoed with humorous asides. It was, for example, the first movie ever made under the overall banner of the Walt Disney studios to feature anal rape. It was also the first to capture John on the john, a scene that, even as it was being filmed, left John quietly musing, "Either this is going to be the best move of my career or the worst, because I have never seen an actor filmed on the toilet, especially somebody who's supposedly a superstar. Is that a low for me?"

But that was only the tip of the iceberg. "There's all kind of stuff behind and between the words. When I walk into Jackrabbit Slim's, the audience is watching both Vincent Vega, who is nobody, and John Travolta, who has been an icon. And obviously the presence of all the other icons—Marilyn, Buddy Holly, Elvis [and frozen into his four o'clock stance, Travolta himself] sets off different echoes at different levels.

"Like in the Twist contest, there's Vincent, barely able to stand up; but there's also the memory of Tony Manero."

The dance sequence took eight hours to shoot and remains one of

John's favorite scenes not merely for the references it made to his own past but also for the freedom Tarantino allowed him once John came to grips with it.

"The script was written with me only doing the Twist. But I said to Quentin that, first of all, we had to find out what kind of Twist we were doing, because Johnny Travolta won, at eight years old, a twist contest in 1962. So there's a Johnny Travolta Twist and a Vincent Vega Twist. We had to find out what Twist we were going to do."

Still speaking from what remained an exhausting memory, John added, "More than that, if you're planning to do a whole song, which he was, we can't do a Twist for five minutes. We had to do other dances and I knew them. I told him that he was maybe two or three years old when I was doing this, but do you know the Swim? I showed it to him, and the Batman. He said, 'What's the Batman?' I said, 'It's this.' Then I asked if he knew the Mashed Potato. These were all the dances I grew up with. I said that I would teach these to Uma because they would make it much more fun. That's how it evolved."

Thurman herself was terrified before the scene, aware not just that she would be dancing with John Travolta, Mr. Dance himself, but also that the sequence ends with her collecting a trophy for her efforts. If she was going to win, she had better dance like a winner.

Tarantino listened to her uncertainties, then he and John hauled her off to Tarantino's trailer, where he had a copy of Jean-Luc Godard's *Bande à Part*. The dance scene in that movie is one of Tarantino's favorites, not because Anna Karina, Claude Brasseur, and Sami Frey dance well, but because they were having so much fun trying. That was what he wanted from Uma and John. Fun.

"The dance number worked on so many levels," John continues. "Here's the deal. It's fun for the audience because they have this picture of me dancing in films. It's fun for me because I get to dance as a heroin addict and a hitman who's a little chunky, which gives me character and makes me dance differently when I have a gut. It's a different way when I can be a character dancing. So everybody gets what they want out of that.

"Then, I've never done those novelty dances on screen. I grew up with the Batman and the Swim. These were dance steps I was doing as a kid. Vincent would also have been the same age and grew up with the same dances. Therefore, it was a blast to do, with everything that was going on in his mind, thinking I have to pull out something. Anyway, it worked on so many levels for everybody. Mind you, anybody written for that part would have done it, but it was more fun that I got to do it."

It was also more fun for the audience—particularly when Thurman, thoroughly into her role, stretched out one hand and pointed a finger at John, aping Olivia Newton-John's *Grease* gestures to a tee.

"For whatever reason, people get so excited when I dance," John reflected. "I'm a heroin-addicted hitman with a gut. It never ceases to amaze me. But at least I didn't have to wear white polyester!"

Work on the movie was completed on November 30, 1993; six months later, in May 1994, *Pulp Fiction* premiered at the Cannes Film Festival, exactly two years after *Reservoir Dogs* had ushered Tarantino into view. But, as one of Tarantino's biographers, Jeff Dawson, noted, "When *Reservoir Dogs* played here. . . it came in with a whimper. *Pulp Fiction*'s bite would be even louder than its bark."

The full cast was present, and Lawrence Bender recalled, "It was like *The Wild Bunch*, and all of a sudden everything started becoming very exciting for us. When we screened the movie. . . Quentin had never been in this much limelight. We get dressed up and we have our dinner and shit and there were twenty-five cars. They basically closed down the Croisette, and it took us half an hour to get from the Carlton to the Palais and it was wild. There were thousands and thousands of people cheering Quentin and all the stars. Extraordinary. It's quite scary if you haven't seen that many people before." The team would leave Cannes the following week with the cherished Palme d'Or, for the best movie of the festival.

The award took Tarantino completely by surprise.

"I never expect to win anything at any festival I go to with a jury," Tarantino admitted in his acceptance speech, "because I don't make the kind of films that bring people together. Usually I make films that split people apart."

In keeping with his usual way of doing these things, John was seeing *Pulp Fiction* for the first time at Cannes. "The buzz on it was extraordinary, and the rumor was that we were going to win the Palme d'Or. I mean, we didn't know it, but that was the feeling. So in that case, I almost had to see it three times before I could form any opinion of it."

Pulp Fiction opened across 1,300 screens throughout America October 14, 1994, following a showing at the New York Film Festival. The following day, John finally guest-hosted *Saturday Night Live*, the show he had tormented with his promise eighteen years before. But it was worth the wait, as John raised to unaccustomed heights a program whose days as a comic power were far behind it.

Dogged by cameras that insisted on focusing on his shoes while the band played "Staying Alive," John proceeded to parody himself and his past to perfection. He appeared in every sketch bar one, including a fabulous Tarantino-style remake of *Welcome Back, Kotter*, and another dragged up as Barbra Streisand for cast-regular Michael Myers' "Coffee Talk" segment.

A mobster scene took one line from *Chains of Gold*, in which the drug baron feigns deafness to discomfort an overzealous employee, hauling it to the height of absurdity. And John finally turned the tables on rumors of his homosexuality (and George Hamilton's *Love at First Bite*), with a sketch about a vampire whose prospective victims are convinced he's gay.

The whole thing was rounded off with a hilarious disjointed impersonation of Marlon Brando's equally precarious appearance on *Larry King Live* the previous week, echoing not merely Brando's discordance but also a twenty-year-old episode of *Kotter* in which Barbarino and Epstein hammed through their own rendering of *The Godfather*.

And all this from a man who opened the show with the pledge that he wouldn't be talking about his old shows and movies, not when he had a new film to talk about.

Not that *Pulp Fiction* really needed him to talk about it.

Riding on a slew of often extravagant reviews ("the reinvention of mainstream American cinema," insisted *Entertainment Weekly*), *Pulp Fiction* was galloping toward an eventual one-hundred seven million-dollar gross, and a mantlepiece full of post-Cannes awards. John himself was up for a Golden Globe and a Best Actor award from the Los Angeles Film Critics Association. Europe, too, fell for his reborn-again charm: Best Actor at the Stockholm International Film Festival, another nomination from the United Kingdom's British Academy Film and Theatre Awards.

At the Golden Globes, he learned of the forthcoming sale of the white suit he'd made so famous. "Gene [Siskel] pulled me aside and said, 'look, I'm having a real moral dilemma. I have an opportunity to make a lot of money on your white suit. But if you feel that it would hurt your feelings, I won't sell it.'"

John responded, "Gene, it's not my suit. It's your suit." Then he asked what Siskel intended to do with the money. When the critic said he planned to buy a cottage, John admits he wondered how a simple suit could be worth the price of a cottage. Nevertheless, he agreed. "I think you should have the cottage. And besides, it's not my suit."

Unfortunately, it wasn't his turn for a Golden Globe, and although he probably deserved it more than anyone in the room, it wasn't his turn for an Oscar, either. Even before it was announced in February, Hollywood took John's nomination for granted, and the pre-awards press made no bones about its preferences. But 1994 was the year of Tom Hanks' over-hyped *Forrest Gump*, and as it romped simple-mindedly home in every category it could find, John took solace in the knowledge that the next day's papers were full of sympathy for him. Many acknowledged that in spite of everything, in spite of *Gump*, he had really been the people's choice.

"The nineties, from *Look Who's Talking* on, there's a new thing that happened. I think a generation denied loving me, meaning they secretly loved me and were afraid to admit it," John mused. *Newsweek's* David Ansen agreed. "There are comebacks, and there are comebacks, and then there are comebacks. John Travolta has known them all. By [his] own count, he's now on his fifth—but this is the best. 'These have been the four most glorious months I've ever known,'[John said]."

John had, in fact, spent some time mulling over the nature of comebacks—again, probably because he had already experienced so many. By his reckoning, *Grease* was a comeback, because it proved there was life after Tony Manero. *Urban Cowboy* was a comeback because it crushed the memory of *Moment by Moment*. *Staying Alive* was a comeback, because it was two years since his last film; *Look Who's Talking* counted because it was his first hit in so long. And now, *Pulp Fiction*.

"I have a theory on it," John explained. "When people refer to a comeback, it doesn't mean you didn't work. It means that you weren't in a film that registered with them on a certain level. I mean, it's like, 'Oh, you think I haven't been doing anything? Well, does that mean the last ten years of my life just disappeared?'

"It's happened to me before, so it's not so surprising as much," he admitted. "But it's been exciting. Sometimes, you go and do your work, and once you're done, you just go home. Then a year later, or nine months later, this thing comes out and has its own life, and you almost feel detached from it. Again, it's something you can't control. It spins in an orbit. I've had this happen before in *Grease* and in *Urban Cowboy*. I've seen it, even in *Look Who's Talking*, although it wasn't performance oriented. So I was familiar with that orbit, but I didn't think that a piece like [*Pulp Fiction*] would have that kind of effect. But when I look at it, I think, 'Why wouldn't it?' because it has a lot of elements that could have that."

Such talk soon bored him, however. By 1995, John simply shrugged such questions off. "It was last year's story, and prior to that it was a story in '89, and prior to that it was a story in '83, and prior to that it was a story in '80. I've never quite figured out why I'm the comeback kid when another actor might just have a normal career of movies that work and don't work."

Quite simply, because other actors were never icons, because other actors weren't symbolic of an age. Because other actors weren't John Travolta. One would have thought he'd have realized that by now.

Still, he did know when to count his blessings. After *Pulp Fiction* aired at Cannes, John remembers, "Everyone who saw it offered me a job—six or seven important directors and producers." Even at the time, he thought, "Oh man, what's going to happen when it comes out?"

What happened? Hollywood virtually stampeded to his door. But this time, he was ready and willing to resist. He told *Newsweek* of a conversation he'd once had with Warren Beatty when he asked the veteran which was more important: having the public love your movie, or having the industry love your movie?

"The industry loving your movie," Beatty replied, "because they're the ones who give you your next job." Now, comparing the response to *Pulp Fiction*, a fair-sized hit with a lot of industry accolades, with *Look Who's Talking*, a monster hit with barely a meaningful plaudit to its name, he knew exactly what Beatty meant. *Look Who's*

Talking made one-hundred thirty-eight million dollars at the box office, but the only other thing it earned him was a couple of sequels. *Pulp Fiction*, which grossed less than half that, produced a phone that never stopped ringing.

Perhaps the greatest accolade came when John was brought face to face with journalist Nik Cohn, the writer who could almost be credited with inventing John Travolta—the icon if not the idol.

Writing in *Vogue* almost two decades after he penned "Tribal Rites of the New Saturday Night," the magazine article that exploded into one of the biggest movies of all time, Cohn said of John, "He never acquired three dimensions in my mind, nor seemed to grow any older. For almost twenty years, when I thought of him, I saw him frozen in the same attitude that had defined him in *Fever*.

"Reality had no function here. From time to time, dim tidings of his progress came to me, and much of the news did not sound good. His lover, actress Diana Hyland, died of cancer, so did his mother, whom he called his luck. Later on I read that he had [gotten] fat, that he was a Scientologist, that he was rumored to be bisexual. [But] in my imagination, he was still Tony Manero—the blue eyes and dimpled chin, the white suit, inviolate forever."

And then came *Pulp Fiction*.

The pair met at the Manor Hotel, the mansionlike guest house on the grounds of the Celebrity Center. John greeted him, Cohn says, as though "we were predestined friends who would not betray each other. 'It's been a long time,' he said, as though we already shared a long and entwined experience, and had been cruelly kept apart. 'I am so happy. Just so thrilled.'"

Just like that afternoon spent in his old apartment in West Hollywood playing with Tarantino's toys, John was coming face to face with a past he alone had experienced, a past that the slightest chance meeting could help him relive, and maybe relieve. Cohn, the man who'd designed the skeleton around which John, Robert Stigwood, and Norman Wexler would fashion an icon, was one of the few who understood that. His meeting with John helped the actor put his past into perspective, to come to grips with it.

"To be honest, I never really had a chance to grasp what was going on, let alone enjoy it." John replied to a question about the impact of the *Fever* years. "It was nothing I ever intended. I was just trying to be an actor. Learn my craft.

"By the time *Fever* came out, I was already working on *Grease*, and then I went straight into *Moment by Moment*, which of course was a disaster. So suddenly the press was killing me, everyone was saying my career was over, and I still hadn't caught up to the last reel, where I'd been the biggest star on earth, blah blah. It was as if everyone experienced the John Travolta craze except for John Travolta. Like I blinked and missed my own coronation."

Now *Pulp Fiction* was giving him a second chance, and this time he could afford the flops—beginning with *Eyes Of Love*.

Directed by Robert Harmon, whose 1986 debut *The Hitcher* made a star of Rutger Hauer, *Eyes of Love* came across as a quasi-*Godfather* modern gangster movie and half Walt Disney's *Incredible Journey*. John is Bobby, another in his series of ex-drunks and losers, who is set up as a thief by his dead wife's racketeer brother, Cissy (Tito Larriva). It's the first round in a no-holds-barred, no-lawyers-necessary custody battle for Bobby's daughter (Ellie Raab).

Into this melodrama is thrown a very large—but to dispell fears of typecasting, a decidedly untalkative—dog, a Doberman that had lost a dogfight at one of Cissy's gambling parties, and had been thrown into the river by its owner.

The daughter (unnamed in the movie, she is simply "the girl" in the credits) finds him, and when she and Bobby split Chicago for L.A. closely pursued by wicked Uncle Cissy, the faithful hound follows, trotting across country and arriving in Los Angeles just in time to thwart the villain's cunning plan.

John would describe *Eyes of Love* as "terrific," presumably only to be nice. Although his own performance wasn't bad, vaguely reminiscent of *Blow Out*'s Jack Teri fallen on harder times, the movie itself landed into that unenviable category of stories that are too long to be properly told in the time available (under ninety minutes) but not nearly good enough to deserve a minute more. Released in early 1995, *Eyes of Love* went straight to video without anyone even noticing. That summed it up, really. No one even noticed. They were too busy watching to see what John would do next.

In fact, two projects interested him now.

To be directed by *Addams Family* mastermind Barry Sonnenfeld, the first was an adaptation of Elmore Leonard's 1990 novel, *Get Shorty*. The other was *White Man's Burden*, which paired him with Andy Lawrence, the younger brother of *Chains of Gold* costar Joey, and Harry Belafonte in an upside down vision of racism and class distinction.

"It's a wonderful risky movie," John raved. "I repeat, it really is. At this point, I don't have to edit my risks. I don't care. I just do whatever's interesting and this one's very interesting. And Desmond McCado is the director. He wrote *Last Exit to Brooklyn*. I think he's very gifted and he wrote a great script."

Lawrence Bender, Tarantino's partner, was coproducer, which may have influenced John, but it was Tarantino himself who turned John on to the film, just as he would eventually influence John's decision on *Get Shorty*.

"We were having a photo shoot for some magazine, and [Quentin] came up to me and said that there was some interesting material that he wanted me to read that doesn't pay a lot of money and is independent, but [he said] I shouldn't be denied good material because I was a hot actor now. I said that I wanted to read it, and I read *White Man's Burden*. He was right. It was one-hundred percent excellent and I hopped on board, as per his suggestion."

He adds, "When I read it, without exaggeration, I couldn't put it down. I stood in my bathroom and read it till it was finished. I knew it wasn't commercial, but I thought 'I know how to play this guy to the hilt. I should do this.'"

Bender was enthusiastic about the chemistry between his two leading men. "It was like watching two kids on their first date. They were blushing. It was like love at first sight, and that chemistry translated on the screen."

Get Shorty, on the other hand, he rejected, even though he knew that Danny DeVito and Gene Hackman had already signed up to play in it. He also knew that the role he'd been offered—the loan shark Chili Palmer—was also of interest to his friend Warren Beatty. As far as John was concerned at that point, Warren was welcome to it.

When the script first arrived, John explains, "I liked it, but I wasn't exactly sure why I should do it." It just didn't seem right. "Then Quentin called me and said that he'd heard I'd turned it down. He said,

'You really have to consider that. You're perfect for it. It's the movie I would put you in next if I were your manager. What's going on? Read the book. Do something that gets you excited. Don't let that one go.' So I read the book, and thought, 'He's got something here.'

What clinched it for John was when Danny DeVito, whose voice had given life to one of *Talking Now*'s speaking dogs, told him virtually the same thing. "Of course you don't get it, you haven't read the book." After he had, John gladly admitted, "I knew exactly why I said no to the movie. All the dialogue in the book was paraphrased in the first draft of the script."

John contacted *Get Shorty*'s producers, DeVito, Michael Shamberg, and Stacey Sher. "I told them, 'Elmore's dialogue is so fabulous, but in the script it's been paraphrased. You've taken off the edge.' Then I gave them an example by reading a whole scene from the book, then from the script. Scott Frank, the screenwriter, got what I was saying immediately. He said he'd go back through the script with my notes."

Tarantino also suggested that John lose fifteen pounds for the part. John says he lost exactly fifteen pounds, and he laughingly continues, "I have a new secret in my decision-making for films I'll be appearing in. The secret is that Quentin is behind all my new movie decisions. He's taken the job as my manager." He paused. "No, not literally." But if a manager's job includes supplying motivation and applying new direction, it was close enough. For the first time since Bob LeMond's death, somebody supported John who not only appreciated his artistic worth but who was also determined to see him maintain it. There would be no more *Perfects*, no more *Chains of Golds*.

Get Shorty was director Barry Sonnenfeld's dreamchild; he had read the book while on a Caribbean vacation and returned home swearing that it was the only thing he had enjoyed about the entire trip. According to legend, he called DeVito and simply told him, "Danny, I just read a book you should buy."

"Okay," DeVito responded. "I'll buy it, you direct it." Two days later, he'd purchased the film rights and rang Sonnenfeld to tell him.

"That's great!" Barry exclaimed. "So what did you think of the book?"

"I don't know. I haven't read it."

Work on *Get Shorty* began January 18, 1995 armed with a cast almost as stellar as *Pulp Fiction*. John's character, Chili Palmer, was a Miami loan shark who travels to Los Angeles to collect on a gambling debt run up by movie producer Harry Zimm (Gene Hackman). He could have broken the old producer's legs; instead, he sells him a movie plot.

DeVito cast himself as Martin Weir, a diminutive megastar actor who is roped into Chili's film in exchange for a coproducing credit; also appearing in the film is Weir's B-Movie scream queen ex-wife, Karen Florres, played by Rene Russo. She'd been a cop in her last big outing, *Lethal Weapon III*, and fifteen years before, she had almost been cast in *Urban Cowboy*. "She was adorable then," John remembered, "and I've always liked her. She has a great sense of humor."

Some critics noted certain similarities between Chili and Vincent Vega, but John was not concerned. There were similarities between all his greatest characters. But, John notes, "Vincent Vega is a heroin addict on his way down, and Chili Palmer is on his way up and clean. There are different ways to portraying different roles."

And successful ways, too. Although John did not receive an Oscar nomination for *Get Shorty*, he was once again the popular choice, and his omission from the nominees only proves the continued shocking myopia of the selection committee.

He did, however, collect a Best Actor Golden Globe, while *Get Shorty* itself surpassed the most extravagant expectations by opening at the top of the weekend box-office list, earning an estimated thirteen million dollars.

Such success, revealed John Krier of the box-office tracking firm Exhibitor Relations, surprised everybody. "It doesn't have that many screens and it's a show business movie." *Get Shorty* could be seen on 1,612 screens across the country; by contrast, the previous week's number one, *Seven*, played on 2,528 screens.

In fact, the one thing that wasn't surprising was the news that John, who had received a respectable 3.5 million for his work on *Get Shorty*, was now commanding offers of twenty-one million for his next movie—or three times the budget for *White Man's Burden*.

Neither could anyone blame him. Talking to *Rolling Stone* shortly before Christmas 1995, John marvelled, "On Friday, I got seventeen offers. I haven't had seventeen offers in my life. Even in my first heyday—*Saturday Night Fever, Grease*, Academy Award nomination, the whole bit—I'd get three offers a year, tops. Either the industry's changed and needs more product, or I'm more valuable to them at this point. I don't know which it is, but it's an extraordinary situation."

He was adamant, though, that he would never take advantage of his status. "In all honesty, I've always been the best deal in town, and now I'm just getting what everyone else is. Well, maybe a little more." In fact, *Newsday* claimed that he would be receiving at least three million more than either Mel Gibson, Tom Hanks, Harrison Ford, or Arnold Schwarzenegger. It was a far cry from the one-third million he'd been paid for *Saturday Night Fever*!

Although it was shot first, *White Man's Burden* trailed *Get Shorty* by several months in the release schedule, finally opening in December 1995. It was an intriguing movie, turning racial stereotypes upside down, and then beating the hell out of them with the biggest stick it could find.

Although its reception was generally warm, *White Man's Burden*'s box-office receipts were laughable. That, however, was not the point. The point was John was enjoying his work again, and his work itself was enjoyable. With that established, nothing else mattered.

Besides, it suddenly seemed that John had so many movies on tap that it didn't matter how any one of them fared. His decade-old dream of returning Hollywood to the values of the '40s and '50s, when a star was judged on a body of work and not simply on whatever he did last time around, a time when one duff movie could not derail an entire career, a time when Gary Cooper could make forty movies in eight years, had finally come to pass.

And with that realization, came another. "I have a better feeling for what I'm doing. I care more." Back then, he would happily take a year off, to become a jet pilot, to study Scientology, to travel the world, whatever. "Now after twenty years, I can honestly say, 'I'm ready to go to work.'"

And for John, "going to work" meant a potential schedule that could make a Trojan blanch. Early in 1996, he confessed, "I spent so long having big time lags between work, and I made my life about what I did between movies. I didn't think I would be working again so easily." Yet he was already filming his fourth back-to-back film, *Phenomenon* for release July 10, 1996.

The movie, he explained, is "about a guy with average intelligence who actually gets struck by a stroke of genius. Throughout the plot you're not sure if it's a UFO that causes this, or possibly some kind of illness. It's up to you to interpret.

"It's beautifully written and it says a lot of what I believe in, you know, about the ultimate generosity of man. In spite of this guy's pain in struggling with this unwanted gift of genius, he still wants to help people. It's a burden for him. It's clever and beautifully done. It's with Robert Duvall, Forest Whitaker, and Kyra Sedgwick." At the wrap party, he continues, all of them wanted to dance with him!

"There's this thing, people feel it would be fun for them to dance with me. And, of course, they'll play some song from *Saturday Night Fever* that I have to deal with. Then I kind of—not cringe—but think 'Okay, once this song is over, I'll be able to have some fun,' because my fear is that they'll clear the floor and I'll have to perform solo. And that I don't want to do. At two-hundred pounds, doing those knee dips is a little tough."

Phenomenon would be followed by Nora Ephron's comedy, *Michael,* the tale of a womanizing, hard-drinking angel who inexplicably materializes in the Midwest, that John had been introduced to by Steven Spielberg. John began the summer of 1996 in Paris shooting *The Double,* directed by Roman Polanski, only to leave the set a few weeks into the filming. At the time of this publication, John was in litigation with the production company. Also on deck were *Lady Takes an Ace* with Sharon Stone and finally, *Dark Horse,* a political thriller he was developing with one-time *Happy Days* hero Ron Howard fourteen years after they were first linked on a movie. He had even raised the necessary financing for a long-dreamed of project of his own, *Fear,* based on a novella by Scientology founder L. Ron Hubbard.

In the meantime, February 5, 1996, brought the premiere of *Broken Arrow,* the seventy-million-dollar successor to Hong Kong-born director John Woo's 1992 effort, Jean-Claude Van Damme's *Hard Target.*

Broken Arrow was one of two projects Woo had presented to him, so that he might pick out the one he liked best. The other was *Tears of the Sun,* "an Amazon River adventure-type thing," as John put it. He was in no doubt, as *Broken Arrow* came together, that he had made the right choice.

"Part of the reason I liked this one the best is because I felt I could do something interesting with the villain, because he was written with an unusual cadence and an unusual style. The writer made him slightly odd, and I thought that oddity in itself could help me perpetuate the character. Because if you know any of these guys in the military who like it just a little too much, you'll know there are eccentricities about them that are kind of interesting and odd."

Besides that, John said as the movie was readied for release, *Broken Arrow* "is wild, just wild. This film will knock your socks off. It's so aesthetic, if that's even possible in an action movie. These characters come alive in a way that it's almost like a Picasso painting or something. It's not like anything you've ever seen before."

Neither was John's role. "I think that audiences will have a lot of fun with the film and with Vic Deakins," he predicted. "They've never seen me be this kind of character. In *Pulp Fiction*, I played a misguided bad guy; but Vic Deakins is definitely more in the tradition of real evil."

Woo agreed. "I enjoyed the contradiction between the real John Travolta, who has such a warm personality and a certain overall twinkle, and the limitless menace of the character of Vic Deakins."

Mark Gordon, the movie's producer, continued, "We wanted to try something different, rather than hiring someone who had played villainous roles before. We all felt it would be really exciting to surprise the audience in the casting and in the action sequences, and make them say, 'I wasn't expecting that.'"

And Woo believed that John really would surprise people. Despite that as Vic Deakins, a B-3 pilot who holds an entire city hostage with a stolen nuclear weapon, John was playing a genuine bad guy for the first time, he was still "a really likeable bad guy, which is a hard thing to do.

"I didn't want this guy to be the typical bad guy. I wanted to make the audience feel like he could be anyone—your neighbor, your colleague, your friend. And John really has a very special gift, especially with his eyes. He can look so charming, but sometimes when he's staring at you he can have the eyes of Satan." Woo, too, must have seen the *Perfect* soundtrack jacket.

This dichotomy, the good-guy bad-guy blend that John so effortlessly captures, powers one of the movie's most stunning scenes—when Deakins lashes out at his partner and friend, played by Christian Slater, who had turned down a starring role in Sylvester Stallone's *Assassins* to work with Woo. The shock in Slater's eyes as his trusted buddy is suddenly revealed to be an absolute lunatic is stupendous. John later praised Slater's talents effusively—especially in that scene.

"He's adorable, funny, smart, a wonderful actor," John raved. "He's such an upstanding, decent fellow. He really tries his hardest to be a good man."

Slater responded, "I've worked with a lot of big stars and he's the only one who's ever knocked on my trailer door just to come in and talk and hang out. He's like an old-time movie star, like the way you'd think Cary Grant would be—smart and funny and fun to be around."

John even taught Slater the hand-jive sequence from *Grease*. He also warned him to keep his head down next time John flew over the set. Gleefully defying the orders of the studio's insurance company, who forbade him to fly while filming, John took to buzzing the Montana set in his Gulfstream II. "The crew came unglued," he chuckled. He added that neighbor Kirstie Alley often got the same treatment when he was at home.

Woo was a director John had been turned on to—of course—by Tarantino, and John understood the attraction right away. "John Woo is—he's an artist in action-drama, which is a genre that normally bores me. It's not that I don't like it, it's just that I don't normally go to see it. But he shakes it up." Before *Broken Arrow* had even wrapped, John and Woo were discussing working together again, possibly on the science fiction adventure *Face Off*.

"I'm very anxious to work with [Woo] again," John says enthusiastically, "because with him, I had one of my favorite rapports with a director. I was so comfortable with John, and happy. He's a happy guy too, not moody. He's a real pro."

Woo tried explaining his approach to filming. "When I was a kid, I was fascinated by cartoons and by musicals—especially musicals. I'm crazy about them. So I've got a very strong feeling for the rhythm and beauty of body movement. When I'm deciding how to do an action sequence, it seems to me that I'm creating a dance scene."

Dance scene or not, *Broken Arrow* involved some rigorous shots. Former world boxing champion Carlos Palamino was recruited to teach John and Slater some basic boxing skills, and the pair was also trained to handle various weapons by Desert Storm veteran weapons specialist Robert "Rock" Galotti, already well known for his advisory work on *Forrest Gump* and *Born on the Fourth of July.*

Broken Arrow, of course, offered a considerably greater challenge than either of those films. "John Woo likes weapons, and he likes gunfire," quipped Galotti. "We had about 60,000 rounds of ammunition—and we shot every single round, if not more."

The movie set was equally stupendous. Designed by Holger Gross, the creator of *Stargate*'s extravagant ersatz-Egyptian landscapes, it included nothing less than a complete indoor mock-up of the abandoned copper mine the crew had used earlier when they were filming on location in northern Arizona. Constructed from wood, fiberglass, and several truckloads of genuine Arizona soil, this mock-up alone occupied most of the airplane hangar-sized sound stage at 20th Century Fox studios. A functioning freight elevator and an underground river completed the illusion.

Another model, much smaller this time but with an equal eye for scale, replicated an entire chunk of desert—one that an underground nuclear explosion ensures is disfigured forever. John could not help but smirk when he was introduced to his stand-in for that scene; it was a Ken doll.

Broken Arrow was to be tragically scarred for John when his father, Sal, died at age of 82, midway through filming. Taking comfort from his family and his faith, and proud that the old man had lived to see his Hollywood rehabilitation, John acknowledges that it was his work, again, that helped him through this latest bout with heartbreak. If Sal had died even two years before, John might not have coped half as well as he did. But still, he will never be able to think about *Broken Arrow* without remembering the pain of his father passing on.

"I had tremendous fun," he reiterated later. But he also had "this overall feeling of losing Dad." It was funny the way fate worked, he mused, because always when he was at his happiest or most successful, she intervened as though to keep him from getting too cocky. When he was high on *Kotter*, Diana passed away. He went up for an Oscar, and his mother died soon after. He won a Golden Globe, and lost his father. It had always been that way, all the way back to when he was a kid posing by the swimming pool, then diving headfirst into the shallow end.

But maybe those checks and balances were necessary, just as he now believes that all those years in relative obscurity were necessary as well. If he hadn't fallen as fast as he did after *Grease*, if he had just kept on rising till there was nowhere left to go, would he still be alive today? Probably not.

Even if he had survived, what would his life be like? Would he still be free to fly his planes? Would he have made the kind of movies—like *Pulp Fiction* and *White Man's Burden*—that filled his heart with joy even though his pockets remained empty? Would he have met and married Kelly and had his wonderful son Jett?

Probably not. It's that knowledge that makes everything else seem worthwhile. It proves that life's really not as aimless as it often seems. It gives him a perspective from which he can look beyond the here-and-now to the personal goals he nurtures that lie far beyond Hollywood.

John is involved, for example, with a multitude of organizations. Through Scientology, he is part of an education group dedicated to redressing America's growing illiteracy problems. He campaigns on the side of various ecological groups, and he is part of a drug rehabilitation group. "I feel that my family's in good shape and my career's in good shape. Now I feel like helping others. I think if you get yourself squared away and you feel good about life, you start wanting to reach out and help others."

Content in every avenue of his life, John Travolta has finally achieved perhaps the only true ambition he ever set himself. On the set of *Grease* back in 1977, he had already tasted fame and fortune, he had already had his talents confirmed by his peers, and he was already the biggest star in the world. But one day, choreographer Pat Birch asked him what he wanted to do when he grew up?

John smiled, and then tossed off the response that has kept him going ever since.

"Well, Paul Newman's had a pretty good career."

Appendices

◇◇◇

FILMOGRAPHY

1975 *Devil's Rain*
Directed by Robert Fuest. Cast: Ernest Borgnine, Ida Lupino, William Shatner, Eddie Albert, Keenan Wynn, Tom Skerritt, John Travolta.

1976 *Carrie*
Directed by Brian De Palma. Cast: Carrie, Sissy Spacek; Margaret White, Piper Laurie; Tommy Ross, William Katt; Billy Nolan, John Travolta; Sue Snell, Amy Irving; Chris Hargenson, Nancy Allen; Miss Collins, Betty Buckley.

1977 *Saturday Night Fever*
Directed by John Badham. Cast: Tony Manero, John Travolta; Stephanie, Karen Lynn Gorney; Bobby C, Barry Miller; Joey, Joseph Cali; Double J, Paul Pape; Annette, Donna Pescow. Best Actor Award, National Board of Reviewers, 1977; Best Actor nominee, Academy Awards, 1977; Best Actor nominee, Golden Globes, 1977.

1978 *Grease*
Directed by Randal Kleiser. Cast: Danny, John Travolta; Sandy, Olivia Newton-John; Rizzo, Stockard Channing; Kenickie, Jeff Conaway; Frenchy, Didi Conn; Principal McGee, Eve Arden; Teen Angel, Frankie Avalon; Vi, Joan Blondell; Vince Fontaine, Ed Byrnes; Coach Calhoun, Sid Caesar; Jan, Jamie Donnelly; Marty, Dinah Manoff; Doody, Barry Pearl; Sonny, Michael Tucci; Putzie, Kelly Ward; Patty Simcox, Susan Buchner. Golden Globe World Film Favorite, 1978.

1978   *Moment by Moment*

Directed by Jane Wagner. Cast: Trisha, Lily Tomlin; Strip, John
Travolta; Naomi, Andra Akers; Stu, Bert Kramer; Peg, Shelley Bonus;
Stacie, Debra Feuer; Dan Santini, James Luisi.

1980   *Urban Cowboy*

Directed by James Bridges. Cast: Bud, John Travolta; Sissy, Debra
Winger; Wes, Scott Glenn; Pam, Madolyn Smith; Uncle Bob, Barry
Corbin; Aunt Corene, Brooke Alderson; Marshall, Cooper Huckabee;
Steve Strange, James Gannon.

1981   *Blow Out*

Directed by Brian De Palma. Cast: Jack, John Travolta; Sally, Nancy
Allen; Burke, John Lithgow; Manny, Dennis Franz; Sam, Peter Boyden;
Jim, Curt May; Jack Manners, Maurice Copeland.

1983   *Staying Alive*

Directed by Sylvester Stallone. Cast: Tony Manero, John Travolta;
Jackie, Cynthia Rhodes; Laura, Finola Hughes; Jesse, Steve Inwood.
Male Box-Office Star of the Year, National Association of Theater
Owners Show West, 1983.

1983   *Two of a Kind*

Directed by John Herzfeld. Cast: Zack, John Travolta; Debbie, Olivia
Newton-John; Charlie, Charles Durning; Ruth, Beatrice Straight; Earl,
Scatman Crothers; Gonzales, Castulo Guerra; Beazley, Oliver Reed;
Stuart, Richard Bright; Oscar, Vincent Bufano.

1985   *Perfect*

Directed by James Bridges. Cast: Adam, John Travolta; Jessie, Jamie Lee
Curtis; Frankie, Anne DeSalvo; Linda, Laraine Newman; Sally, Marilu
Henner; Roger, Matthew Reed; Charlie, Stefan Gierasch; Mark Roth,
Jann Wenner.

1989   *The Experts*

Directed by Dave Thomas. Cast: Travis, John Travolta; Wendell, Ayre
Gross; Bonnie, Kelly Preston; Jill, Deborah Foreman; Yuri, James
Keach; Illyich, Jan Rubes; Mr. Smith, Charles Martin Smith.

1989 *Look Who's Talking*
Directed by Amy Heckerling. Cast: James, John Travolta; Mollie, Kirstie Alley; Rosie, Olympia Dukakis; Albert, George Segal; Grandpa, Abe Vigoda; Voice of Mikey, Bruce Willis; Rona, Twink Caplan. Male Box-Office Star of the Year, National Association of Theater Owners Show East, 1989.

1990 *Look Who's Talking Too*
Directed by Amy Heckerling. Cast: James, John Travolta; Mollie, Kirstie Alley; Rosie, Olympia Dukakis; Stuart, Elias Koteas; Rona, Twink Caplan; Voice of Mikey, Bruce Willis; Voice of Julie, Roseanne Barr; Voice of Mr. Toilet Man, Mel Brooks.

1991 *Chains of Gold*
Directed by Rod Holcomb. Cast: Scott:, John Travolta; Jackie, Marilu Henner; Tommy Burke, Joey Lawrence; Carlos, Benjamin Bratt; James, Ramon Franco; Mrs. Burke, Conchata Ferrell.

1991 *Shout*
Directed by Jeffrey Hornaday. Cast: Jack Cabe, John Travolta; Jesse Tucker, James Walters; Sara Benedict, Heather Graham.

1992 *Boris and Natasha* (cameo)
Directed by Charles Martin Smith. Cast: Boris, Dave Thomas; Natasha, Sally Kellerman; John Travolta as himself.

1993 *Look Who's Talking Now*
Directed by Tom Ropelewski. Cast: James, John Travolta; Mollie, Kirstie Alley; Albert, George Segal; Dog, Diane Keaton; Stray Dog, Danny DeVito.

1994 *Pulp Fiction*
Directed by Quentin Tarantino. Cast: Vincent Vega, John Travolta; Mia, Uma Thurman; Jules, Samuel Jackson; Butch Coolidge, Bruce Willis; Lance, Eric Stoltz. Best Actor nominee, Academy Awards, 1994; Best Actor, British Academy of Film and Television Arts, 1994; Best Actor nominee, Golden Globes, 1994; Best Actor nominee, Screen

Actor's Guild, 1994; Best Actor Award, Chicago Film Critics, 1994; Best Actor nominee, Comedy Awards, 1994; Best Actor Award, L.A. Film Critics, 1994; Best Actor Award, Stockholm Film Festival, 1994; Best Actor Award, London Film Critics Circle, 1994.

1994   *Eyes of Love*
Directed by Robert Harmon. Cast: Bobby, John Travolta; The Girl, Ellie Raab; Cissy, Tito Larriva; Goon, Richard Edson; Georgie, Jeffrey DeMunn; Georgie's Wife, Lisa Ziegler.

1995   *Get Shorty*
Directed by Barry Sonnenfeld. Cast: Chili Palmer, John Travolta; Harry Zimm, Gene Hackman; Martin Weir, Danny DeVito; Karen Florres, Rene Russo; Ray Barboni, Dennis Farina; Bo Catlett, Delroy Lindo; Ronnie Wingate, Jon Gries.

1995   *White Man's Burden*
Directed by Desmond Nakano. Cast: Louis Pinnock, John Travolta; Thaddeus Thomas, Harry Belafonte; Louis, Kelly Lynch.

1996   *Broken Arrow*
Directed by John Woo. Cast: Vic Deakins, John Travolta. Riley Hale, Christian Slater; Terry Carmichael, Samantha Mathis.

TELEVISION APPEARANCES

December 14, 1972   *Owen Marshall, Counsellor at Law*
one episode, "A Piece of God"
Regular cast: Owen Marshall, Arthur Hill; Jess Brandon, Lee Majors;
Melissa, Christine Matchett; Frieda Krause, Joan Darling. Danny
Paterno, Reni Santoni.

October 1, 1973   *The Rookies*
one episode, "Frozen Smoke"
Regular cast: Terry Webster, Georg Brown; Willie Gillis, Michael
Ontkean; Mike Danko, Sam Melville; Jill Danko, Kate Jackson; Eddie
Ryker, Gerald O'Loughlin.

December 16, 1974   *Medical Center*
one episode, "Saturday's Child"
Regular cast: Paul Lochner, James Daly; Joe Gannon, Chad Everett;
Nurse Courtland, Chris Hutson; Nurse Wilcox, Audrey Totter.

September 9, 1975–August 10, 1979   *Welcome Back, Kotter*
Regular cast: Gabe Kotter, Gabriel Kaplan; Julie, Marcia Strassman;
Vinnie, John Travolta; Epstein, Robert Hegyes; Washington, Lawrence-
Hilton Jacobs; Horshack, Ron Palillo; Mr. Woodman, John Sylvester
White.

November 12, 1976   *The Boy in the Plastic Bubble*
TV movie directed by Randal Kleiser. Cast: Todd, John Travolta;
Johnny, Robert Reed. Mickey, Diana Hyland; Roy Slater, John
Friedrich; Tom Shuster, Kelly Ward; Bruce Shuster, Skip Lowell;
Deborah, P.J. Soles.

May 12, 1987   *The Dumbwaiter*
TV special directed by Robert Altman. Cast: John Travolta and Tom
Conti.

STAGE SHOWS

1967   *Who'll Save the Plowboy?*
                    cast not available

1970 (summer)   *Gypsy*
                    cast not available

1970 (summer)   *Bye Bye Birdie*
                    cast not available

1971   *Metamorphoses*
                    cast not available

1971 (summer)   *The Boyfriend*
                    cast not available

1971 (summer)   *She Loves Me*
                    cast not available

1972 (March)   *Rain*
                Astor Place Theater, New York. Cast: Mrs.Horn,
                Antonia Ray; Private Griggs, John Travolta; Corp.
                Hodgson, Richard Ryder; Sgt. O'Hara, Beeson
                Carroll; Joe Horn, Ben Slack; Mrs. Davidson,
                Patricia O'Connell; Dr. McPhail, Paul Milikin; Mrs.
                McPhail, Elizabeth Farley; Quartermaster Bates,
                Bernie Passeltime; Sadie Thompson, Madeleine
                LeRoux; Rev. Davidson, James Cahill; Policeman,
                Bob Parlan.

December 1972–September 1973   *Grease*
                National touring company. Cast: Miss Lynch, Leslie
                Nicol; Patty Simcox, Carol Culver; Eugene, Stephen
                Van Benschoten; Jan, Rebecca Gilchrist; Marty,
                Marilu Henner; Betty Rizzo, Judy Kaye; Doody,
                John Travolta; Roger, Ray DeMattis; Kenickie, Jerry
                Zaks; Sonny, Michael Lembeck, Tommy Gerard;

Frenchy, Ellen March; Sandy, Pamela Adams,
Candice Early; Danny, Jeff Conaway, Barry
Bostwick; Johnny Casino, Mike Clifford; Cha Cha,
Judith Sullivan, Vivian Fineman; Teen Angel, Mike
Clifford.

March–September, 1974 *Over Here*
Schubert Theater, New York. Cast: Norwin
Spokesman, Douglass Watson; Make-Out, Jim
Weston; Father, MacIntyre Dixon; Mother, Bette
Henritze; Rankin, William Griffis; Donna, Marilu
Henner; Wilma, Phyllis Somerville; Maggie, Ann
Reinking; Mitzi, Janie Sell; Misfit, John Travolta;
Utah, Treat Williams; Lucky, John Mineo; Sarge,
William Newman; Sam, Samuel E. Wright; June,
April Shawhan; Bill, John Driver; Pauline De Paul,
Maxene Andrews; Paulette De Paul, Patty Andrews.

1976 (summer) *Bus Stop*
East Coast Touring Company. Cast not available.
Starring: John Travolta, Ellen Travolta, Ann Travolta,
Anita Gillette.

1982 (July) *Mass Appeal*
Cast not available. Starring: John Travolta, Charles
Durning.

DISCOGRAPHY

U.S. Singles
Let Her In/Big Trouble, Mid Int 10623, 1976
Whenever I'm Away From You/Razzamatazz, Mid Int 10780, 1976
All Strung Out On You/Easy Evil, Mid Int 10907, 1977
Slow Dancing, Mid Int 10997, 1977
Razzamatazz, Mid Int 11206, 1978
Sandy/Blue Moon, RSO 930, 1978
You Set My Dreams To Music/It Had To Be You, Mid Int 72007, 1980

U.S. Singles with Olivia Newton-John
You're the One That I Want/Alone At a Drive-in Movie
   b-side performed by Louis St. Louis, RSO 891, 1978
Summer Nights/Rock 'n' Roll Party Queen
   b-side performed by Louis St. Louis, RSO 906, 1978
Twist of Fate/Take a Chance
   a-side performed by Olivia Newton-John, MCA 52284, 1983

U.S. Singles with Jeff Conaway
Greased Lightning, RSO 909, 1978

Albums
Over Here: Original Broadway Cast, Columbia 32961, 1974
various artists: includes "Dream Drummin'/Soft Music" (w/Phyllis
Somerville, Big Band and Company)

John Travolta, Mid Int BKL-1 1563, 1976
Let Her In/Never Gonna Fall in Love Again/Rainbows/A Girl Like
You/Razzamatazz/I Don't Know What I Like About You Baby/Big
Trouble/Goodnight Mr. Moon/Baby I Could Be So Good at Lovin'
You

Can't Let You Go, Mid Int BKL-1 2211, 1977
Slow Dancing/Can't Let You Go/Easy Evil/Back Doors Crying/What

Would They Say/Moonlight Lady/Settle Down/You Set My Dreams to Music/Whenever I'm Away From You/All Strung Out On You

Grease: The Original Soundtrack, RSO RS2-4002, 1978
various artists: includes Summer Nights (w/Olivia Newton-John) /You're the One That I Want (w/Olivia Newton-John)/Sandy/Greased Lightning (w/Jeff Conaway)

Travolta Fever, Mid Int MTF 001, 1978
Let Her In/Never Gonna Fall in Love Again/Rainbows/A Girl Like You/Razzamatazz/I Don't Know What I Like About You Baby/Big Trouble/Goodnight Mr. Moon/Baby I Could Be So Good at Lovin' You/Slow Dancing/Can't Let You Go/Easy Evil/Back Doors Crying/ What Would They Say/Moonlight Lady/Settle Down/You Set My Dreams to Music/Whenever I'm Away From You/All Strung Out On You/Right Time of the Night

Sandy, Polydor (UK) 5014, 1978
Sandy/Slow Dancing/You Set My Dreams to Music/Whenever I'm Away From You/Settle Down/Back Doors Crying/Greased Lightning/ Moonlight Lady/All Strung Out/Can't Let You Go/Easy Evil/What Would They Say

Two of a Kind: Music from the Original Motion Picture, MCA 6127, 1983
various artists: includes "Take A Chance" (w/Olivia Newton-John)

20 Golden Pieces: John Travolta, BDL (UK) 2021, 1993
Let Her In/Never Gonna Fall in Love Again/Rainbows/Razzamatazz/ I Don't Know What I Like About You Baby/Big Trouble/Goodnight Mr. Moon/Sandy/Baby I Could Be So Good at Lovin' You/It Had To Be You/Slow Dancing/Can't Let You Go/Easy Evil/Back Doors Crying/ What Would They Say/Right Time Of The Night/Moonlight Lady/ Greased Lightning/Settle Down/You Set My Dreams to Music

Sandy, Emporio (UK) EMPRCD 524, 1993
Let Her In/Never Gonna Fall in Love Again/Rainbows/Razzamatazz/

I Don't Know What I Like About You Baby/Big Trouble/Goodnight
Mr. Moon/Sandy/Baby I Could Be So Good at Lovin' You/It Had To
Be You/Slow Dancing/Can't Let You Go/Easy Evil/Back Doors Crying/
What Would They Say/Right Time of the Night/Moonlight Lady/
Greased Lightning/Settle Down/You Set My Dreams to Music